ONCE UPON A WINDOWSILL

ONCE UPON A WINDOWSILL

A

History

of

Indoor Plants

BY

TOVAH MARTIN

TIMBER PRESS

Portland, Oregon

ISBN 0-88192-120-3
Printed in the United States of America
Designed by Sandra Mattielli

TIMBER PRESS
9999 SW Wilshire
Portland, Oregon 97225

Library of Congress Cataloging-in-Publication Data

Martin, Tovah.
    Once upon a windowsill : a history of indoor plants / by Tovah
Martin.
        p.   cm.
    Bibliography: p.
    Includes index.
    ISBN 0-88192-120-3
    1. House plants--United States--History. 2. Indoor gardening-
-United States--History.   I. Title.
SB419.M32   1989
635.9'65'0973--dc19   88-31499
                                                                CIP

303p., illus.

CONTENTS

To
Geoffrey

INTRODUCTION

HAVE YOU EVER PAUSED to ponder how the Boston Fern stationed serenely in the corner and the African Violet perched pertly on your windowsill came to share your home and hospitality? Probably not. Houseplants have become so firmly entrenched in the North American scene that they are rarely given a second thought. We take the Weeping Fig by the window and the jasmine on the porch completely for granted. But it was not always so. There was a time, and it was not so long ago, when we dwelt completely separately from members of the botanical kingdom. Plants lived outdoors, and we lived indoors.

The cultivation of houseplants is a relatively recent event. Until the last century, the typical North American home contained no resident botanicals lurking on its windowsills. However, that state of affairs was destined to change with the dawning of the Victorian Era.

Early in the 19th Century, plants wandered into our abodes. In retrospect, it is easy to speak of the occurrence casually. And, in fact, that fortuitous entry was not the result of a sudden, dramatic incident. Instead, it was a gradual infiltration. Nevertheless, the entry of plants indoors was an event of enormous import for the horticultural world. It also constituted a landmark triumph in the age-old endeavor to create a more comfortable and meaningful environment in our dwelling places. And it was a lasting victory. The entry of houseplants was accomplished so efficiently and effectively that plants simply melted comfortably into the indoor scenery, where they remain as permanent fixtures.

The houseplant you harbor on your windowsill owes a deep obligation to the unique historical circumstances of the 19th Century Western world. It was no accident that houseplants were invited into our dwellings just as the Victorian Era was dawning. At that moment in time, an incredible and auspicious constellation of artistic, social, moral, political and economic factors came together leading to a set of conditions admirably suited to the entry of plants into our homes. In that singularly favorable environment, the lives of people and plants

1

became intimately entwined. Never before, and never again, would the stage be so auspiciously set.

The people, the times and the technology of the 19th Century all favored the arrival of plants in the home. But, in addition to a receptive audience and a friendly welcome, plants needed an appropriate point of entry. They found that nearly faultless environment awaiting them in the Victorian front parlor.

The parlor provides an excellent starting point to trace this remarkable sequence of events. Not only did that room witness the arrival of an endless stream of plants, but it is an annex that remains locked in time with no specific role in modern daily life. Enter a restored or preserved front parlor and you are instantly drawn back to a by-gone era. In the parlor, you can hear the sounds, touch the textures and inhale the scents of the 19th Century. In that room, you can imagine the world as it was on the eve of the entry of houseplants.

Setting the Stage

The front parlor complete with its horsehair furniture, souvenirs and resident houseplants.

CHAPTER I

THE FRONT PARLOR

TIME STANDS STILL in the front parlor. Nothing moves, not the clock which ceased its labor decades ago, nor the humid air. Although it is a dimly lit room, the shades are usually drawn, more to preserve the austere atmosphere than to protect the furniture.

It is a solemn scene composed of heavy mahogany and draped in dark velvet. A marble-topped table, a claw-legged sofa, a few stiff chairs and a sizable oval mirror are among the notable accouterments of the scene. Year in and year out, the furniture stands sentinel—heavy, haughty and dormant.

Facing in from the entryway, where the hall floorboards meet once-plush carpet, it is nearly impossible to peer completely across the room. But, if one strains, a fern is barely visible standing solitary vigil in its jardiniere by the window. Heedless of the dim atmosphere, the plant calmly coexists with its neighboring antiques. Given to neither pageantry nor acrobatics, it simply survives.

Closer inspection might reveal that the fern's delicate fronds have swept past its territorial table, encroaching onto the domain of a neighboring chair. As the lacy fronds cascade lazily over tapestry and woodwork, they fall gently upon a pattern carved in the nearby chair back, brushing a whimsical wooden crozier etched in the deep, mellow wood. One quick glance sent wandering around the room reveals a similar motif throughout the furnishings. Fiddleheads are etched deep in the furniture. They are molded onto the gilded mirror frame and pressed into the lampshade. They dance laboriously across the wallpaper in repeated patterns. The carpet underfoot is a befuddlement of fanciful fernery.

This is the story of that fern, and a million similar ferns, and how they came to send their croziers crawling onto marble tables and nearby chairs. This is the account of the ivies, citrus, palms, cacti and Flowering Maples which came to share the front parlor with the ferns, incumbent what-nots, souvenirs and horsehair furniture. And this is the history of the room which played host to those plants, the front parlor, and its evolution. But, most importantly, this is the story of the people who brought those plants indoors—this is the biography of the middle class Victorian family.

Our account begins in the 1830s when the Victorian Era was born. Some historians argue that the era did not commence in this country until after the Civil War. Other students of history avow that North America enjoyed no Victorian Era whatsoever, although they will allow us the associated Industrial Era. However, for our purposes, we can easily follow the contingent of historians who count the dawning of the Victorian Era in North America as coinciding with the birth of that era in Britain, citing the changes in technology and lifestyle which were rapidly transforming both countries simultaneously.

The scene of our narrative could take place in any town born a century or more ago. Take a walk down Main Street and you will doubtlessly find tucked close to the heart of the community, nestled against the town's throbbing center, a row of grand Victorian houses—all trimmed, all corniced, and all once claiming a parlor which nurtured within its bosom an array of carved, velvet-seated furniture and incumbent plants.

The houses along Main Street may vary in size and grandeur—they were not the best homes in town nor the worst. They were the residences of the professionals, the tradesmen and merchants, the average citizens in the area. They were constructed, decorated and inhabited by families who had come a long way, but still had much further to travel. Their original occupants toiled long hours to provide the wherewithal to finance such a home and furnish such a room. Those abodes embodied every man's little piece of Paradise—his personal Eden.

An invitation to enter such a house would reveal sequestered within its dark, cavernous confines a front parlor very much like the one which I describe. The vintage of the particular room I have in mind is 1880, by that year the Victorian Era had ample time to gain personality—it was nearly 50 years young. But, the front parlor was not born high and mighty. It did not suddenly hatch upon the scene complete with ornate furniture and luxuriant houseplants. Rather, it evolved slowly from humble origins and grew gradually to become the focal point of family life. So our story actually begins a century before the parlor was accepted and embraced as an integral part of our residences. We harken back to the 1700s, when the household was witnessing a metamorphosis which eventually led to the parlor's reign of glory.

The early Colonial home was simple and barren; it was a modest dwelling which claimed few rooms. In families of average or meager means, weaving, cooking, eating and sleep were all realized in sections of a common area; whereas, wealthier homes boasted several rooms and occasionally a separate story for the bedchambers. Since fashion is typically set by the wealthy, it was in those affluent homes that the first evidence of the parlor appeared.

Upon opening the front door to one of the more sumptuous early Colonial dwellings, the guest was greeted in an entry hall. That hall was later expanded into an alcove which served as a reception area for visitors, equipped with a fireplace and furnished with a few stiff chairs. Although Spartan, the annex was generally more decorative and formal than the remainder of the dwelling. However, it was characteristically a bare room, naked except for a few essential pieces of furniture bearing straight, terse, "honest" lines, and the relatively elaborate hearth which dominated the scene. A guest was forced to glean warmth from the gathered family and fire in the hearth; certainly the furnishings offered little solace for the visitor. The other rooms conformed to a similar theme, entirely bereft of any ornamentation or creature comforts. Such a home reflected the Colonial penchant for utilitarianism and the Puritan ethic.

Gradually that entry room was converted, expanded and endowed with a distinctive personality. The room became more cordial, inviting visitors to tarry for a while within the home. And yet, it still held the outside world at arm's length. The parlor kept the world at bay, and for good reason, as architectural critic Russell Stergis explained in 1893, "tradesmen and visitors, however welcome, cannot be dropped in the midst of the family group."

The entire house was beginning a slow but definite metamorphosis, evolving from a plain to a sumptuous entity. The country was travelling the road toward embellishment, and the ramifications of that inclination were evident everywhere—in the garden, in wearing apparel and, of course, in the home.

The early examples of this trend were confined to upper class homes, especially those in urban areas. The houses in the flourishing towns of Boston, Providence, New York and Philadelphia were among the first to experiment freely with the addition of relatively elaborate floor plans and spacious rooms. Carved woodwork appeared at key focal points, especially on door and window frames or surrounding the hearth. Toward the latter part of the 18th Century, this ornamentation spread throughout the home, and floral motifs became a common theme. Garlands and festoons of trailing leaves and flowers were carved in the wood moldings and stenciled on the walls offering a subdued hint of the future vogue in design. Relatively elaborate curtains draped the windows. Upholstery began to include ruffles and skirts of lengthy fringe, while the wallpaper became astonishingly merry and garish. The reign of the Victorian Era was creeping slowly in.

There were also botanical hints of things to come. Flowers were introduced into the late Colonial home. Cut flowers were displayed in large urns stationed in front of mirrors or standing in solitary splendor on a table. Generally, these flowers were gathered in the field; rarely was a garden devoted solely to their supply. But, nonetheless, blossoms were considered to be an important element in the interior decor. During the winter, dried flowers replaced fresh arrangements in the same prominent positions.

The middle class merchants and tradesmen, the common men, were reluctant to embrace this new inclination toward finery. Slow to abandon doctrines which were deeply ingrained as national tenets, the middle class family was understandably suspicious of this unprecedented direction in fashion. Caution ruled the average home. Embellishment was introduced only with the greatest of prudence.

However, change is inevitable, especially in matters of fashion—and it came rushing in toward the end of the 18th Century. By that time, the design of the typical house had improved greatly over the original Colonial box. A late 18th Century middle class home usually contained several family-oriented rooms on the ground floor, each entertaining a distinct living function. There was an area devoted to cooking, a separate space for slumber, and often, a less functional gathering room as well.

In the late 18th Century, all of the rooms in the home devoted to family life were collectively termed "living rooms" regardless of the specific functions which they served. Of those living spaces, the gathering or common room (as it was sometimes called) eventually evolved into that entity which we have come to call "the parlor" from the French *parler*—to speak.

Although the parlor could claim some American roots, most of its personality came from farther afield—it was strongly affected by foreign influence. In *The Decoration of Homes*, written in 1902, Edith Wharton and Ogden Codman, Jr. traced the front parlor's origins to Medieval France.

During the French Middle Ages and early Renaissance, the upper classes conducted all their social and domestic entertainment in the bedchamber. Only state business was administered in the *grand salle*, the great hall. With their heavy burden of duty, the sleeping quarters eventually spawned a separate space devoted solely to social affairs. Interestingly, that annex still contained its traditional bed. This room was ultimately split into two chambers, the *salon de compagnie* and the *salon de famille*. The former was utilized only for the entertainment of guests, its decor being more formal and also more ostentatious than any other room in the building. On the other hand, the *salon de famille* was devoted to family use and was furnished with more comfortable, plainer furniture. The erstwhile bed, which had remained in these chambers throughout the metamorphosis, developed into the "day bed" which later became our couch or sofa.

Throughout the centuries, the room remained locked in the European tradition, and in that form was eventually adopted into the wealthiest homes in this country. By the time the parlor was accepted into the average American home, it had acquired a very pronounced personality.

With the advent of the Victorian Era, the American front parlor was already too formal and delicately balanced for daily family usage. It was employed for "state occasions" only. Weddings, funerals, christenings and moments of similar weight were entertained in that forbidding atmosphere, although such events occurred infrequently in the life of the typical bourgeois family. Nevertheless, people were fascinated with the novelty of their new showpiece, and so refrained from altering the function, or lack of function, of such a unique room.

Not everyone approved of that sedentary and little-used annex. The plight of the parlor was a topic frequently addressed in period magazines. This paragraph from *The Home-Maker* is typical of the criticism which that superfluous "living" space attracted,

> Who ever heard of decent people living without a 'best room'? Our notable housekeeper makes hers 'a very best', maintains a sharp look-out for moth and dust, and never sits down in it except when there is 'company'. Company is the fetish of her class. To propitiate it, Brussels and brocatel, varnish and veneer, chromos and curtains, horse-hair and hard finish are set continually in order... The room is darkened by closed blinds and lowered shades, and the corpse of dead comfort lies here in state from Christmas to Christmas.

An elaborate mantle from Clarence Cook's *The House Beautiful*.

Despite pleas for a more livable milieu from every major architect and many respected literary figures, the parlor generally remained too grand and too aloof for such mundane chores as daily existence entails. As Edith Wharton commented, the parlor was "considered sacred to gilding and discomfort, the best room in the house, and the convenience of the inmates, being sacrificed to the vague feeling that no drawing-room is worthy of the name unless it is uninhabitable."

Following the French tradition, another room assumed the responsibilities for daily family function. This room was referred to as the "sitting room" or, if connected to the front parlor (as was most often the case), it was known as the "back parlor". Very frequently, that room discharged other duties as well, doubling as a dining area or library.

The back parlor was generally described as the coziest room in the home, and most architects felt that it deserved a command of the most cheerful exposure in the floor plan. In summer, it was sun-filled, while winter found it warmed by a sizable and often elaborate hearth containing a roaring fire. Partitioned off from its formidable counterpart, the back parlor harbored easy chairs, writing tables and lamps. In general, it possessed a far less intimidating personality than the front parlor.

Among the back parlor's main attractions was its hearth. At one time, the sitting room fire was paramount in American life. Eventually, the fire became the symbol of the family bond, a value which was widely and strongly held by the general public and extolled by contemporary authors. Victorian literature never tired of invoking the fireside as a symbol of the comfort and meaning of family ties. In fact, the fire was so frequently employed to connote security that it is difficult to imagine "Home, Sweet Home" without its traditional flame.

The mantelpiece borrowed some of the prestige. Clarence Cook's *The House Beautiful* written in 1873, describes the importance of the glowing mantel,

> The mantelpiece ought to second the intention of the fireplace as the center of family life—the spiritual and intellectual center as the table is the material center. There ought thereon to be gathered on the shelf or shelves, over the fireplace, a few beautiful and chosen things—the most beautiful that the family purse can afford.

Toward this end, the mantel frequently held cut flowers and displayed forced bulbs.

When the fire was confined to a stove in mid-century, that technological advance provoked an understandable widespread fear that the family might dissipate into moral corruption without the uniting force of its inspirational hearth. However, time and technology cannot be halted in their unrelenting march forward. Eventually, the central furnace replaced the stove, leaving the occupants of the back parlor entirely bereft of an object on which to focus their attention. They were left to stare blankly at the purely ornamental mantel which remained.

The literary world reacted immediately. Having cultivated the connection

The fireside symbolized "Home Sweet Home". Illustration from Clarence Cook's *The House Beautiful*.

between fire and family, they were hesitant to relinquish the metaphor. Influential authors invoked every possible method to reinstate the fireplace, but the propaganda was doomed to failure. As a poor compromise, they advocated adorning the grates with sham flames to simulate the cozy fire and, hopefully, to imbue the family with memories of the moral warmth which the bonafide fire had provided.

Inevitably, nostalgia was sacrificed to convenience and the open hearth disappeared, leaving the fire's former ethical role open to other objects with uplifting moral qualities. This was the position that houseplants would eventually fill both in the front and back parlors.

So a golden opportunity presented itself. Coincidence had provided the perfect setting for the entry of houseplants. Now all that was needed was an advocate to advance the cause.

We can proceed no further into our account without invoking the name of Andrew Jackson Downing. His was perhaps the most prominent, and certainly the most unrelenting, voice influencing and defining Victorian ethics. And his theories eventually led to the entrance of plants into the parlor.

Born into a family of nurserymen, Downing was a combination gentleman, landscape designer and architect with a strong penchant for preaching. He stood accused of being snobbish and aloof, and his critics often complained that his ideas were too unattainably grand for the common householder. This may have been the case, but Downing's theories would eventually influence the design of American homes for all economic classes.

Andrew Jackson Downing.

Downing aired his views on lifestyles in four books which used architecture as a vehicle to convey moral and aesthetic dictums. He also served as editor and contributed numerous articles to one of America's first horticultural magazines, *The Horticulturist*, self-described in the subtitle as a *Journal of Rural Art and Rural Taste*. Downing presided over *The Horticulturist* from its birth in 1846 until his tragic death in 1852 when a Hudson River steamboat caught fire while racing another passenger vessel to their destination. His magazine became sufficiently popular and influential in those brief six years to continue publishing until 1876.

Do not be misled by the magazine's subtitle, Downing was not advocating a return to life on the farm in his journal—far from it. "Rural Taste" was a quality to be captured in country villas to which the inhabitants of the city fled seasonally as a retreat from urban existence. "Rural Art" was the essence of pastoral beauty as incorporated into homes throughout the nation, rural and urban alike. These concepts became so popular that every family, no matter how humble their abode, sought to invoke a rural flavor in and around their home.

Downing preached the doctrine of Beauty with a fervor and conviction that most men reserved for expounding the gospel. In so doing, he successfully imbued architecture and landscape design with religious connotations. He inveighed in a thunderous and righteous voice against the popular and traditional reigning utilitarianism. The Useful was adequate only for people of "undeveloped natures". Such insufficient creatures could in no way compare to those souls "who yearn with an instinct as strong as life itself, for the manifestation of a higher attribute of matter—the Beautiful."

According to his premise, when people are surrounded with Beauty, they are necessarily favorably influenced and can hardly fail to be rendered ethically superior to those persons who dwell in unadorned residences. But, Downing did not dare leave the terms Beauty and Good open to popular definition. Objects which embodied these qualities were carefully prescribed. The illustrations in his books provide graphic examples of homes which, when transformed architecturally from simple to embellished, rescued their resident families from moral and spiritual disrepair.

Downing introduced a gardening style referred to as "the Beautiful" wherein nature was respected and revealed but not left uncontrolled. The rural scene gained its "Beauty" only with the aid of human hands. This partnership of man and nature which eventually became known as "the rustic scene" was a popular theme for horticultural design outdoors. It also formed the theoretical basis for the incorporation of living plants into the interior decor.

As Downing repeatedly explained—in no uncertain terms—nature was a redeeming factor of crucial importance in daily family life. The goal was to live as intimately as possible with nature, while still carefully controlling its wildness. Given this assumption, Downing and his disciples had only to hint that plants might be incorporated into the home, and hundreds of households throughout the country immediately invited botanicals to come and share their

According to Downing, when houses were transformed architecturally from simple to embellished, they elevated the morals of the incumbent family. This farmhouse, illustrated in *The Architecture of Country Houses*, was improved by vines, brackets and a bay window.

dwellings. And the parlor, with its great accumulation of pomp and ceremony, was the room deemed most suitable to entertain houseplants.

So keenly was the reign of the rustic felt that eventually every nook of the home harbored one of nature's creations. Those corners not kindly disposed to the cultivation of houseplants were adorned with imitation wax flowers (generally contained in bell-jars), carefully carved wooden flowers (typically dipped in gilt) and cut leather leaves twirled around table legs, picture frames, mirrors, clocks and shelves. A guest must never be allowed to doubt, even for an instant, that the benevolent forces of nature were close at hand.

Nature was not the only entity to be well represented in the parlor. As the era progressed, furniture became more complex in design, full of dysfunctional garnishment. Not only did each piece of furniture gain breadth, but the quantity of furniture residing in the parlor also multiplied. As the years passed, chairs, tables, lamps, cabinets, stools and stands were all wedged in. The front parlor

A plant-adorned window from Edwin A. Johnson's *Winter Greeneries at Home*.

The parlor soon became an unnavigable maze. Illustration from Henry T. Williams' *Window Gardening.*

was rapidly being rendered an unnavigable maze. Looking back on the development of the clutter, a critic lamented in 1896,

> The usual drawing room grew, from a funereal and awesome mystery opened on state occasions, to an inextricable mass of curios, heaped up without rhyme or reason on cabinets, what-nots, tables, door frames, mantles, brackets—until the general appearance of the place resembled a junk-shop more than a reception room for friends, and the slightest movement was actually dangerous. The eye found no satisfaction, the body no comfort; even the bric-a-brac was at a disadvantage from its very superabundance.

Furniture comprised only a small fraction of the paraphernalia in the parlor. There was an awesome collection of various and sundry possessions. The front parlor was the only "living room" to fully reflect feminine taste, all the other rooms were devoted to the male head of household and his comfort. The library was devoted to books and their study and the dining room was dedicated to the consumption of dinner, the parlor alone was a void with no specific function at all. Given its ostentatious tradition, the lady of the house opted to fill it with the family's treasures. Apparently, she simply did not know where to stop.

Victorian literary luminaries took great pleasure in providing graphic descriptions of parlor scenes—and their comments were rarely charitable. Nearly every contemporary author took a stab at the front parlor. Even those writers who did not normally dabble in satire brandished their pens and attacked that room. Edgar Allan Poe offered one such uncharacteristically comic portrayal of the Victorian vogue in interior design. His article on furnishings, published in an 1840 *Burton's Gentleman's Magazine*, begins with this discourse,

> In the internal decoration, if not the external architecture of their residences the English are supreme. The Italians have but little sentiment beyond marbles and colors. In France... the people are too much a race of gad-abouts to maintain household properties of which, indeed, they have a delicate appreciation. The Chinese and most of the Eastern races have a warm but inappropriate fancy. The Scotch are poor decorists... The Yankees alone are preposterous.

Many contemporary authors blamed the parlor's fate on its feminine influence. But, Poe pointed the finger accusingly at American capitalism,

> We have no aristocracy of blood, and having therefore as a natural, and indeed inevitable thing, fashioned ourselves an aristocracy of dollars, the display of wealth has here to take the place and perform the office of the heraldic display of the monarchic countries.

Mark Twain also objected to the current vogue in parlor decor. But, he chose only to rail against those aspects which he considered to be a blasphemy of Beauty. Apparently, he was no less a victim of the ethos of his times than any of his fellow North Americans. It was the specimen confined "under glass French clock dome", the bogus "large bouquet of stiff flowers done in corpsy white wax" and the endless collection of meaningless bric-a-brac that he found offensive, not the bonafide living houseplants and elegant mahogany furniture. In *The Gilded Age*, which Mark Twain coauthored with Charles Dudley Warner, a model parlor was described. It was cluttered, but only with "meaningful" paraphernalia,

> Every room had its book-cases or book-shelves, and was more or less a library; upon every table was liable to be a litter of new books, fresh periodicals and daily newspapers. There were plants in the sunny windows and some choice engravings on the walls... the piano was sure to be open and strewn with music; and there were photographs and little souvenirs here and there of foreign travel.

Although the tastemakers may have disagreed on the vagaries of fabrics, lighting fixtures, mirror arrangements and mantel designs, they were unanimous in supporting one element of parlor decor. Houseplants were always tasteful in

Although the parlor may have been cluttered, it was only filled with "meaningful" paraphernalia. Illustration from Edwin A. Johnson's *Winter Greeneries at Home*.

the front parlor—the more, the merrier. Not only did that room claim the proper ambiance for botanical characters, it also contained many other auspicious conditions which fit the purpose admirably.

As the front parlor evolved, its physical environment was continually rendered more propitious to the health and welfare of living plants. But, the parlor had not always been a climatically appropriate spot for botanicals. Even if women were previously disposed to embark upon the houseplant hobby, their efforts would have been thwarted due to inclement conditions. Although the changes which the front parlor witnessed during the first decades of the Victorian Era may not have been provoked by the desire to incorporate living botanicals into the scene, they certainly aided to further that end.

Perhaps most crucially, the windows in the front parlor were enlarged early in the century to brighten the atmosphere and gain the benefit of the rustic view. A room's importance was often denoted by the number and size of its windows, and the parlor was the home's most prominent sector. In addition, the front parlor was constantly cool in winter, and that chilly atmosphere was ideal for the first garden transplants which took up residence. Due to the lack of heat, the parlor was invariably damp and often dank. The environment may not have lent itself to the comfort of human residents, but botanicals found it quite suitable.

The windows in the parlor were enlarged early in the century. Illustration from Jonathan Periam's *The Home and Farm Manual*.

Other rooms in the house were also assessed for their suitability to harbor houseplants. Many Victorian homes incorporated houseplants into the back parlor. A botanical collection often dwelled alongside the many accouterments of daily family life, amidst the musical instruments, the artwork and the leather-bound volumes. However, just as the back parlor was less formal than its partner, so the plants were less ostentatiously arranged.

Practically speaking, the back parlor possessed both advantages and disadvantages compared to its formal counterpart as a suitable environment for plants. Architects prescribed that the back parlor should command the best exposure in the house, which meant that the room received an abundance of sunlight. However, in its capacity as the family's meeting area, the back parlor was typically overheated. Some Victorian horticulturists charitably labelled this stifling atmosphere as ''hothouse-like''. In truth, it was generally very arid previous to the introduction of steam heat in 1870.

Although the back parlor was toasty by day, the fires were usually neglected overnight. A botanical inhabitant would therefore be subjected to wide variations in temperature and some very chilly winter morns. Considering the rigors which they endured, it is amazing that botanicals managed to survive at all.

Occasionally, plants dwelled in other chambers of the house, or in a foyer or hallway. Bedrooms infrequently harbored plant life due to the popular belief that such a sleeping situation was unsuitable for the human occupants. Throughout the century, horticultural writers tried in vain to dispel the erroneous rumor that the carbonic acid emitted by plants caused illness to human cohabitants dwelling in closed quarters.

In *Winter Greeneries at Home*, Edwin A. Johnson suggested the kitchen as a suitable environment for houseplants. Johnson argued that the kitchen was moist, the air was continually circulated by the frequent comings and goings typical of that busy workspace, and the plants would be left in darkness to ''rest'' after the completion of the evening chores. In turn, the addition of plant life might render scullery drudgery more pleasant to the women whose lives were confined to that labor. Although the argument was compelling, the kitchen rarely housed plants. It provided far too mundane a setting for the display of the family's treasured botanicals.

The front parlor remained the mainstay of the botanical exhibition indoors, unsurpassed by other rooms in the house. True, it was not granted the best exposure. But, it held a superior strategic position, aloof to all of its surroundings and yet effected by them all.

When the front parlor reached the zenith of its splendor in the latter half of the Victorian Era, its botanical inhabitants were of equal magnificence. The single fern which remains in our parlor is but a token reminder of the plant life which once ran rampant in that room. Vines scrambled up the walls, over the window casements and around pictures portraying appropriate rural scenes. Hanging plants showered luxuriantly from their baskets, twining rambunctiously from ceiling to floor. The maze of furniture was complemented by an entanglement of coexisting plant life replete with orbs, topiary, and desultory festoons of ivy. The room contained more than just one fern or palm, there were palms galore, each displayed in its own formidably adorned jardiniere.

For our purposes, the parlor bears watching. Every aspect of that room—its furniture, draperies, bric-a-brac and houseplants—all recorded the changes in the times. Although the front parlor claimed a dark and dreary presence, within its walls we find documentation of advances in the worlds of technology, science and horticulture.

CHAPTER II

THE AGE OF TECHNOLOGY

THE PARLOR WAS EVOLVING. It gathered strength, it gained definition and it acquired breadth. It reflected the fads and fancies of the times. But, stylish though it may have been, the parlor was actually a formidable and protective force created to buffer the family against a world which was in a precariously tenuous state. If the parlor appears cold and stern to us today, it is because that room was once the chilly barrier developed to shield the family from a storm of change.

And the world was changing. As Queen Victoria ascended to her throne in 1837, the pace of the world simultaneously began to quicken. It was a time of motion and then speed, of wonder and then discovery, and a time of ideas that matured into inventions. Science experienced a second renaissance. And, with it, horticultural pursuits also came of age. Prior to the Victorian Era, horticulture was in its infancy in North America, due partly to our lack of technology. But, that situation was destined to change dramatically in the 19th Century.

The home changed, the town changed and the world changed. With the arrival of the 1830s, most North Americans were profoundly aware that they were entering a new era, and that it would certainly be the Age of Transition.

The previous century had witnessed its fair share of excitement. And yet, in the 1700s, North American energy was expended mainly in developing a virgin land. If Europe was making technological advances, the settlers in this country had barely time to take notice. We exhausted our strength in growth.

However, at the turn of the century, there were many indications that the next 100 years would be a century of unprecedented development. The 1800s opened with a massive effort to link the countryside by improving transportation. The Lancaster Pike in Pennsylvania was built in 1792. And, following that lead, Congress authorized construction of the Cumberland Road in 1806 to traverse the treacherous Appalachian Mountains. That single Congressional Act incited a contagion of road construction. In Connecticut alone, no fewer than 50 turnpike companies were incorporated by the 1830s.

Waterway transportation had also come alive just prior to the dawn of the Victorian Era. Flatboats and keelboats navigated the rivers in continually increasing numbers. Of course, boats had been employed for trade since the first settlers arrived in America, but they did not serve the general public. The first publicly advertised, commercial venture to exploit the rivers in this country was officially heralded in a notice placed in the *Kentucky Gazette* in 1793. Jacob Myer offered to carry passengers, letters or cargo from Pittsburgh, Pa. to Limestone, Ky. His was a popular and profitable idea, prompting other enterprising carriers to follow suit. Later in the same year, a regular passenger line opened from Cincinnati to Pittsburgh advertising weekly scheduled trips. However, the fare was expensive and water travel was time consuming. In 1800, the cost of travelling from Pittsburgh to New Orleans by flatboat was $160.00 and the freight tariff was $6.75 per 100 lbs—a steep fee when the dollar was worth 4 to 5 times what it is today.

The arrival of the steamboat heralded a new age of water transportation. It also caught many North Americans completely off guard. This colorful account of one family's initial introduction to steam appeared in *The Gilded Age* by Mark Twain and Charles Dudley Warner,

> A deep coughing sound troubled the stillness . . . All in an instant a fierce eye of fire shot out from behind the cape and sent a long brilliant pathway quivering athwart the dusky water. The coughing grew louder and louder, the glaring eye grew larger and still larger, glared wilder and still wilder. A huge shape developed itself out of the gloom, and from its tall duplicate horns dense volumes of smoke, starred and spangled with sparks, poured out and went tumbling away into the farther darkness. Nearer and nearer the thing came, till its long sides began to glow with spots of light which mirrored themselves in the river and attended the monster like a torchlight procession.
>
> "What is it! Oh, what *is* it, Uncle Dan'l?" With deep solemnity the answer came: "It's de Almighty! Git down on yo' knees!"

In 1817, 17 steamboats were working the inland waters and a typical trip from Pittsburgh to New Orleans required 2½ months. However, passage could be had for half the price of the earlier flat and keelboats. By 1830, 228 steamboats puffed their laborious way up and down the eastern rivers, hurrying both people and trade back and forth in a fashion previously undreamt.

At the same time, trans-Atlantic transportation was also improving. By 1818, sailing vessels were scheduling regular trips between North America and Europe. Commerce improved and trade became brisk and more profitable. Many people took advantage of those trans-Atlantic crossings. By the 1830s, there were approximately 20 commercial lines navigating the Atlantic.

So, when the Victorian Era officially commenced in 1837, the pace of life had already quickened sufficiently to affect the average citizen. Indeed, the enhanced pace was beginning to cause uneasiness. When Washington Irving wrote *The Legend of Sleepy Hollow* in 1820, he already sensed the passing of the Homespun Age. In the introductory pages of that story, he reminisced about Sleepy Hollow, an idyllic community in New York state. He wrote,

> I mention this peaceful spot with all possible laud; for it is in such little retired Dutch valleys, found here and there embosomed in the great state of New York that population, manners, and customs remained fixed; while the great torrent of migration and improvement, which is making such incessant changes in other parts of this restless country, sweeps by them unobserved . . . They are like those little nooks of still water which border a rapid stream . . . undisturbed by the rush of the passing current. Though many years have elapsed since I trod the drowsy shades of Sleepy Hollow, yet I question whether I should not still find the same trees and the same families vegetating in its sheltered bosom.

A decade later, it would be difficult to find a town like Sleepy Hollow, untouched by the times. By the 1830s, the pace, which had been quickened to a stride, accelerated to a gallop. No nook nor cranny in the country was spared from the march of progress. Life and manners began changing at a phenomenal velocity. The nation was being forced forward by steam.

The locomotive was single-handedly responsible for violating the slumber of many Sleepy Hollows. In fact, the "Puffing Billy" threw the country into turmoil. In 1828, the Baltimore & Ohio began service as the first passenger rail line in the United States. And, from that date onward, track was laid with lightning haste. Meanwhile, engines were being improved both in speed and horsepower.

Those engines awed the average citizen. To people accustomed only to the speed which they could achieve on horseback, the pace of the early locomotives was unbelievably swift. In Twain and Warner's *The Gilded Age*, Si Hawkins described the phenomenon to his wife,

> There's a bigger wonder—the railroad! . . . Coaches that fly over the ground twenty miles an hour—heavens and earth, think of that, Nancy! Twenty miles an hour. It makes a man's brain whirl.

In 1829, the highest speed that an engine could achieve was 29 mph, which was reduced to 10 mph drawing the short train typical of the time. However, the November 1848 issue of *Scientific American* proudly reported that a locomotive had attained 75 mph, with the far more impressive working speed of 55 mph. Tracks crisscrossed the countryside. People, parcels, letters and freight were being whisked from one place to another as never before.

Backwoodsmen described those new machines as "pandemonium in harness," and that may have been a fair characterization of the first steaming, roaring, whistling locomotives. But, those thundering monstrosities were, by and large, accepted and adored by early 19th Century citizens eager for an easier life. In fact, Emerson commented in 1846 that "the Americans take to this little contrivance, the railroad, as if it were the cradle in which they were born."

The railroad forged a new way of life for North Americans. Most obviously, it expedited land travel. John Quincy Adams reported with respectful wonderment that the trip from Boston to New York which had encompassed 4 days of arduous and hazardous travel in 1826, could be accomplished in a brief 41 hours in 1832. There was great optimism about the future of train travel. Everyone sensed that they were merely sampling a preview of forthcoming advances in technology. Hopes ran high and speculation was keen. In fact, in 1833, Simon Cameron had the foresight to predict that, "A child born within this decade will, before he dies, be able to eat breakfast in Harrisburg, and take supper in Philadelphia on the same day, almost 100 miles away."

The trains sent goods and letters speeding across the countryside, and they hastened the movement of live plant material from one collector to another. In addition, they also facilitated the journeys of gardeners to and fro. According to the pundits who wrote for *The Horticulturist*, the acceleration of motion was responsible for the proliferation of the popular outdoor sport known as garden touring. This item, entitled "Railroads from a Social Point of View" appeared in the January 1856 issue,

> Everybody now expands, if not their minds, at least their travel . . . till the number of people in motion every day in this Union would make a very respectable army to subdue the Russians at Sebastopol.
> What motives call so many people from home I shall not endeavor to inquire; nor shall I condemn any, for I confess I travel hundreds of miles myself for no other object than to see a good garden, nursery, or state or county fair.

The "Puffing Billy" was carrying horticultural knowledge far and wide. But, the going was still not easy. Although early steam transportation was definitely more rapid than the pace of any horse-drawn vehicle, the travelling horticulturist did not necessarily enjoy a more comfortable or safer trip than previously. According to an 1852 *Scientific American* report, a trip on the young railroads was not the delightful experience that it is today,

> It is really afflicting to ride on the Hudson River Railroad at present. The passengers, when they land . . . look as if they had been working all day in a plaster mill; their clothes are spoiled, and in every sense of the word they look as if they had been doing some dreadful penance.

Throughout the century, however, inventors labored to remedy those shortcomings, and horticulturists reaped the rewards of their efforts as this note in an 1860 issue of *The Gardener's Monthly* illustrates,

> A. L. Barber, Quincy, IL. sends us an account of a new invention which prevents cars and locomotives from being thrown from the tracks in case of meeting with obstructions. As Horticulturists are among the greatest travelers in the community, it is hoped that for their sakes at least, the invention will be speedily applied . . .

Steam not only conveyed horticulturists and their bounty around the country, it also carried them across the oceans. The nations of Europe had been regularly deploying botanical explorers since the 18th Century, and those collectors returned home bearing new introductions of tropical plants. Although some of these plants had arrived on American shores prior to the introduction of steamships, when Atlantic travel was expedited, their importation increased commensurately.

In 1838, the steamships *Sirius* and *Great Western* began regular Atlantic crossings. Naturally, it was an auspicious moment for North Americans eager to augment links with the older, and perhaps wiser countries across the ocean. Americans no longer harbored the bitterness of revolutionaries, although they were deeply inflicted with the spirit of competition. They were eager for European/American interchange of trade, knowledge and visitors.

Prior to the introduction of steam, an eastern voyage between Europe and North America averaged 24 days. But a trip on the new steamships reduced travel time to 15 days. The duration of the western voyage was even more dramatically reduced. The voyage consumed a lengthy 34 days under sail, but the new steamships cut that time by half, delivering their passengers and cargo to North American ports in 17 days.

As improved transportation systems were speeding plant material and horticulturists back and forth between counties, countries and continents, new communication systems were simultaneously being developed. The horticultural word was spreading further afield and into more homes than ever before.

In 1798, Nicholas Robert invented the first web papermaking machine in France which was later improved by the Fourdrinier brothers. By 1830, a team of two men and two girls could turn out no less than 24 miles of paper daily. The newly introduced steam-driven printing presses consumed this mountain of paper with untiring voraciousness. Finally, books, magazines and newspapers could be distributed widely and sold cheaply. At last, printed material was within the budget of the common man.

According to an 1840 census, there were 1400 papers and periodicals in circulation in that year within the U.S. alone. And those periodicals obviously reached an eager public—The New York *Sun* boasted a circulation of 40,000 daily readers. That growth rate continued unabated throughout the era. *The Ladies' Floral Cabinet*, which owed its birth to the new and inexpensive paper/printing boom, reported that in the years 1883 and 1884 no fewer than 1600 periodicals were born. And no class benefited from this form of cheap education more fully than the middle class. The newly founded public libraries, filled with books, magazines and newspapers freely available to the citizens, richly deserved their designation as "the poor man's college".

Of course, the proliferating horticultural societies and nursery businesses were eager to exploit this effective means of reaching an augmented mass market. In the 1830s and '40s, several horticultural magazines came into print including A. J. Downing's *The Horticulturist*, Thomas Hibbert and Robert Buist's

American Flower Garden Directory and Charles Mason Hovey's *Magazine of Horticulture*. They were the forerunners of a myriad of similar publications. In fact, by 1860, no fewer than 40 horticultural periodicals were in circulation.

But the spectacular increase in the extent and speed of communication was not confined to the public media. The horticultural word was also being disseminated through the mail service, which was equally indebted to steam for its rising prominence. Special mail and cargo carrying steamships began making regular runs across the Atlantic, keeping horticulturists abreast of happenings, introductions and discoveries in Europe. Letters were also flying to and fro between North Americans. By the 1830s, the Eastern states had developed a reliable mail system. And, as settlers pushed into the western frontiers, the Postal Service moved westward with them, linking the Atlantic and the Pacific. However, early in the era, not everyone agreed that the effort to settle or communicate with the Wild West was worthwhile. Daniel Webster was a formidable opponent of the Senate Bill which proposed the expansion of frontier posts. "What do we want with this vast, worthless area?" he ranted.

Although Daniel Webster swore that he would never vote a single penny from the public treasury "to place the Pacific Coast one inch nearer Boston than it is now," the Bill eventually passed without Webster's support. And, by 1861, *The Press* of Philadelphia was jubilantly proclaiming the arrival of the first letter from the West Coast via overland mail. "We were shown last evening... the first letter received in this city by overland mail under the new arrangement of a daily mail to and from California... being 22 days on the route."

The marching order of the Victorians was clearly "Progress," and there was no resisting the tide. By mid-century, the technological strides of the era had transformed the lifestyle of the common man. The citizenry had grown accustomed to change. They looked back at their forefather's circumstances and gloated over the improvements that modern genius had wrought. Naturally, the newly born magazines were quick to extol the blessings of progress. In 1851, *Scientific American* gleefully recounted the highlights of the first half century,

> We live in an age of wonders, and the last half of the century has witnessed a succession of the most mighty events and the most astounding discoveries which have ever been made. If in 1800 there were no steamships in the world, where is the country now where they are not seen? If the steamship has revolutionized communication by river and sea, the locomotive has done more to revolutionize travel by land... There cannot be less than 20,250 miles of railroad in operation in Europe and America.

On the surface, the general population appeared to respond to the profound changes of the era with wholehearted support. However, an undercurrent of doubt flowed beneath the prevailing enthusiasm. No one questioned that progress was inevitable, but everyone worried about its ramifications. Where would it all end? Would they be forced to pay for the luxuries of progress? And would the price be extracted from the warm bosom of the family? The citizens of the 19th Century had an awesome number of questions and painfully few answers.

The housewife's plight was particularly problematic. In that fast-paced world, she could not be sure where she would be tomorrow, what she would be doing, or how she would be doing it. The only certainty was change: Things would definitely be different.

Anxiety lay beneath the rejoicing. And, as the era advanced and the pace accelerated, the feeling of uneasiness increased proportionally. Everyone welcomed change, but most people also felt the inevitable pressure that accompanies alterations. The world was moving forward so rapidly that there was hardly sufficient time to take stock of it all. "Life at High Pressure", a panic-stricken essay penned by William Rathbone Greg in 1875, attempted to put the prevailing mood into words. He characterized Victorian existence as life "without leisure and without pause—a life of haste—above all a life of excitement such as haste inevitably involves—a life so full . . . that we have no time to reflect where we have been and whither we intend to go."

The Rev. C. L. Dodgson, alias Lewis Carroll, must have been plagued by similar pangs of inadequacy while attempting to keep abreast of the times. He described the prevailing fatigue with typical allegorical subtlety in an oft-quoted scene from *Alice Through the Looking Glass*. The Red Queen and Alice had been running at high speed for an uncomfortably long time. And yet, the scenery around Alice had not moved. Exhausted, they finally stopped to rest when Alice took stock of the situation.

> Alice looked around her in great surprise, "Why, I do believe we've been under this tree for the whole time! Everything is just as it was!"
>
> "Of course it is," said the Queen, "What would you have it?"
>
> "Well, in our country," said Alice, still panting a little, "you'd generally get to somewhere else—if you ran very fast for a long time as we've been doing."
>
> "A slow sort of country!" said the Queen. "Now, *here*, you see, it takes all of the running *you* can do, to keep in the same place. If you want to get somewhere else, you must run at least twice as fast as that."
>
> "I'd rather not try, please!" said Alice.

Apparently, our British cousins were also feeling the same growing pains that we were experiencing. But the British had developed a means of partially pacifying their inclination to panic in the face of unrelenting change. Citizens of the United Kingdom traditionally looked toward their Monarch as a source of solace in an age of flux. Solid, stalwart and strong, Queen Victoria was a bastion of comfort. If all else failed, the Monarch would remain.

Unfortunately, we had no comparable role model to turn toward on this side of the Atlantic. As a consequence, North Americans turned inward, clinging to the family and its sheltering "Home, Sweet Home."

The home was a buffer to barricade the family from the rush of the outside world, and the front parlor was the home's most impenetrable component. Dark, stern, clad in heavy furniture and draped in yards of thick fabric, the parlor presented a very impressive and impregnable façade against the uncertain world outside.

When sheltered in their parlor, the family could hold the world at arm's length. And, hopefully, when viewing the world from a distance, they could sort out the good elements from the bad.

But, life within the home was also changing, impelled by the forces of technological change. The new technology, with its railroads and magazines, was drawing the world closer to the family while, at the same time, it was spiriting the family out of its home into the world. The structure of daily life was being transformed and the very roots of the family were being shaken. North Americans, with their fluid social structure, felt the pangs of novelty even more acutely than their British counterparts. In a democracy, any man could become President, or a millionaire, or a vagrant for that matter. James Fenimore Cooper described the situation with characteristic pith in a letter to Horatio Greenough, the American sculptor,

> You are in a country in which every man swaggers and talks, knowledge or no knowledge; brains or no brains; taste or no taste. They are all *ex nato* connoisseurs, politicians, religionists and every man's equal and all men's betters.

In America, there was always hope for a better future, especially in a period of change. Naturally, when the door of opportunity opened, the 19th Century youth rushed in. They recognized the possibility for self-betterment, and eagerly embraced it. The era offered the promise of a different life for those who possessed the courage needed to leave the parental farm behind. Many young people were clearly in possession of that courage.

Fortunately, the city-ward shift in population came when machinery could replace field hands. A steam plow from Jonathan Periam's *The Home and Farm Manual.*

With the industrialization of the country came a major city-ward shift in the population. The great metropolises of the country matured during the Victorian Era. As the continuing flood of inventions created jobs in the cities, farmers' sons left their quiet, rural homes to earn better wages in the factories. In 1850, 6.2 million Americans lived in towns and cities. By 1900, the urban and suburban population had risen to 30.1 million. Certainly, this increase in population was due in part to the massive immigration which was simultaneously occurring. However, native Americans migrating from the farm made up a large percentage of those new urbanites. Fortunately, they left the land at a time when new farm machinery could effectively replace their hands in the field.

That city-ward migration shook the foundations of family life. The roaring railroads and the puffing steamboats were tolerable, and even enjoyable innovations. But, when they threatened the home, suddenly the Age of Transition and all of its ramifications took on a personal and fearful meaning.

Many journalists and moralists foresaw the wave of the future and predicted its effect on the family. They warned mothers to draw their children close lest they be snatched away by the city, which was considered to be the root of all evil. *The Ladies' Floral Cabinet* was among those who struck an alarmist's note alerting the mothers in the audience to the out-going tide,

> Why are all the farm-houses so deserted? Where are the bright young creatures who should be the light and joy of cottage homes? . . . Look for them not amid rural haunts, but at the railroad termini which open to the great cities . . .

The Ladies' Floral Cabinet was not alone in its cry of panic. Nearly every horticultural, agricultural and ladies' journal adopted a similar stance. But they fought a losing battle. The city drew people with a magnetic attraction. They left their rural haunts despite the admonitions of their parents, and against the advice of most religious leaders. The tastemakers of the times were ambivalent about the city. The city was not considered to be a healthy environment. Even Frederick Law Olmsted, a strong proponent of city development, admitted to doubt about the long-term effects of the new cities. He warned that "the average length of the life of mankind in towns has been less than in the country, and . . . the average amount of disease and misery and vice and crime has been much greater in towns."

And yet, despite these vices, Olmsted and some of his contemporaries found many reasons to recommend city life. In his 1870 proposal for a public park in the city of Boston, Olmsted explained the attraction of the city. Quoting from a survey of professional seamstresses taken by the New York *Tribune*, Olmsted concluded that the attraction was primarily,

> A frantic desire to escape from the dull lives which they have seen before them in the country, a craving for recreation, especially for some companionship in yielding to playful girlish impulses, innocent in themselves, drives more young women to the town than anything else.

The new railroads allowed farm folk to sample the city when they came into town to enjoy its shops and markets, buying goods previously produced on the homestead. And, once given a taste of the exciting city, there was no keeping the children back on the farm. Before long, the flight of young people from the country became a cause for alarm, despite the introduction of new labor saving farm machinery. It became increasingly difficult to find help in the home or fields. Olmsted noted that " . . . only the poorest, who cannot find employment in the city, will come to the country, and these as soon as they have got a few dollars ahead, are crazy to get back to the town."

Eventually, the family's inevitable dispersal became an accepted fact of life. Mothers no longer fought the tide, but faced the idea with resignation. As youngsters reached adulthood, it was assumed that they would leave their childhood farm behind. Therefore, male or female, children were taught to withstand the evil temptations inherent to the cities. Victorian mothers had great faith in the strength of "moral fiber." If raised correctly, a child might face the changing world and remain morally untainted.

Of course, it is easiest to instill an abstract idea when symbols are employed. The most frequently invoked symbol used to represent the simple pleasures of family life and the warmth of familiar faces was embodied in the crackling, dancing, open hearth. The cozy fireplace of "Home, Sweet Home", with its attentive,

A cozy fireplace from Clarence Cook's *The House Beautiful.*

cohesive family gathered closely around, was a picture employed long after the hearth was rendered functionally obsolete by the adoption of stoves. There was something inherently good about the hypnotic open fire. It inspired everyone within its influence to pause, day-dream and escape the pace of the times. It warmed the hands and the heart. When the family was gathered around the fire, all was well.

Second in popularity only to the concept of the fireside was the symbol of nature. If the city was evil, then its wickedness was due, in part, to the absence of nature within its confines. Nature had long since established its reputation as the embodiment of goodness. In fact, all the creations of the Almighty were inherently good, it was only in straying from the natural order of things that people courted the forces of evil. And plant life was the work of the Creator in its purest form. If a person lived intimately with plants, the goodness of nature would certainly become instilled in him. The argument was appealingly simple. Surely, the remedy for the temptations of the city lay in nature.

Resigned to the inevitable exodus city-ward, rural folk were determined that their off-spring would not leave the farm without a strong affection for nature. "Don't cultivate your farms and gardens and neglect your children," became the battle-cry. It was essential to expose youth, at a tender age, to floral beauty.

However, the definition of floral beauty was also being refined. Tastes were growing more sophisticated. The farmyard, with its austere charm and unadorned simplicity was undoubtedly a reflection of nature in the raw, but it was no longer considered to be a thing of Beauty. However full of nature the farmer's fields might be, they were not of sufficient inspiration to instill goodness in anyone—or, at least, that was the prevailing opinion voiced by 19th Century magazines. *Vick's Monthly* patiently explained that inspiration and beauty were not to be found in acres of corn or rows of potatoes. Beauty never appeared accidentally—it came only as a result of careful and deliberate planning and planting. It came by invitation only. Beauty was found by those who beautified their homes. And further, according to *Vick's Monthly*, the rural folk were in sore need of coaching on the topic. Farms were in need of improvement,

> There is very little attempt here to beautify with flowers, or vines, or shrubbery. There may be, perhaps, a few who know nothing of these ornamentals. This is to be deplored, as there are so many hardy shrubs, vines, and bulbs that would be ornamental in such places, and would require very little care . . . These things, so simple and yet so beautiful, are not only a constant pleasure to the children while growing up on the farm, but their fragrance comes to them in after years, when their feet are weary far from the old farmstead.

So, with the love of nature firmly instilled in their breasts, the youth packed their bags and travelled city-ward, leaving the country life forever. There was no going back. For, if rural folks were convinced that the city was evil, the inhabitants of the cities were equally certain that life in the country was a thing of thin gruel. They had discovered a better, more enlightened way of life. The *Overland Monthly* gave voice to the prevailing opinion of 1870, "only an inferior class of people can be induced to live out of towns. There is something in the country which repels men. In the city alone they nourish the juices of life."

Although the affection for the old homestead may have turned sour, the love of nature stood firm. The new urbanites were convinced of the city's superiority, but they still found it difficult to exist in an environment so totally devoid of nature. They wanted to own a piece of nature, to work it, and to mold it into a form which would reflect the fashionable concept of Beauty. They strove to possess the best of both worlds: a place where they might enjoy the sophistication and salaries of the city, while experiencing the Goodness of nature as well.

If the railroads had nurtured the cities, they also fathered the suburbs. No sooner had the Victorians reached the cities, then they fled from its crowded, polluted, noisy streets. They moved into the suburbs, an opportunity made possible by the newly laid tracks linking the city with its outskirts.

The railroad allowed the citizenry to reap the benefits of the city daily, but it also provided escape at day's end. Men could easily travel from the bustle of the city into the quiet, tree-lined, nature-filled streets in the surrounding towns. Invention became the servant of aesthetics, as well as the slave of industry.

It seemed as though everyone was willing to make the commute. The suburbs proliferated. And the tastemakers revelled. In 1858, *The Gardener's Monthly* extolled the manifold virtues inherent in the suburbs,

> Since the introduction of railroads . . . a very large proportion of the population of our large cities have sought relief from the noise and heat of the city in the many beautiful, cool, and shady retreats by which our cities are surrounded. Boston has its Roxbury, Dorchester, Cambridge, &c.; New York its Yonkers, Harlem and both banks of the noble Hudson; Philadelphia its Frankfort, Germantown, and the banks of the rivers Delaware and Schuylkill . . . all of them abounding in elegant and, for the most part, tasteful villas. In these "homes of taste", far from the many temptations and dissipation of city life, and under the refining influences of horticulture, music and social intercourse are being trained and educated the children of our most influential citizens.

Not only did the suburbs provide an escape from the hustle and bustle of the city, they also afforded the opportunity to work the soil. The beauty of the suburbs lay partly in the fact that nature could be enjoyed to its fullest. But, the suburbs differed dramatically from the farm. Nature was no longer an adversary, it was an ally. A man could toy with nature and its design without fearing the consequences. Nothing of earth-shattering importance was at stake. No one would go hungry if the tomato crop failed, or if a hedge of boxwood was planted instead of a stand of blueberries. The suburbs introduced the concept of gardening for pleasure in North America. And, as Frank J. Scott, a contemporary landscape architect explained, the key to suburban gardening lay in the fact that, unlike farming, it was practiced in moderation,

A tree-lined suburban street.

One panacea for the town-sick business man who longs for a rural home, whether from ennui of the monotonousness of business life, or from the higher nature-loving soul that is in him, is to take country life as a famishing man should take food—in very small quantities.

Gardening gained an entirely new status with the coming of the suburbs. Gardens were beautiful and healthful, and now they were pleasurable as well. The possession of a fine garden became one of the goals of successful males. According to Charles Dudley Warner, author of *My Summer in the Garden*, and a particularly colorful Victorian, the garden offered a man salvation as well as freedom,

The love of dirt is among the earliest passions, as it is the latest. Mud-pies gratify one of our first and best instincts. So long as we are dirty, we are pure. Fondness for the ground comes back to a man after he has run the round of business and pleasure, eaten dirt, and sown wild-oats.

Women were also allowed to sample the pleasures of gardening. And, naturally, they took that opportunity to cultivate a little Beauty for the family's benefit. Whether out of choice or compulsion, a woman's place was in the flower garden, and not in the vegetable patch where her husband toiled. And, apparently, the arrangement was an amicable one for both partners.

As women's interaction with flowers increased, so did their affection for blossoms. Eventually, women began to feel the first rustlings of a desire to bring plants indoors over the winter. However, whether or not women loved flowers, it is certain that plants would have remained steadfastly in Mother Nature's care outdoors had it not been for the arrival of labor saving household inventions.

When the family moved from its rural home, men were freed from the pressures of maintaining a farm. They were no longer the slaves of livestock and crops which monopolized every minute of their waking hours and frequently infringed on their sleeping time as well. The city employee worked by the company's clock, not to the measure of nature's call. When the whistle blew at the end of the working day, a gentleman was free to pursue his own pleasures.

But housework was never done. An overlooked speck of dust was invariably lurking behind the sofa, and the rug could always benefit from a shaking out. Housekeeping remained arduous, full-time work throughout the 19th Century. And yet, the female's burden was significantly lightened by the arrival of new technology in her home. Her job was still full-time, but the overtime hours were reduced.

Even before inventors put their minds to easing the feminine work load, an invaluable tool entered the home. As printing became less expensive, a bevy of housekeeping manuals appeared on the scene filled with detailed instructions on how to perform household chores efficiently. The advice was clear, orderly, and presented by experienced and practical matrons. Through those books, housewives gained a sense of camaraderie with other kindred spirits. Housekeeping manuals became important sources of information for every wife and mother, but they were absolutely indispensible to the novice homemaker who might otherwise spend years developing an efficient regimen.

One of the most popular and comprehensive of these manuals was authored by Catherine Ward Beecher. Written in 1868, its soothing introduction must have been music to the harried female ear,

> Neither your parents, teachers, or husband have *trained* you for the place you fill, nor furnished you with the knowledge or assistance needed to enable you to meet all the complicated and untried duties of your lot. A young woman who has never had the care of a child, never done housework, never learned the numberless processes that are indispensable to keep domestic affairs in regular order, never done anything but attend books, drawing, and music at school, such an one is as unprepared to take charge of a nursery, kitchen, and family establishment, as she is to take charge of a *Man-of-War*.

But sympathy and advice alone could not ease the housewife's burden, she needed new tools to shoulder some of the labor. Fortunately, those tools arrived on her doorstep *en masse* with the coming of the Age of Transition.

When the Victorian Era opened, women were no longer the slaves of the open hearth with its unpredictable moods. They no longer dipped candles or spun their own thread. New technology had rendered those major chores outdated by the late 1830s.

As the era progressed, other inventions appeared. In 1846, Elias Howe designed a workable sewing machine, a little invention that promised to revolutionize the world. Initially, his invention was more readily accepted in Europe than in North America. But Isaac Singer soon remedied that situation by deploying an army of 3,000 salesmen to work the virgin territory on this side of the Atlantic.

Another labor saver to help turn the tide of housework was developed in 1825 when Thomas Kensett preserved oysters and fruit in a tin canister. Although North American women did not jump to adopt the new canning process, it proved its worth dramatically when the army successfully fed the Union troops on canned goods throughout the Civil War.

The invention of the ice cutter paired with the development of an improved design for ice storage houses also had a dramatic effect on the home. After the system of ice acquisition and storage was perfected in 1827, the cost of ice fell by 60%, making ice affordable for most families. Finally, perishable food could be preserved throughout the summer months.

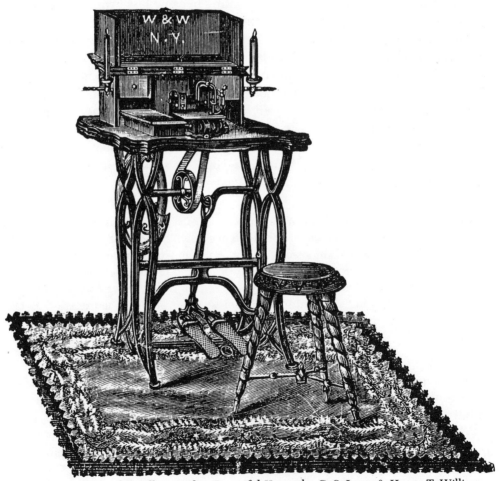

An early sewing machine illustrated in *Beautiful Homes* by C. S. Jones & Henry T. Williams.

APPLE PARER.

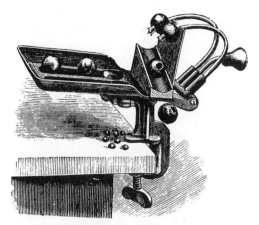

CHERRY STONER.

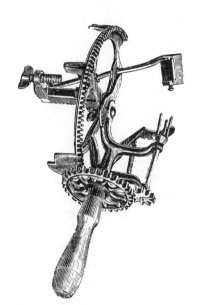

SLICER.

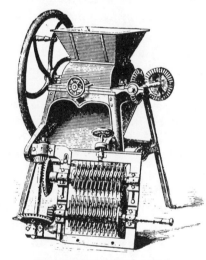

IMPROVED ICE CRUSHER.

POTATO PARER.

CAHOON BROAD-CAST SOWER.

Six new inventions featured in the Women's Pavilion at the Centennial Exposition.

As the century progressed, enterprising and imaginative inventors kept the home well stocked with novelties, both large and small. Less dramatic, but equally helpful, were the endless supply of small, labor saving gadgets which inundated the kitchen. When the Centennial Exposition at Fairmount Park opened its doors in 1876 to provide a showcase of the century's inventions, exhibitors proudly unveiled the fruits of 19th Century domestic progress. On display in the Women's Pavilion were such little wonders as the Lightning Apple Corer, the Family Cherry Stoner, the Improved Ice Crusher as well as the Bay State Paring and Slicing Machine, to mention only a handful of the miraculous devices on exhibition to tempt the lady of the house.

She was duly tempted. Every woman longed for a personal collection of gadgets. And she often indulged in buying a few. Although trains, telegraphs and steamboats all had their vociferous opponents, even hardcore traditionalists rarely opposed the introduction of housekeeping aids. A clean, well-organized home was a happy home. And so, the newly proliferating women's magazines almost invariably came out in support of household machinery. In 1872, *The Household*, a periodical published briefly in Vermont, began an article on machinery with apparent mixed emotions,

> Her daily life runs on wheels, and a little machine oil is substituted for the old-fashioned "elbow grease." By these untiring and dumb (if not exactly noiseless), domestic helps, her yarn can be spun, her clothes stitched, washed, wrung and mangled.

But, to the relief of all, the article's conclusion fully supported the use of the housekeeper's new helpers, offering this advice to readers, "Make some sacrifice of expensive amusements, or outward adorning, in order to procure as much labor-saving machinery as can be afforded."

The new machinery effectively freed some leisure time for the grateful housewife. But, in the Age of Transition, even leisure time became a burden. Instead of soothing the pangs of concern inflicted by momentum, those newly vacant minutes added to the prevailing anxiety. What should they do with those empty hours? George Eliot mourned the loss of innocence with her fellow females,

> Even idleness is eager now,—eager for amusement; prone to excursions—trains, art-museums, periodical literature and exciting novels; prone even to scientific theorizing and cursory peeps through microscopes.

Women suffered from a particularly confounding dilemma. Those leisure hours which were a much-deserved godsend to the lady of the house, were not so eagerly welcomed by her male partner. Husbands were suspicious of those unfilled moments. Surely, idle hands would do the devil's work. Moralists fretted about the future of the "weaker sex". No one would rest easily until a suitable substitute was found to occupy those bits of time once filled by housework.

Rather than causing an upheaval in tradition, the 19th Century female chose to take the path of least resistance to her ultimate liberation. She merely reallocated her time, finding acceptable pursuits in and around the home to fill the leisure hours. She turned to nature. What could be more laudable than spending one's free time and talents cultivating plants and providing the family with an abundance of beneficial influences?

In choosing horticulture as a hobby, the nature-loving wife and mother was remaining true to her traditional role (much to her husband's relief) and, at the same time, she was broadening her horizons. Although the menfolk might debunk the importance of that new-found hobby and mumble about the dollars spent on horticultural supplies, for the most part, they were consoled. Julius Heinrich, a contemporary nurseryman and author, voiced the typical male reaction,

> Probably no other occupation or amusement is more innocent in itself, or more devoid of injury or annoyance to others, than the cultivation of flowers. The pleasures arising from the culture of flowers, are harmless and pure . . .

At first, this newly adopted pastime was practiced out-of-doors. The beauty of the suburbs lay partly in the fact that it allowed both Charles Dudley Warner and his sister Polly "To own a bit of ground, to scratch it with a hoe, to plant seeds and watch their renewal of life—this is the commonest delight of the race."

Women lavished on their flowerbeds a tender loving care and determination akin to that which men spent coaxing forth the fruits of their vegetable patches. Although flower beds produced no economically important crop, they were nonetheless an important element of the home scene. Everyone in the family was encouraged to participate in the garden, and the work was considered to be healthy as well as therapeutic. The youngsters, especially, were sent to play amongst the flowers.

Soon, it was not sufficient to hand the children their own set of gardening tools and point them in the direction of the garden. The gardening season was brief—too brief, in fact, to produce permanently beneficial effects on the family.

Houseplants entered the scene. The entry of plants into the parlor came in answer to many of the pressing needs of the day. Most importantly, it calmed the anxiety of the era. Houseplants symbolized a conviction that nature, with its inherent goodness, would prevail against all the evils and pain of transition. Flowers are cheerful and hopeful, they speak of the renewal of life, they are the antithesis of evil. When change was awesomely omnipresent, threatening life and morals, the family could look toward their plants as the embodiment of the purity of nature. And, thus inspired, they gained assurance that the eventual outcome of their topsy turvy existence would be Good.

Although women had originally embraced horticultural pursuits primarily as an antidote for leisure-time boredom, the hobby was soon magnified in importance. A windowsill bereft of houseplants symbolized a barrenness within the home. Good, moral people grew houseplants while poor, unenlightened souls

Flowers calmed the anxiety of the era. Illustration from Margaret Sangster's *Home Life made Beautiful*.

did not. Most citizens of the 19th Century were accustomed to building their lives based on such broad generalizations.

If indoor horticulture was first practiced to fill the leisure hours of women who enjoyed spare time, it was eventually pursued by all, regardless of whether they enjoyed leisure time or not. Growing houseplants was seen as an important investment of time and effort, to be wedged into the busiest schedule. Most notably, magazines urged women to grow plants when their children were young and impressionable. *The Ladies' Floral Cabinet* wrote,

No doubt it is oftenest in childless homes, or those in which the children are nearly grown, that we see large and flourishing collections of plants . . . But not only does the mother, who forgoes the culture of flowers for the children's sake, lose the interest and enjoyment it might afford her busy life, but the children themselves lose something from their childhood which cannot well be spared.

Naturally, indoor gardening gained its most enthusiastic following in the city. The residents of the city were acutely aware of the prevailing opinion concerning the metropolis and its morality. If they could stave off the devil by merely introducing a few flowers into their parlors, then they were more than willing to adopt that easy and inexpensive means to salvation. Even if the project entailed knocking out a wall or two and adding a small window greenhouse or bay window, the investment was negligible in view of its rewards.

Botany was warmly welcomed in the city. The appreciation of nature instilled in the youthful hearts of rural expatriots was not forgotten. In fact, those new urbanites were deeply homesick for the sight of trees, fish and birds. At first, a few plants on the windowsill satisfied their hunger for nature. But, eventually, the plant alcove was expanded until it contained all sorts of natural ingredients distilled into a minuscule environment. In fact, John Claudius Loudon, a celebrated British horticulturist, went so far as to design a window apiary where guests could sip their afternoon tea and watch as the industrious insects went about their work. If nature they must have, then nature they would get—with a vengeance.

As horticulture entered the city, it sparked the birth of a bevy of plant-inspired inventions. Most particularly, plants piqued the female imagination. While men were preoccupied inventing new reapers and improving mowing machines, women were busy designing contraptions for their houseplants.

Here was a chance to exercise the female's innate sense of creativity. The Women's Pavilion at the Centennial Exposition at Fairmount Park featured a popular display of inventions by American women. No fewer than 74 unique items, most of which were designed to assist in the essential daily chores of housekeeping, were amassed for the public's scrutiny. But, interestingly, the award committee chose to honor the designer of a plant stand with a prize.

Another major attraction at the Centennial Exposition was the magnificent Horticultural Hall. Inside that prodigious building was a collection of inventions designed to astound and entice every gentleman in the crowd. The newest farm machinery was on display including all of the state-of-the-art reapers, sowers and mowers the century had produced. However, even in that building, the accompanying wives were not neglected. Several commercial exhibits in the Hall were devoted to the gentle art of window gardening and to promoting new fads associated with the cultivation of flowers. On display were terra cotta pots, an array of ferneries, as well as plant tables of all sorts. But, the item which completely stole the show was the newly introduced aquarium. Racine Manufacturing Company of Wisconsin explained the purpose of that novelty from Great Britain,

These articles are specially adapted for the home cultivation of flowers during the winter season, and the aquaria are beautiful ornaments for the home, and a perpetual source of amusement and instruction. They have the peculiar advantage of making us acquainted with forms and habits of animated existence which are commonly hid from our inspection. Thus their influence upon the family circle is wholesome and elevating, tending constantly to awaken in all the members both young and old, an increased love for the contemplation of the wondrous skill and wisdom of the great Creator.

In addition to playing host to a bevy of new, plant-related paraphernalia, the home was witnessing a multitude of major changes, each abetting the smooth addition of plant care into the daily schedule and rendering the home environment more suitable to the cultivation of plants. As the century progressed, more inventions which indirectly benefitted houseplants appeared in the home.

A great moment for people and plants alike occurred when middle class homes saw the introduction of indoor plumbing in the 1870s. Municipal water supplies were pressed into operation in the 1830s, although in many cases the sources of supply were woefully insufficient and often unsanitary. Most gardeners relied primarily on rainwater until the latter part of the century. However, when indoor plumbing was improved, a great deal of bucket lugging back and forth was avoided.

Another product of the new technology was thinner, better quality and less

Plant stands on display.

A "rustic aquarium" from *The Gardener's Monthly*.

expensive glass. Traditionally, America trailed Europe in the quality of its glass. An improved glass pressing process had originated in the United States in 1826. However, France and Belgium succeeded in producing a far superior product than we could manufacture until after the Civil War. Of course, quality glass was a crucial element in providing plants with a suitable indoor environment. And, as glass became less expensive and more common, it was employed in many plant-related contrivances such as aquariums and terrariums. Eventually, greenhouses and conservatories would also benefit from the prevalence of inexpensive glass.

Simultaneously, heating systems were improving. Although no one would dare to argue the virtues of the open hearth's aesthetic superiority, the enclosed stove was obviously more efficient for practical purposes, hence its broad acceptance. By the 1860s, when architect Henry Hudson Holly wrote *Country Seats and Modern Dwellings*, central heating was already well established in many homes. Hot air systems, fueled by a central furnace and circulated through ducting systems, were the most common method of central heat. However, Holly advocated the use of steam as a healthier alternative. Apparently, however, his ideas were treated as the rantings of a maverick, and therefore met with potent opposition. In his book, he conceded that "Nervous people might, with some degree of reason, protest against the presence of a steam-boiler in their cellars." In time, fears were soothed, and steam became the system of choice in North

An ornate aquarium for "the home of taste".

America by the 1880s. Houseplants reaped the benefits from that more humid source of heat.

When Henry Hudson Holly wrote his popular two-volume book, *Country Seats and Modern Dwellings* in the 1860s, electricity was already being harnessed for new and imaginative uses. Although he may have been a maverick, Holly was prophetic in his foresight. He predicted with incredible prescience some of the future uses of electricity,

> A guest arriving at the porter's lodge would be signalled in advance, and the gardener, could not allow the greenhouse to cool, on a freezing night, without this little sentinel proclaiming the neglect. In fact, we may soon expect to see electricity so trained to our domestic service that it will announce when the baby wakes up, or the pudding is done.

Twenty years after his book was published, the incandescent light bulb was incorporated into domestic architecture, effectively rendering nighttime hours into time for work or leisure.

As the era progressed to its end, technology kept up its frenzied pace. More inventions arrived on the scene to aid in the dissemination of horticultural knowledge. One little machine, whose value was undoubtedly appreciated by horticultural writers, was the typewriter. Finally, the menial labor of writing was lessened by the type-machine, as it was then called. However, the machine required a little perfecting before it was actually a help rather than a hindrance. Mark Twain claimed to have purchased the first typewriter on the market in 1873. And he did not harbor a very high opinion of its value,

> That early machine was full of caprices, full of defects—devilish ones. It had as many immoralities as the machine of to-day has virtues. After a year or two I found that it was degrading my character, so I thought I would give it to Howells [William Dean Howells, humorist and critic]. He was reluctant, for he was suspicious of novelties and unfriendly toward them . . . but I persuaded him. He had great confidence in me, and I got him to believe things about the machine that I did not believe myself. He took it home to Boston, and my morals began to improve, but his have never recovered.

Mark Twain also took credit for being "the first person in the world that ever had a telephone in his house for practical purposes." Although he proudly boasted of being the machine's first private owner (a telephone was installed in his Hartford home in 1876), he despised the talking instrument with a passion.

Mark Twain was extraordinarily precocious in his adoption of new inventions. In fact, his telephone was installed in the same year that Alexander Graham Bell patented the new machine. Telephones would not make their debut in the average home until the 20th Century. Meanwhile, most people realized the benefits derived from the rapid worldwide deployment of the telegraph.

The telegraph began to unite the nation as early as 1877, and people rushed to send messages through wires that linked city to city. In that year, the *Scientific American* documented the existence of 780 telegraph machines. By February of 1885, there were no fewer than 325,574 instruments busily relaying messages.

However, not everyone agreed that the new technology was a good thing. Henry David Thoreau not only voiced skepticism about rail travel, he was also opposed to the effort to wire the world with telegraph. He wrote,

> We are in great haste to construct a magnetic telegraph from Maine to Texas; but Maine and Texas, it may be, have nothing important to communicate . . . We are eager to tunnel under the Atlantic and bring the Old World some weeks nearer the New; but perchance the first news that will leak through into the broad, flapping American ear will be that Princess Adelaide has the whooping cough.

History proved him wrong. The people of Maine and Texas, as well as in Philadelphia and London, did have a great deal to say to one another, and not least about horticultural matters. And, with the aid of the new technology, their words, letters, wisdom and botanical discoveries flew back and forth as never before. In fact, the Age of Transition ushered plants into the parlor.

CHAPTER III

THE RISE OF HORTICULTURE

MANY TERMS OF ENDEARMENT were attached to various elements of the 19th Century. For Mark Twain, the century climaxed in the Gilded Age. To Edith Wharton, it was the Age of Innocence. And it was known to the art world as the Dawn of Impressionism. Ernest H. Wilson, the great plant explorer, dubbed it the Age of Travel, while other contemporary writers saw it under a variety of guises including the Age of Veneer and the Age of Optimism. But, to Shirley Hibberd, author of the popular *Rustic Adornments for Homes of Taste*, it was the Age of Toys. He was not alluding to the bounty of new inventions which had suddenly besieged the world, but rather, he was speaking primarily of the new-found fascination for horticulture.

New fashions rarely arrive unannounced. For those astute observers who intently monitor the murmurings in the air, it is always apparent which way the wind is blowing. Long before ornamental plants were elevated to the position of cohabitants in the front parlor, a discrete but deliberate chain of events was slowly but inevitably leading to that grand moment. Although social and technological changes played a prominent role in the preparation of the scene, the entrance was actually fathered by a unique series of circumstances in the horticultural world.

Dozens of random botanical and scientific discoveries preceded the entrance of houseplants. For Americans, whose traditional interaction with plant life was agricultural, it was a gradual awakening. The early murmurs of the 19th Century horticultural renaissance were first heard overseas, and only later echoed on this side of the Atlantic. Concern with matters horticultural had been growing in Europe for at least a century, but only in the 1830s were Americans finally prepared to listen.

With the beginning of the Victorian Era, America was no longer the solitary, introspective country of Colonial times. Quite abruptly, America had come of age. In their youth, the Colonies spent their energy taming the wilderness of the

46

An Algerian queen immersed in gardening.

continent, completely engrossed in self-preservation and unable to devote time or consideration to any endeavors other than utilitarian enterprises. With the dawning of the 19th Century, the East Coast was sufficiently tamed to afford inhabitants with an easier existence, and the advancing technology of the subsequent years provided labor saving inventions further alleviating the daily burden of the populace.

Life had eased, and the average citizen was able to find a few precious moments for pleasure—a luxury unknown in previous generations. Finally, there was leisure time to enjoy the home, the parlor and the family. There was time to contemplate less pressing matters than the necessities of survival. There was also time to think—and, where there is thought, there is also doubt. Inevitably, American gardeners found moments to compare their horticultural accomplishments with those of Europe and Asia.

Popular magazines of a culturally uplifting nature were, by the 1830s, flowing from the presses in ever increasing numbers. Dozens of periodicals, containing colorful tales of the tropics illustrated with intricate drawings depicting such esoteric themes as the epiphytic vegetation of Barbados, the forests of Nicaragua, or the overhanging rock formations of the Central Province of Ceylon, had sprung into life to entertain and educate the American family. Subscribers were able to scrutinize detailed engravings representing the delicate features of an exotic Algerian queen watering terrace plants from a jug balanced precariously on her veiled shoulder. Or they could gaze upon drawings of European nobility disporting themselves in elaborate formal gardens.

Victorians were intrigued by any fragment of knowledge dealing with the secrets of foreign lands. The jungles of Africa, the deserts of Australia and the mountains of the Andes—all were of interest to people eager to attain worldliness.

Although Victorian Americans were curious about all worldly topics, they were particularly intrigued by news of their European peers. A competitive relationship, almost akin to sibling rivalry, developed between Britain and America. Competition raged on nearly every economic, social, political and cultural front. However, in the increasingly significant realm of horticulture, America was very much Britain's inferior. This obvious deficiency precluded any notions of competition. So, in matters horticultural, American remained the obedient students

Magazines and books brought news of the people and plants of distant lands such as this Turkish beauty pictured in Frances & Harriet Clark's *Our Journey Around the World*.

of their parental mentor. Britain set the standards, and America followed—at a somewhat lethargic pace.

Americans were embarrassingly slow in developing any semblance of interest in their gardens. Traditionally, Colonial gardens were simple affairs, devoted to providing the essentials of life. Little, if any, attention was paid to the aesthetic potential of a scene. In 1705, Robert Beverley, author of *The History and Present State of Virginia*, noted American disinterest in ornamental gardening as compared to the enthusiasm evident in Europe. He wrote, "A garden is nowhere soon made than ther . . . yet they han't many gardens in that country fit to bear the name gardens."

The first hint of design crept into American landscapes when gardens became more specialized and a separate plot was devoted to the cultivation of herbs. Herbs are handsome plants. Their physical attributes almost insensibly lead to the creation of a pattern. The American herb garden was at first a geometric, but simple affair, constructed with an eye only to practicality. And yet, the sections of the herb patch were traversed by more paths than ease of cultivation dictated. The colonists had obviously taken a cautious step toward ornamentation.

Throughout the 18th Century, American gardens continued to evolve, but at a sluggish pace. Gradually, flowers were incorporated into the garden, to be appreciated solely for their aesthetic value. However, by the end of the century, we could claim little in the way of progress in the planning of our gardens save for the single major step of dividing the flower and kitchen gardens. At last, ornamentals were given a bed of their own. The end-of-the-century flower garden may not have been as quaint or coddled as the corresponding English cottage garden, but the plot was obviously intended to please the eye. The ornamental garden provided a bright note in the yard, although it could never be accused of ostentation.

The early flower patch was situated in the front of the home, intended to greet visitors as they arrived. For its commanding position (both socially and physically), as well as its lack of utility, contemporary writers referred to that ornamental plot as the "parlor garden." Like its namesake in the interior of the home, the parlor garden was destined to evolve into an entity of some magnificence and of great importance. It marked the gradual trend from Puritan simplicity toward an era of embellishment. It was the beginning of a long journey along a slow and winding road.

With the exception of a few minor refinements, the gardens of the New World stood virtually stationary while the European landscape witnessed the arrival and departure of many continent-wide horticultural trends. By the 18th Century, England had completely abandoned the stiff symmetry of the "ancient system", with its neat but convoluted geometric beds, and embraced instead the cult of the "Picturesque" garden. The latter system was championed by the dynamic Lancelot "Capability" Brown, a man famous for his dramatic landscape overhauls.

The Picturesque landscape was created by moving earth to form hills and valleys studded with groupings of trees and traversed by waterways rerouted into serpentine contortions. All was designed to provide a series of dramatic scenes unfolding before the viewer enjoying the "pleasure grounds" on foot.

So radical was Brown's effect on the British landscape, that it provoked this anonymous quip. A gentleman is said to have approached "Capability" with the comment

> "Mr. Brown, I very earnestly desire that I may die before you."
> "Why so?" was Brown's reply.
> "Because I should like to see heaven before you have improved it."

Brown's artificially pastoral creations survived into the 1880s under the direction of his protégé, Humphrey Repton, whose main alteration to Brown's basic principles was to "prettify" the scene with the addition of flowers. Although this was but a slight modification, it proved to be most propitious. Repton's designs provided the opportunity to incorporate the new botanicals which botanists and plant explorers were retrieving from all parts of the world including North America. Ironically, Europeans discovered the ornamental value of many North Americans plants which were merely weeds to the settlers of the New World.

The reign of the Picturesque enjoyed a prolonged popularity in England. In time, the style evolved and began to degenerate into absurd flights of the designers' imagination. Artificial grottoes, craggy rock formations, hidden wild scenes and other imitations of nature at her most extreme were all incorporated into the formerly subdued Picturesque scene. Britain was clearly becoming bored with the prolonged reign of the Picturesque style. In fact, they were so bored that, when critics called for landscape reform, the public eagerly agreed.

The movement was led by John Claudius Loudon. Never a man to mince words, Loudon irreverently described Repton's typical creation as "a round lake, an open lawn and a copse of trees." However, the Picturesque landscape was so all-pervasive that more than mere sarcasm was required to create a change. Loudon finally resorted to a direct attack to win his battle. He pointed out the regimental aspects of Repton's so-called Picturesque creations, and then publicly extending his sympathy to any gentleman who had the misfortune of hiring Repton to improve his grounds. Loudon won his battle.

Having deposed Repton, J. C. Loudon took the throne to become one of the most influential voices in establishing Victorian taste. Although his main forum was in British gardening circles, his influence eventually floated across the Atlantic. His extensive writings were uniformly enthralling and his energies were boundless. At one point in his career, Loudon successfully edited four horticultural periodicals simultaneously. Inevitably, his clear vision of the nature of a fine landscape convinced the gardening public to replace the Picturesque style with his own "Gardenesque" design.

A garden, he argued, was by its very nature a man-made creation. Any attempt at "naturalness" was a contradiction in terms, and thus, bound to fail. It followed that a garden could be executed in a completely contrived design. Loudon's gardens were profusely adorned with flowers, statues, temples and beds of foliage designed in geometric patterns.

America entered the gardening scene at that point in Loudon's apotheosis. Carried by the vastly improved communications systems, his fervent writings reached America's shores where they fell on fertile ground. Loudon's design ideas had no previously endorsed style to overthrow in North America. His only battle here was against ignorance—and that obstacle proved to be a substantial barricade.

As the 19th Century dawned, North Americans were well aware that their gardens were bleak in comparison to those of Europe. In the past, we had rested on strongly held religious traditions of utilitarianism to rationalize our unadorned countryside. However, time had washed away the fervor of Puritan conviction. The Age of Rebellion had passed, and citizens of the 19th Century sought mainly to keep abreast of their changing world. In addition, the fire of conformity was fanned by the regular exchange of information between America and Europe as steamships carried letters, periodicals and visitors back and forth. Suddenly, Americans were beset by the opinions of the world.

By the 1830s, Americans were experiencing all of the bewilderment of an Adam who suddenly discovers that he is naked. Visitors from Europe flooded our shores in astounding numbers and with great regularity. They came, they saw, and they commented.

Throughout the 19th Century, innumerable travel books and articles authored by European travellers appeared. And, in those publications, the citizens of Europe took the opportunity to candidly, and often condescendingly, describe their impressions of the New World. Their accounts were rarely charitable. They were the slightly jaded perceptions of travellers accustomed to the carefully clipped, grand estates of Europe. They were critical. In fact, their remarks were sufficiently searing and derisive to cause Washington Irving to complain, "It has been the peculiar lot of our country to be visited by the worst kind of English travellers."

Simultaneously, Americans set off to see Europe and view the scenery on that side of the ocean. And they, too, recorded their impressions. The resulting relationship was one of smug dismay on the part of the British, and reverent awe on the American side of the exchange. True, this country was indubitably endowed with a generous profusion of natural wonders. But, at the beginning of the 19th Century, America was largely naked of embellishment, especially in the adornment of home grounds. The shame of our bareness was infinitely confounded by the realization that the rest of the world was clothed.

As with all trends, the arrival of landscape architecture on the American scene had forerunners. Long before most citizens showed the slightest concern for the beauty of their immediate surroundings, a few visionary Americans were attempting to import European ideas. Most notably, George Washington at Mount Vernon and Thomas Jefferson, at Monticello, studied and embraced the

18th Century British gardening vogue. But, their estates were exceptional; the average man was woefully ignorant of horticultural pursuits.

In 1822, William Cobbett was prompted to sum up the prevailing horticultural atmosphere here with the comment, "Some persons may think, that flowers are things of no use, that they are nonsensical things." And that situation was not destined to change overnight. For the next half century, writers railed against our insensitivity to all aesthetic endeavors. The tastemakers of the times saw their task primarily as a battle against widespread ignorance.

If Americans found themselves trailing Europe in horticultural matters, there was an obvious remedy. From the 1830s onward, Americans were subjected to an onslaught of consciousness-raising publicity aimed at educating the masses about the pleasures of ornamental gardening. The battle had its inevitable ups and downs—Americans displayed a distressing tendency to revert back to their traditional Puritan doctrines if they were not continually coached by vigilant gardening advocates. As late as mid-century, Andrew Jackson Downing was provoked to remind his fellow Americans that, "All persons of good taste agree that however necessary, satisfactory and pleasant a thing a good kitchen garden is, it is not, aesthetically considered, a beautiful thing."

The cause was not progressing with the proper swiftness. The average citizen remained largely unconcerned with the state of American home grounds. Toward mid-century, garden writers grew perturbed, and their message became more agitated and critical of their fellow citizens. Geo. Jaques, an authority on landscape design in Worcester, MA., was an established master of the fine art of horticultural criticism. And he found plenty to criticize when contemplating the abysmal state of landscape art in New England. He painted a dismal portrait of the northeastern countryside when he wrote in *The Horticulturist,*

> . . . in this section of the country, whenever a contest takes place between economic advantage and good taste, the latter is sure to find some apology for making a hasty retreat.

Jaques complained that, regardless of wealth, the typical Yankee would never consent to appropriating more than half an acre to merely ornamental purposes,

> . . . even having forced himself to acquiesce in such like 'wasteful' embellishments, he does all the work grudgingly, counting (and if a profane man, cursing) the cost.

Although landscape design had not reached the level of excellence which its proponents would have hoped by mid-century, the tastemakers could congratulate themselves on one victory. The American penchant for utilitarianism had been markedly eroded due, in part, to the cajolery of garden writers. Apparently, Americans were putting some thought into gardening, though few critics agreed that the prevailing affinities lay with the correct style. Jaques wrote in *The Horticulturist,*

The American Colonial style of gardening according to Bailey's *The Standard Cyclopedia of Horticulture* published by MacMillan.

. . . the taste of New England people generally; for the beautiful and picturesque in rural scenery is either vitiated, or totally uncultivated. Hence, the mass of the people prefer symmetry, stiff formality, straight lines, and the geometric forms of the ancient and artificial style of laying out grounds. Nearly all our first class places in Yankeedom are so arranged.

The time had clearly come to choose an American style. Jaques favored the Picturesque scene, but few of his fellow countrymen shared his views. North Americans leaned toward the Gardenesque style.

It was not purely coincidental that America's entry on the gardening scene transpired at the exact moment when the Gardenesque style was born. Although "Capability" Brown's artificially created pastoral scenes and Humphrey Repton's abrupt landscapes suited the wealthy class of Britain, they had little potential for enlisting converts in this country. The Picturesque scene was too closely akin to the untamed American wilderness to be considered a step toward improvement here. In addition, practically speaking, the Picturesque design required too expansive a parcel of land to be realized successfully in a country with stiff property taxes. Wealthy Americans had scarcely enough acreage to do a Picturesque scene justice, for the typical citizen, it was completely unattainable. Downing succinctly identified the problem,

. . . here the rights of men are held to be equal; and if there are no enormous parks, and no class of men whose wealth is hereditary [there is] the almost entire absence of a very poor class in the country, while we have, on the other hand a large class of independent landholders.

Andrew Jackson Downing, arbiter of taste and advocate of morals, was willing to address the unique needs of Americans. He developed a specific mode of landscape design based on his theory of the Beautiful. Having already established the importance of the Beautiful in the architecture and interior design of homes, it took only a short leap of the imagination to encompass the surrounding grounds in the theory. However, Americans were unsure of who held jurisdiction over the home's acreage—man or nature. Downing's first task was to establish the distinction between rude nature and the garden. This concept came easily—a garden was man's domain, and therefore, by definition, it was a contrived environment. A garden was a work of art, and should be approached artistically.

Actually, Downing's gardens were quite similar to those designed by Loudon, although they possessed a more intimate appeal. When describing his style, Downing liked to say simply, "It is, in short, the Beautiful, embodied in a home scene." Downing did for the home grounds what had already been accomplished in the parlor, he made them an essential part of the family's domestic heart, and a thread in the nation's moral fiber. A Beautiful garden was crucial to the morality of every American man, woman and child.

An enterprise so important to the nation's morality could not be left to chance. Downing was quite specific about who should create a garden. Not every man was born a landscape gardener—it was a gift given only to a chosen few. And here Downing identified a major hurdle. In a democracy, everyone can entertain delusions of grandeur. Downing complained,

> . . . professional talent is seldom employed in Architecture or Landscape Gardening, but almost every man fancies himself an amateur, and endeavors to plan and arrange his own residence. With but little practical knowledge, and few correct principles for his guidance, it is not surprising that we witness such incongruity and great waste of time and money.

Downing was not the only advocate for a professional approach to landscape design, other nurserymen eagerly added their voices. In 1852, Thomas Meehan of Philadelphia wrote in *The Horticulturist*, "Were every man born an artist, any one might justly deem himself capable of laying out his own place in a manner capable of affording ultimately the highest pleasure; but it is not so."

To succeed, a garden must embody a set of principles executed by the correct use and balance of botanicals, statuary and patterns. A poorly conceived garden was spiritually worthless. Meehan explained, "There are innumerable instances of gardens which afford no pleasure to anyone."

But Downing's campaign for professionalism was doomed to failure. We are not inherently a nation of gardeners. For many years after Downing's untimely death, the only professionals to design the American landscape were a handful

According to Andrew Jackson Downing, there was little comparison between the orderly Beautiful landscape and the rude Picturesque landscape. Illustration from Downing's *The Theory and Practice of Landscape Gardening*.

Downing waged an on-going campaign for professionalism in landscape design. Illustration from *Suburban Home Grounds* by Frank Scott; first printed in 1870, reprinted by the American Life Foundation, Watkins Glen, NY in 1982.

of immigrants trained as gardeners overseas, but attracted by the prospects of tilling American soil.

Few Americans were cut of the cloth necessary to provide the nation with native-born professional gardeners. According to the 1852 edition of *The Horticulturist*, only 3% of the working gardeners in this country were native. Most nurserymen and gardeners in America were Irish, followed by those of Scottish, English and German descent. Of course, no one objected to the employment of foreign talent. In fact, it was an indication of status to import a gardener. However, there were simply not enough gardeners to go around. And obviously, few American citizens could afford to hire an extra hand solely for the purpose of adorning the yard.

Most garden writers immediately saw that the nation would remain naked if we were to rely solely on professional talent. Instead, more realistic writers made a concerted effort to enlist anyone who was ready, willing and able. Granted, the end result would not be comparable to the estates abroad, but untrained local talent was all that was readily available. This was the audience at which Robert Morris Copeland aimed his book, *Country Life*, written in 1860,

> To all Lovers of Nature and to all engaged in cultivating and adorning the Earth, This book is Dedicated, with the Earnest hope that it may attract to the Practice of the Arts of culture some who will see that the pursuit is full of pleasure, with no more than a healthy amount of labor. And also, with the hope that some who earn their bread with the sweat of their brow, and look upon their calling as a treadmill of drudgery and endurance, may here learn that within the round of their daily duties they have everything which can expand the mind and ennoble the soul.

Further in his book, Copeland wrote, "I shall confine myself to the wants of men with small fortunes, as our country must always be principally inhabited by that class." Obviously, he was anxious to gain as many converts as possible. Although his intentions were sound, when he proceeded to put his ideas into practice with plans for gardens, it was clear that the author had no notion of what the average home was like. Copeland's description of the "average" estate (situated in the Boston environs) consisted of no less than 60 acres; 20 of which were farmed, ½ planted to flower gardens, 3 dedicated to a kitchen garden, 11 in orchard and the remaining acres devoted to stable, greenhouses, grapehouses, hotbeds, nurseries, dwelling houses, lawns, woods and ponds. He obviously entertained a slightly glorified vision of the average man. His garden plans were of no use to the middle class citizen.

By mid-century, the typical homeowner had moved into an urban area, or into one of the rapidly developing suburbs. His needs and tastes were notably different from those of either the rural farmer or the proud owner of the ornée fermé. The suburban gardener had ample leisure time, an average income and a modest but malleable estate. With those basic ingredients, he lacked only the instruction necessary to direct his progress in horticultural pursuits.

In 1870, the needs of that suburban gardener were finally addressed in a book authored by Frank J. Scott entitled *Suburban Home Grounds*. In it are found concepts which many consider to be America's first truly unique contribution to landscape design. The book was composed to "aid persons of a moderate income, who know little of the arts of decorative gardening."

Scott held a more realistic picture of the average family situation. His typical house was located on a ½ acre suburban lot, buffered by trees and within view of several neighbors. And he proceeded to demonstrate that it was entirely possible to reach the heights of perfection on that pocket-sized parcel. Scott revealed how a suburban gardener could realize a scaled-down scene similar to the landscape created on much larger estates. By way of encouragement, Scott casually mentioned that the poorer class in Britain had successfully accomplished the beautification of their suburbs no less than 30 years prior to the American horticultural awakening. That was just the kind of competitive encouragement the American public needed to hear.

For his gardening style, Scott chose a reduced version of Loudon's Gardenesque scene. But modifications were necessary to condense Loudon's ideas into the confines of an American suburb. As Scott humbly explained, "His works are too voluminous, too thorough, too English, to meet the needs of American suburban life."

Scott also recognized the lack of professional native talent. Apparently, the situation had not improved in the 20 years that elapsed between Downing's death and the publication of *Suburban Home Grounds*. Scott wrote,

> . . . the number of such men, devoted to this profession, is so small, that we have not heard of more than half a dozen skilled, professional gardeners among our thirty millions of native Americans; and not more than double that number of educated foreigners.

The typical suburban home was on a ½ acre lot, buffered by trees and within view of several neighbors. Illustration from Scott's *Suburban Home Grounds*.

Scott had an answer. His idea was to educate the masses. And his definition of education was not a lackadaisical, unstructured impartation of knowledge. He had a very specific plan in mind,

> If we can induce every family who have a home to adorn to study the art of planning and arranging of their own grounds, the seed will be planted that will germinate, in another generation, in a crop of gardeners of such high culture, and of such necessity to the educated community, that it will be one of the honored professions of our best collegiates.

Not only did Scott introduce a broader audience to the pleasures of gardening, he also exposed many previously unenlightened homeowners to the plants of the tropics. The Gardenesque style utilized tender plants in ornamental displays, a practice which became known as "bedding out". Scott brought this concept to every home. Hundreds of tender annuals were germinated from seed in mid-winter and raised in small pots until spring when they were amassed outdoors in geometric designs such as paisleys, spirals, triangles, spheres, etc. In such a display, the emphasis was on the total effect rather than on its specific components. Of course, a huge vista planted to beds of flowers was an awesome sight, but Scott demonstrated how a small garden could be equally intricate and impressive.

Not only were Victorians developing their skill and interest in the garden as a whole, they were also acquiring a heightened appreciation for plants. Americans were learning to assess plants for their ornamental usefulness rather than their culinary or economic value.

By mid-century, plants were accepted simply for their beauty. Plants possessed innate value. Their uplifting aura permeated the surroundings—they bestowed beauty on the garden, and on any human who trod the garden's path. Certainly, such a liberal attitude toward ornamentals was not easily adopted by a formerly Puritanical public. But, Victorians were learning to appreciate many cultural pursuits in their new-found spare time. Art, music, literature and dance were all thriving fine arts in the 19th Century. In fact, by the 1850s, the editors of the popular rural paper, *Coleman's Agricultural Tour*, felt that even the farm folk were ready for some lessons in cultural elevation. They wrote,

> I have said and written a great deal to my countrymen about the cultivation of flowers, ornamental gardening, and rural embellishments; and I would read them a homily on the subject every day of every remaining year of my life, if I thought it would induce them to make this a matter of particular attention and care. When a man asks me, what is the use of shrubs and flowers, my first impulse is always to look under his hat and see the length of his ears. I am heartily sick of measuring everything by a standard of mere utility and profit; and as heartily do I pity the man, who can see no good in life but the pecuniary gain, or in the mere animal indulgence of eating and drinking.

The Victorian fascination for plant life was neither a casual nor a fleeting affair. By mid-century, the love of plants had become a way of life in America. Not only did that theme resound from the pulpits of such ardent flower aficionados as Henry Ward Beecher, but it was also a concept often intoned around the family hearth and a matter of frequent discussion in nearly every periodical which arrived on the doorstep. It was obvious that Downing and his colleagues had captured their audience. However, it is one thing to enlist botanical recruits, and quite another and more difficult task to maintain their ardor. Having gathered the flock, the last half of the era was devoted to maintaining interest and involvement.

The most efficient means to this end was to provide a constant flow of new botanical material from far away shores. Toward this end, explorers were dispatched to strange and little known places on long and much-glorified journeys with the introduction of rare plants as their primary goal. Americans followed these expeditions with anticipation, breathlessly awaiting the latest treasures captured by an intrepid band of Victorian plant hunters.

The Victorian Era was the Golden Age of Plant Hunting. Never before, and never again, would plant hunting reach the frenzied tempo of the 19th Century. So avid was the Victorian urge to investigate the corners of the earth, that by the end of the 19th Century, few regions were left unbotanized.

Naturally, the typical American took a keen interest in the progress of exploration. Even the horticulturally ignorant citizen could scarcely escape exposure to the proliferating expeditions sent to scour the earth's edges. The ventures received immense publicity. And every expedition which journeyed forth, regardless of its goal, included a botanist in the crew. In many cases, expeditions were mounted solely for botanical pursuits.

On the earliest voyages, the botanist's duty was primarily to obtain herbarium specimens and seeds. Due to the problems associated with keeping plant material alive on long sea journeys, few living plants were collected. In the 19th Century, glass plant cases, known as Wardian cases, were invented to facilitate the maintenance of living plant material. At last, explorers could collect growing plants to be cultivated in the heated "stove" greenhouses back home.

The world immediately sat up and took notice as those strange plants were introduced. Stranger still were the stories of tangled and exotic plant life, extreme temperatures and unique native customs encountered on the treks through heretofore fabled lands. The Victorians were thoroughly enraptured by any word of that brave new world.

Although plant hunters sent home romantic tales of life in pursuit of strange and wonderful plants, their fare was actually one of daily hardship, disease, discomfort and mortal danger, all endured for a trifling monetary recompense. A plant hunter's mission could only be called successful if, struggling against nearly insurmountable obstacles, he introduced a handful of exotic plants into Europe and North America. Having risked life and limb for the sake of botany, he was then paid a fixed sum for each case successfully delivered, regardless of the value of the material which it contained.

Plant hunters never acquired significant wealth from their employment, but they often secured substantial fame. Upon returning with their botanical booty, the more flamboyant explorers were embraced and enshrouded in an aura which approached deification. That moment of glory, and perhaps the honor of having one's name immortalized in a Latin binomial, constituted the plant hunter's fundamental reward.

The hunters throve on the mood of romanticism which permeated the era. And they, in turn, lent their hardships and discoveries to heighten its intensity. One of the earliest plant hunters, Carl Thunberg, summarized the magnetism of the hunt, "... I met the dangers of life, I prudently eluded ferocious tribes and beasts, and for the sake of discovering the beautiful plants of this Southern Thule, I joyfully ran, sweated and chilled." In other eras, such a confession might easily be classified as the rantings of a lunatic.

Whether insane or not, the fever continued throughout the century. Plant hunters traversed Africa, the Indies, South America, China and Japan. Wherever there were unexplored regions, they went. And wherever they went, they sent back cases filled with exotic flora.

North American interest in plant hunting peaked with the opening of China to trade. One of the most popular mid-century explorers was Robert Fortune, who embarked on his Chinese expedition in 1843, immediately after China signed the treaty which closed the Opium Wars and opened their doors to trade. Of course, Fortune's progress was followed religiously in the pages of *The Horticulturist*. Andrew Jackson Downing, master of the art of suspense, wrote a stirring introduction to Fortune's journals, and promised his audience the entire account in serial form. Furthermore, he pledged that the China serial would be every bit as intriguing as any adventure which had "the opium trade or the spread of cheap calicoes" for its motive. The account followed Fortune's trek through China, depicting in glorious detail every collecting point that the expedition visited. This dramatic introduction to exotica not only heightened North American esteem for those botanical "denizens of the deep", but such accounts also added to the mounting anticipation for those who awaited the fruits of the expedition.

By the 1830s, plant hunting was big business. Hunters no longer depended solely on the largess of kings and their courts to fund expeditions. Private entrepreneurs were increasingly willing to gamble on the commercial yield of botanical booty. Nurseries sent out expeditions to augment the offerings in their catalogs and provide a regular supply of novelties to stimulate an easily bored public.

By mid-century, hundreds of rare plants had already been plucked from their native tropics and successfully reestablished in European and North American greenhouses. Each plant was a challenge, especially at a time when greenhouse management was in its infancy. Typically, a 5 to 15 year hiatus intervened between introduction and popularization of a new ornamental. And not all initial introductions were successful. Several attempts were often made before growers understood the eccentricities of each exotic and were able to provide the correct environment and culture.

Establishing optimal growing conditions for the new exotics was only one problem faced by horticulturists. It was also necessary to search out profitable, ornamental uses for the rapidly increasing roster of beautiful plants. The obvious solution was to incorporate the plants into the garden.

The idea caught hold like wildfire, and kindled the imagination of landscape designers such as J. C. Loudon. Exotic plants provided a strong incentive for the development of the Gardenesque style. And, in North America, Downing's

The Victorians acquired a heightened appreciation for plants—especially tropical plants. Illustration from *Suburban Home Grounds* by Frank Scott.

Beautiful garden style—replete with abundant beds of bright heretofore unknown species—provided employment for the exotic plant material which arrived daily from foreign shores. Victorians saw this as a unique opportunity to share in the excitement of exploration, as well as a means of adorning the home grounds.

In the garden, compact newcomers provided fillers in beds of colorful geometric designs, while larger plants furnished an exotic accent or focal point in the display. The more elaborate specimens were employed in urns that stood sentinel flanking the entryway of the House Beautiful. Plants and people were establishing a relationship which was growing increasingly intimate.

Botany took on a new significance with the burgeoning 19th Century interest in plants. Prior to that century, science was a domain reserved for a handful of eccentric gentlemen, the common man never dabbled in that esoteric hobby. However, times had changed. And the influx of new plant material encouraged a popular interest in science, especially plant science.

Naturally, people began to display a healthy curiosity about those new exotics which contemporary writers urged them to cultivate at an increasingly close proximity. While gazing at those rare botanicals, one could not help but ponder the plant's internal and external workings. Innumerable books were written to aid the observer in his musings.

Americans found the unique physical attributes peculiar to exotics to be a particularly engrossing topic of study. They noted the differences between tropical plants and the native flora, and wondered why there was such a great diversity in physical appearance. The topic engaged authors throughout the century as theories flew back and forth. In *Wonders of the Plant World*, a popular little volume written and published by D. Lothrop and Company of Boston in 1872, the unique physical endowments of rare plants were explored,

> The leaves of Tropical trees and shrubs, as far as I have observed are very much larger than those of trees and shrubs of England and Europe. This would seem to be a provision of a merciful Creator to enable them to receive upon their broad surface whatever humidity the atmosphere contains. A narrow leaf, moreover, would sooner be shrivelled and scorched by the brazen sunshine of a torrid clime.

Wonders of the Plant World provides an excellent example of the typical 19th Century popular presentation of plant morphology. The theories were logical, although Victorians had a tendency to jump to conclusions based on limited evidence. Whether faulty of fact or not, such books greatly stimulated the popular study of a previously unexplored field.

Generally, scientific concepts were carefully simplified and made more palatable for the audience. A favorite and frequently employed method of explaining the functioning of botanicals was accomplished by drawing correlations between the plant and animal kingdoms. For example, *Wonders of the Plant World* drew a parallel between resinous, aromatic herbs and polar bears. Both were provided with thick layers of fat, which served as protection and as a

Tropical leaves from *Wonders of the Plant World*.

source of nourishment in severe climates. Less imaginative, but easier to envision was Grant Allen's simple summary of plant physiology in *The Story of Plants*, "Plants Eat with their Leaves—the Leaves are, in fact, their mouths and stomachs." Although such statements were, at best, gross oversimplifications of fact, the terms were easily understandable and slightly entertaining. Such books were immensely popular with a public seeking an easy education.

As with most horticultural subjects, Europe was far ahead of us in their pursuit of botany. Not only had scientists already spent long decades seeking botanical truths, but the public had also adopted botany as a new method of providing an evening's entertainment. After dinner, family and guests gathered around the microscope and explored the minute world which it revealed.

The microscope was a primary tool in the popularization of botany. Of course, the microscope had been in use since the 17th Century, and its lens had fostered several important discoveries. But, in Europe, the ingenious Victorians recognized an amusing toy embodied in that magnifying instrument, and so began the vogue of microscopic scrutiny as a common after-dinner amusement.

By the mid-1800s, Americans were also becoming excited by the microscope, although theirs was a tame curiosity compared with the fanatical rage which that tool incited in Europe. *Wonders of the Plant World* speaks with enthusiasm about the potential of that instrument,

> Talk of spells and talismans, which open up the depths of treasure caves. What are they to the microscope, whose powerful lens people a drop of water with a thousand strange and beautiful beings.

On a more practical vein, *Godey's Lady's Book*, a very widely read 19th Century periodical filled with tantalizingly romantic stories and trivia, carried the following item concerning the microscope,

> This valuable instrument has long been one of the principle aids of the druggist and physician, and essential to a student of many sciences such as chemistry, geometry, botany and physiology. Perhaps the time is not distant when every good housekeeper will think it necessary to be armed with one of these detectors.

The microscope was the tool which laid bare the study of plant classification. The British passionately pursued the pleasures of classification. In contrast, although Americans were keen explorers of morphology, they paid little or no heed to its kindred pursuit—taxonomy. The complete disinterest with which Americans greeted plant classification was at such marked variance to the European fashion, that it provoked comment abroad.

For the British, one of the chief pleasures in travelling to this country was the joy of sending searing criticisms back home. And they found a great deal to criticize about our deficiency in botany, a subject which they had embraced and mastered with dogged devotion. The era's most notorious travelling critic, Frances Trollope, mother of Anthony Trollope, the well-known Victorian novelist, published a diary of her North American journey which was particularly frugal with its compliments. Mrs. Trollope's main topic of concern was social customs, but she did not fail to take a swipe at the state of American botanical achievement. In *Domestic Manners of the Americans*, written in 1832, she delivered America a most underhanded compliment,

> Let no one visit America without having first studied botany, it is an amusement . . . that helps wonderfully up and down the hill, and must be superlatively valuable in America, both from the plentiful lack of other amusements, and the plentiful material for enjoyment in this; besides, if one is dying to know the name of those lovely [botanical] strangers; it is a thousand to one against finding anyone who can tell you.

In Britain, a working knowledge of plant names had become one of the social graces. A young lady of genteel origins was expected to be capable of reeling off, without hesitation, the Latin binomial for any given popular flower. However, in this country, members of the gentler sex were not as eager to embrace any sort of scholarly endeavor, preferring to remain blissfully and beguilingly ignorant. Here, people held the prevailing opinion that a woman should react to plants with warmth and sentiment, not with cold scientific analysis. At the beginning of the era, the American feminine ideal still held that a lady ought to be coy and cute. A segment from a romantic story in *The Ladies' Floral Cabinet* illustrates the typical American reaction to botanical pursuits. Reata, our young heroine, has just been approached by a solicitous suitor,

> "You should study botany," said Otto.
> "I tried to do so once, but I shall never try again, I hate botany . . . I shouldn't care for a flower a bit better for knowing how it is constructed. Only fancy, on the first page the book told me to cut up an anemone. I couldn't do it—it went to my heart; so I cut up the book instead and threw it in the kitchen fire. Now I have made a botany of my own, and divided off the flowers into far more satisfactory classes. There is a sentimental class, a fierce class, a silly class, there is a silly-sentimental, a fierce-sentimental, and so on."

Although the passage aptly described the popular female reaction to any suggestion concerning the study of botany, if one reads between the lines, it also subtly reveals the fact that botany had become one item on a very restricted list of acceptable pastimes for young ladies, placed right alongside the study of music, poetry, literature, homemaking and crafts. Although it may not have been an avenue frequently trod, it was now open for travel.

Botany was offered as a hobby for ladies with one reservation—the topic of sexuality was not to be touched. Sex was generally not a subject of frequent deliberation during the prudish Victorian Era. So, naturally, it was a matter of slight discomfort for the Victorians. In particular, the British were extremely uneasy about encouraging women to examine the sexual activities of any organism—botanical or whatever. John Ruskin, the popular British essayist, feared the moral ramifications inherent in the study of botanical sexuality and voiced his hope that the "gentle and happy scholar of flowers" would remain ignorant of the "obscene processes" of nature. Apparently, the ladies did not heed his warning for, undaunted by his words, they continued peering into their microscopes.

Ruskin need not have worried. Somehow, plant sexuality was treated as a hermetic science lacking any connection to other organisms. Cloaked in the pure innocence of nature, a working knowledge of "the birds and the bees" was not generally considered harmful, even to children. In fact, *Vick's Monthly Magazine* published by the James Vick Seed Company, featured a section entitled "Botany for Little Folks" aimed at educating "Our Young People" concerning the sexual parts of each flower.

The study of plant parts may have given the young scholar some intimation of his (or her) own bodily functions, but the topic was always approached from the most analytic of angles. Nature, being morally perfect, was incapable of wrong. Plant sexuality was restricted solely to the reproduction of the species, which was an unarguably laudable activity. A treatise on botany was generally prefixed by a benevolent explanation such as Grant Allen's introduction in *The Story of Plants*, "Plants also marry and rear families." When swathed in such prosaic innocence, the discussion of botanical behavior was perfectly acceptable, even to the staunchest Victorians.

It was clear that plants could do no wrong. Without reservation, plant study and cultivation were endeavors recommended to all age groups. Anyone might benefit from the uplifting influences of plants, especially when their beneficial effects could be enjoyed at a close proximity to the family's hearth.

So, the groundwork was laid for the blossoming of indoor horticulture. By the beginning of the Victorian Era, exotics had entered the country and the garden. The time was growing ripe for their entry into the home as well. However, that occurrence also required preparation. The country had established an acquaintance with botanicals. But, at the dawn of the Victorian Era, that relationship had not yet developed into intimacy. From the progress of events, that intimacy was bound to blossom.

The horticultural renaissance crept upon this country discretely, foreshadowed in dozens of subtle ways. It was evident in the garden, which was developing at a deliberate pace, and in the avid study of plant life, which had taken the country by storm. The trend was evident in the proliferation of plant expeditions and the enthusiasm which greeted the fruits of those journeys. There were indications everywhere, so that no astute observer could doubt the general inclination toward horticultural interest.

All of the era's horticultural happenings set the stage for the entry of plants indoors. Each had its direct or indirect effect on the public perception of plants and their willingness to embrace them as housemates. When it happened, the houseplant fad was the crescendo of decades of horticultural awakening. But, like all of the era's other occurrences, the entry of houseplants did not arrive completely unannounced. In fact, there was plenty of forewarning.

Although houseplant cultivation, like so many other horticultural trends, was a fashion that crossed the ocean from Europe, the practice of growing a plant in the house did not lack precedent on these shores. The Colonists had wintered favorite herbs in their homes long before the Victorians began coveting ornamentals as houseplants.

Most of the herbs which were cultivated in the simple Colonial gardens outdoors were not native to North America, but had arrived with the settlers, travelling across the Atlantic as seed. And, many of those plants could scarcely tolerate the cruel North American winters to which they were suddenly subjected. The settlers considered most herbs to be sufficiently indispensable to warrant special attention in inclement weather. After all, herbs provided the basic ingredients for household necessities such as soap, polishes, moth repellents, etc. But, most fundamentally, they were valued medicinally. Herbs constituted the sole and entire pharmacopeia for the ailments and injuries suffered by early Americans.

The Colonists were practical people with no time for frivolities. In their view, the place for plants was indisputably in the garden patch. However, the harsh northern climate necessitated some precautionary measures to protect tender plants over the coldest winter months, and so the most valuable herbs were wintered indoors. Those herbs could actually be called the first houseplants in this country.

However, herbs were wintered out of necessity rather than choice. And protection was all that the plants were afforded. In fact, during the early winter, the plants were generally shocked into a state of dormancy to be stored during the coldest season and revived the following spring. Just barely alive, a dormant plant provided little aesthetic pleasure.

Actually, a botanical could only endure the environment typical of a Colonial home in a semi-alive state. Eighteenth Century houses went below freezing every bitter winter night. In addition, Colonial gardeners might have preferred to sequester dormant plants in their homes. There were obvious advantages in tending a sleeping plant rather than a growing specimen. While resting, herbs require little sunlight, and light was a valuable commodity in those sparsely windowed dwellings. In addition, a dormant herb does not require water, and fetching water was a laborsome chore before the advent of indoor plumbing. So the plants rested, out of sight and mind until spring, at which time they were again transported outdoors where nature could awaken the sleeping botanicals and tend to their needs.

Although North Americans wintered their plants indoors out of necessity, Europeans showed more interest in exploring the possibilities inherent in the undertaking. As early as the 1600s, Europe was feeling premonitions of the future houseplant fetish. However, even the precocious Europeans confined the practice of growing plants indoors principally to the cultivation of herbs.

One of the earliest literary allusions to indoor herbal cultivation in Europe appears in Izaac Walton's *The Complete Angler*, written in the mid-17th Century. He mentions the comforting sight of lavender in the windows of rural English inns, set there to assure the weary traveller that the tavern offered clean rooms for a good night's repose.

Although a few herbs and primroses may have been grown in the windowsills of rural European towns, window gardening was not a prevalent practice in Europe until the 19th Century. W. Caret Hazlitt commented in *Gleanings in Garden Literature*, published in London in 1887, "The taste for window-gardening is of very remote antiquity." Later in the text he provides a description of the conditions which barred the broader cultivation of houseplants, "But the facilities for rendering a windowsill a receptacle for flowers scarcely existed until apertures for the admission of light and air into dwellings were placed on a more or less modern footing." The desire to grow houseplants may have been strong, but early architecture simply did not provide the opportunity, in either Europe or North America.

As the Victorian Era dawned, the premonitions of the future fad multiplied on this side of the ocean. Just as Thomas Jefferson and George Washington had the foresight to follow European landscape styles long before most of their fellow citizens exhibited the slightest inclination to harken to those voices, there were Americans who grew ornamentals in their homes years before Victorian fashions hit the American scene.

Every trend is heralded by a handful of visionary citizens who foresee the future import of their interests long before the general populace awakens to its call. So it was with houseplant cultivation. The first Americans to receive exotic botanical material were wealthy estate owners and people of prominence with connections and correspondents in Europe. And, of course, their wealth allowed them to provide suitable well-lit locations for plants indoors at a time when glass was still extremely expensive. They were the tastemakers who set the pace for the nation, and their homes were the envy of their countrymen.

Throughout our Colonial history collectors of plants, both men and women, laid the agricultural and horticultural foundations necessary to the growth of the nation. In their gardens, and later, in their windowsills and greenhouses, trials were undertaken. At a time when worldliness was a new concept, those citizens of wealth and position rendered the trend all the more tantalizing to their fellow Americans.

So, when visitors called on Lady Skipwith's Colonial Virginia mansion, they rarely neglected to comment on the unique display in her home. The front hall of her salubrious house was filled with a collection of citrus trees being wintered from the garden and basking happily in the warm sun. The collection was particularly worthy of comment because it was gathered decades before the popular cultivation of houseplants.

Lady Skipwith, William Hamilton, Thomas Jefferson, George Washington, John Bartram and a handful of other serious colleagues devoted their efforts to the horticultural growth of North America. They found time and space to experi-

Tulips from Dingee & Conard's *Success with Flowers*.

CHAPTER IV

FORCING BULBS

THE DESIRE TO GROW plants in the parlor may have warmed the heart of every Victorian in the country—but where should they begin? Obviously, the first houseplants had to be foolproof. Certainly, if the confidence of the masses was to be bolstered, then facility was a fundamental requirement. The easily disenchanted middle class needed a resounding success in their first attempt at growing houseplants. They expected plants to grow, flourish and blossom rapidly, painlessly and with the same spontaneity as garden-grown specimens.

The first plants to enter the home had to possess a stoic fortitude. Although domestic architecture and fittings had evolved far beyond the original Colonial box, the average home still fell short of the ideal environment for botanicals. Before central heating systems were perfected and popularized, the parlor froze frequently, especially around the room's periphery and near the windows. In addition, although the room's windows had grown larger, the incoming light remained greatly reduced due to the thick and uneven glass available at the time. Such low light levels were not sufficient to support the demands of sun-loving plants. The first houseplants had to be capable of enduring and per-forming in spite of the people's fumbling ignorance and the home's less than ideal environment.

Fortunately, the Victorians began with bulbs. Whether the tradition of forcing bulbs was a happy accident or a carefully engineered plan is a detail lost to history. However, the process did not lack precedent. Like many other customs which we borrowed from overseas, bulb forcing came from Europe. Naturally, the first citizens in this country to pursue the European trend were wealthy Americans with trade connections abroad. But, eventually, bulbs managed to wander into the homes of the masses. And, once they entered, bulb forcing became a wintertime ritual observed with religious regularity.

Success was inevitable. Bulbs are virtually indomitable. They are invulnerable to the caprices of human nature and the vagaries of fluctuating stoves and fireplaces. They offered the ideal vehicle for a complete novice to enter the horticultural scene. And yet, growing bulbs was an immensely rewarding endeavor. With minimal exertion and scant knowledge, anyone could place a hyacinth in a glass of water and experience quite spectacular results. A bulb provided all manner of entertainment for the Victorian family—including the element of drama. Within a few weeks of planting, a squat, ugly tuber sprouted, grew blades of fascinating form, sent forth a floral stem and bore an impressive bouquet of flowers. The whole thing hinted of legerdemain.

Not only did bulbs furnish instant gratification, but they also offered the possibility of prolonging the pleasure of floral company throughout the long, dark winter by staggering the cooling and warming cycle. It was a simple feat to choreograph a succession of flowers in the parlor so the room never lacked blossoms, not even for a day.

The tradition of forcing bulbs probably began quite casually. The Victorians were already familiar with hardy garden bulbs such as hyacinths, narcissus, tulips and crocus. In fact, bulbs were among the first living plant specimens to be successfully imported from abroad. Garden bulbs, later dubbed "Dutch bulbs", entered Europe as early as the 16th Century, and from that date onward, they were regular commodities in the brisk trade with the Levant.

North America's first plant collectors received bulbs from Europe in exchange for their consignments of native American flora. John Bartram (1699—1777), a North American botanist, acquired Dutch bulbs from Peter Collinson, his correspondent in England. Eventually, Bartram was appointed Botanizer Royal for America, a position which brought Bartram fame, but not fortune. Bulbs were frequently sent to assuage the American collector while he awaited recompense from a king who was rarely punctual in paying his accounts. Fortunately, Collinson was generous in his botanical compensation. One shipment sent to Philadelphia included 20 crocus and 20 narcissus, as well as generous allocations of martagons, lilies, gladiolus, ornithalgums, iris and *Allium moly*.

The Collinson/Bartram exchange was informal, so no fixed rate was set on the value of each plant. But, bulbs had long since established a reputation as commodities of value. In fact, the North American/British exchange was not the first instance in which bulbs were substituted for legal tender. A century before bulbs entered America, they were the subject of brisk speculation and trade in Holland. During the height of the bulb frenzy, popularly known as 'Tulipomania' which peaked between 1634 and 1637, tulips gained an astounding monetary value. Tulip bulbs were swapped for property and offered as dowries for daughters. Fortunes were created and destroyed in their exchange, and Dutch bulbs established a firm affiliation with affluence.

By the early 1800s, the fires of Tulipomania had long since cooled, but Dutch bulbs were still extremely valuable to early plant collectors in North America. In fact, John Custis, renown for his avid botanical correspondence, posed for his portrait with one hand clutching a book entitled *Of the Tulip*. And, to prove that

Custis had acquired the bulbs themselves as well as knowledge of their existence, the artist also laid a cut tulip bud beside the volume. He was in the very best of company, George Washington, Thomas Jefferson and Lady Jean Skipwith of Colonial Williamsburg shared an interest in collecting bulbs.

Bulbs did not immediately fall into the hands of the common man. Long before the ordinary North American invited bulbs into the parlor, Dutch bulbs were forced in cool greenhouses where they comprised the bulk of the botanical collection. When greenhouses made their debut among wealthy Americans in the 1700s, temperature control was provided by primitive heating systems which were only partially effective in preventing frosts. Bulbs were among the few plants which could provide a winter floral display under such difficult conditions. The environment in those prototypical greenhouses was perfect for growing bulbs, giving them a splendid opportunity to strut their winter glories. Inevitably, word of those near-failure-proof winter blooming plants spread, and the less affluent citizenry saw no reason why they could not attempt a little magic in their parlors. In fact, the only hindrance precluding the bulb's entry into the home was cost—a substantial impediment indeed.

A windowbox of hyacinths, tulips and crocus from *The Ladies' Floral Cabinet*, Oct. 1886.

Bulbs could not grace the common parlor until the expense of importation moderated. The first bulbs to be cultivated commercially were grown in Holland by nurseries that catered to the tastes of tulipomaniacs. The price of those collectors' items was much too steep for the average purse. However, the introduction of steamships radically altered trade in all manner of products— including bulbs. The price fell dramatically until, in 1825, bulbs were common on the market. Noting the simultaneous relationship between the popularity of bulbs and the dawning of the Age of Technology, *Vick's Monthly Magazine* reported,

Years ago, when Hyacinths were still so high in price that they were only to be had by the rich, there were just a few gardens around Haarlem where these bulbs were grown, and the stock was small at the time. Since the railways and the steamers go direct to nearly every part of the world, the nurserymen of Haarlem are producing more stock.

Haarlem bulbs eventually found their way to American shores, and the burgeoning nursery and seed houses eagerly added them to their lists. Stock was amassed quickly in response to public demand. Landreth's Nursery, one of the earliest seed companies in Philadelphia, offered no less than 50 varieties of hyacinths in 1832.

By mid-century, the most popular bulbs could be obtained at quite reasonable prices. A collection of mixed hyacinths was available for approximately $1.50 a dozen, while choice named varieties sold for prices up to $8.00 a dozen. Although the cost had declined, flowers were still costly considering that a hoe could be purchased for 53¢ and Henry David Thoreau spent only $2.00 for an 8 month supply of lamp oil.

The obvious connection with the advent of the steamship does not aid us in affixing a firm date on the entry of bulbs into the home. Although the exact moment of the popularization of indoor bulbs eludes us, an item in an 1870 issue of *Vick's Monthly Magazine* offers some insight into the chronology of the event. The author, reminiscing on her childhood, recalls the arrival of a new schoolmaster who came to board with her family. When the gentleman appeared, he carefully carried a mysterious parcel from his carriage into the parlor and unwrapped it with great ceremony. As he peeled back the paper, he revealed pots of hyacinths and Lily of the Valley, both in full bloom,

> In those days window-plants were not cultivated as they are now, and this plant, with its waxy blossoms, and bright foliage, seemed like a piece of summer come into our house, or a visitor from some tropical clime. Mr. Ellison asked permission to leave the plants in the sitting rooms until the weather should be warm enough to place them outdoors. Aunt Mary gladly consented, and we girls were highly pleased at the idea of their remaining where we could enjoy the sight and smell of their beauty.

Mr. Ellison proved to be a kindly schoolmaster who maintained classroom discipline with good-natured rebukes rather than inflicting the rod. His students were encouraged to study plant life and undertake horticultural projects—the boys in the garden, and the girls in the home. And the story ends happily—as a result of their benevolent intellectual and moral tutelage, the children grew up to be model citizens who, when the time came, entrusted their children's education to the hands of Mr. Ellison.

On the surface, this saccharin story can be viewed as just another sweet Victorian fable. However, the tale also speaks of the development of a new vista for women. From childhood onward, the art and skill of growing plants became an important part of a woman's education. It was one domestic chore which proved infinitely more fulfilling and enjoyable than sweeping and washing. Women gained a great deal more than merely a few pretty petals in the parlor with the popularization of Dutch bulbs.

Bulb forcing became the American woman's wintertime hobby. In fact, North Americans embraced the fashion with a more fervent attention than bulbs found among Europeans. And, Northerners took to Dutch bulbs with an intensity unknown in the South. Of course, many plausible social and economic explanations can be formulated for this phenomenon, but the Victorians chose to blame it on the weather. *Vick's Monthly Magazine* adopted a simple climatic explanation for the geographic trends in houseplant popularity. According to *Vick's*, bulbs were a panacea for winter's doldrums. Their prevalence indoors increased in direct proportion to the severity of the climate outdoors:

> In countries where the winters are short and comparatively pleasant, Bulbs that are suitable for flowering in the house, in fact all houseplants, are of far less importance than in the North, where we have to endure five months of winter... Nothing renders winter so endurable as a little summer life and beauty indoors in the form of House Plants, none are more easily grown and more certain to reward the care of the cultivator, than those produced by Bulbs, generally known as Holland Bulbs...

So the need for beauty, beneficence, personal achievement and seasonal escape provided the soil in which the tradition of bulb forcing flourished. And these same powerful incentives moved the public to study the culture of bulbs with a fervent devotion and fascination. Bulbs helped create a middle class audience of avid horticultural readers. The first indoor gardeners gratefully devoured article after article addressing the specifics of bulb forcing. Eventually, the parlor was not only filled with pots of bulbs, it was also scattered with numerous periodicals discussing their care and maintenance.

Eben Rexford, a popular 19th Century horticulturist, commented that, "there is nothing simpler in all flower growing than the cultivation of many kinds of bulbs in the house in winter." Although this claim may have been well-founded, people still depended upon the encouragement found in step-by-step instructions describing how to force bulbs. And, of course, magazines congenially supplied these directions in abundance. Almost every issue of the popular 19th Century horticultural magazines contained some item about bulbs. They recommended the best species and cultivars, offered cultural instructions, discussed new introductions, revealed hoaxes and noted the winners of exhibition premiums.

Horticultural knowledge became a valuable asset in daily life. Those gardeners who studied current magazines and books were kept abreast of "tasteful" home decoration. They mastered the proper sequence of events, and prepared for the seasons ahead. Forcing bulbs was so much a part of the Victorian home that *The Ladies' Floral Cabinet* had nothing but disdain for any female who lacked the organization necessary to keep the tradition. They addressed the wayward gardener with this scornful rebuke, "Next year comes, always on time, and finds those who would have hyacinths and other flowering bulbs this spring just as they were last, one day too late."

If the empty-headed female was popular as a single young lady, she was not the ideal wife and mother. Creating the proper home atmosphere required forethought and planning as well as skill and culture. How could one better demonstrate these qualities than by forcing bulbs? Bulb forcing became another indispensable duty for the busy housewife, ranking in importance right alongside ministering to the health of the family and providing clean clothes and wholesome meals. Those women who had previously failed to take bulb forcing seriously were embarrassed into growing bulbs by the implicit rebukes of their peers.

Magazines were not the only enterprise to benefit from the growing interest in bulbs. The increasingly vigorous publicity devoted to promoting bulbs put many commercial greenhouses into business, as well as expanding the clientele of those seedsmen already open to trade. Throughout the era, there was an extremely close link between educators and the horticultural industry. In fact, quite often, purveyors and publishers were one and the same. Many of the largest nurseries published their own periodicals, interspersing advertisements throughout the pages and promoting their stock in the text. *Vick's Monthly Magazine* was an organ of the James Vick Seed Company of Rochester, NY; Thomas Meehan of Meehan's Nursery near Philadelphia edited the *Gardener's Monthly* and Dingee & Conard of West Grove, PA published *Success with Flowers*, to mention only a trio of the many companies which utilized this incredibly effective ploy. Of course, there was no attempt to mask the truth, everyone was willing to read a nurseryman's advice on what should be grown and how it ought to be cultivated. The readership was contented, and the companies were able to control the direction of taste, insuring that the bulb business would remain profitable.

Undoubtedly, bulb dealing was lucrative. Every major city on the East Coast had a few resident purveyors of bulbs. If a gardener did not happen to reside within city limits, no matter, bulbs could be obtained by mail. Bulb growers issued profusely illustrated catalogs replete with enticing engravings depicting resplendent potted bulbs blooming in profusion. Actually, those illustrations could easily be accused of presenting an overly optimistic rendition of blossoming potential. The gross exaggerations illustrated in those catalogs probably hooked more clients than any modern brochure armed with full-color photographic reproductions. And the effect of those catalogs was compounded immeasurably by the fact that seed companies kept their presses at the very forefront of printing technology. Their pamphlets were more profusely illustrated than those of any other industry and color printing was introduced into the horticultural field before it infiltrated most publishing houses.

The circulation of those bulb catalogs was truly phenomenal. The James Vick Seed Company of Rochester, NY claimed a catalog circulation of a quarter of a million in the mid-1870s—an impressive figure, even by present standards. However, the magnitude of that statistic can only be fully appreciated in view of the fact that the population of this country was only about 30 million at the time. The same seed, flower and bulb company also claimed that the postman delivered approximately 3,000 pieces of mail daily to their Rochester offices during the busiest season. And Vick's further boasted that the in-coming mail consisted mostly of orders.

Obviously, the market for bulbs had been successfully won. Considering the prices, the victory was probably an easy conquest. In the 1880s, a housewife could order an array of 6 double snowdrops, a pearl tuberose, 2 lilies, a single jonquil, 4 narcissus and a dozen crocus from Schlagel & Fottlers of Boston and spend less than a dollar. By the turn of the century, the price had plummeted even further. Good & Reese, a bulb firm located in Ohio, listed a collection of 60 forcing bulbs including an Easter Lily for $1.00. One wonders how the bulb purveyor could realize a profit.

In fact, Dutch bulbs opened the avenue not only for good, honest tradesmen, but for charlatans as well. At about that time, a breed of men known as "door-to-door salesmen" appeared on the scene. Perhaps there were honest gentlemen pursuing that calling. If so, they were apparently in the minority. Most travelling salesmen were referred to as "a class of itinerant swindlers"—or worse. Their business ethics were notoriously unprincipled.

Unfortunately, bulbs provided an easy product with which to deceive the public. One bulb looked much like the next, especially to an inexperienced eye. Who could tell positively if a bulb was a rare lily worth $1.00 or a less valuable variety? Of course, the salesman had completely vanished from the scene before his client discovered the hoax. Time and again, gullible housewives fell prey to the schemes of street vendors and transient rogues.

It was truly the Age of Innocence if we can judge from the scenario related by Peter Henderson in *Garden and Farm Topics*. Apparently, a certain charlatan had wreaked havoc selling bogus goods in towns and cities throughout the country. Henderson heard tales of his exploits far and wide. But this item in a San Francisco paper topped all the other stories. In California, the huckster was going under the name of Carlo Corella, introducing himself to perspective customers as the "Botanist to the Court of Brazil",

> He said to each that a failure of remittance compelled him to sell some rare bulbs of Brazilian lilies, which he had intended to present to Mrs. R.B. Hayes [then First Lady of the United States]. "The flowers," says the Chronicle, "were to be a great Scarlet bell, with ecru ruchings on the petals, a Solerino frill around the pistil, and a whole bottle of perfumery in each stamen." He sold about 50 worthless bulbs at $4.00 each.

Mr. Henderson himself was not immune to the wiles of travelling salesmen, although, as the owner of one of the largest mail-order companies in the country, he certainly should have known better. In *Garden and Farm Topics*, he recounted an incident in which he was offered bulbs of the rare, gold-banded Japan Lily from a pedlar who agreed to take only half payment until the flower had blossomed and proved to be true to name. Henderson naively purchased 100 for a $50.00 down payment. When the blossoms appeared, they proved to be the common white variety, normally sold for $5—$6 per 100. Obviously, the salesman never returned to collect the balance due on the sale.

Of course, such salesmanship cast doubt on the claims of honest tradesmen. Magazines and nurserymen were eager to expose the perpetrators of hoaxes. In their view, every transient dealer was suspect. At best, they accused door-to-door salesmen of offering inferior goods. Unfortunately, the credibility of their warnings was somewhat diluted by the fact that they accused one another of the same faults.

In truth, every 19th Century seedsman was guilty of gross exaggeration. Mankind had yet to invent the concept of truth in advertising. The engravings in 19th Century catalogs were preposterous renditions of fact. And, to those trumped-up pictures, many firms had the audacity to add a note explaining that the illustration was not nearly as grand as the genuine article. The enhanced pictures always did their subject scant justice in the eyes of the proprietors. In view of the claims, one may well wonder if customers were disappointed when their mail-order bulbs blossomed with a single flower rather than two dozen as depicted in the catalog. Apparently, they were neither seriously disillusioned nor permanently disheartened, for the market continued to gather strength throughout the century. Dutch bulbs of all descriptions attracted a strong following.

It should not surprise the reader to learn that hyacinths were the most popular bulbs for forcing. Hyacinths, with their full head of colorful bells emitting a distinctive, strong, heady fragrance, were considered to be the embodiment of every quality thought valuable in a flower. And, forcing hyacinths was a singularly simple chore. Mrs. Loudon (wife of the British horticulturist, John Claudius Loudon) explained the reason for the hyacinth's popularity in her book entitled, *Gardening for Ladies*, imported into North America in 1843 by Andrew Jackson Downing,

> *Hyacinthus orientalis*, is one of the most beautiful as well as the most fragrant flowers; and to a certain extent is also one of the easiest of culture for the amateur gardener. The reason for this is that the bulbs are generally to be purchased at an easy rate in the seed-shops, and the leaves and flowers being prepared in the bulb during the previous year, it is only necessary to place the bulbs in soil of any kind, or even on the surface of vessels of water, to produce a fine flower.

Americans needed little convincing. That thick, musty perfume peculiar to hyacinths was the perfect remedy for winter's bleak weather. The effusive aroma bound the disparate elements of the parlor together. Throughout the century, North Americans inhaled deeply of the strong, sweet perfume and revelled in its beneficence, wallowing in the assumption that the more fragrance a blossom emitted, the more thoroughly its goodness permeated the family. However, as always, the British remained a little more conservative in their tastes and affections. British-born Mrs. Loudon remarked, "In choosing Hyacinths for water-glasses, the red and blue are preferable to those which are white or yellow, the latter two have a fragrance too powerful for rooms, and besides, they

A slightly inflated rendition of the scilla's blooming potential from A. Blanc's *Hints on Cacti*.

generally flower weaker in glass than others." However, the North American audience showed no sign of discriminating against white or yellow hyacinths indoors—in fact, they preferred the more redolent varieties.

When Mrs. Loudon spoke of placing bulbs on the surface of vessels of water, she assumed that her audience had knowledge of the practice of forcing hyacinths in specially designed glass vases. The forcing vase had a wide mouth which held the bulb, then tapered to a thin waist which, in turn, flared into a large base which held the water. In fact, the vases boasted the same hour-glass shape so fashionable for the Victorian female figure. The bulb rested in the cup, only barely touching moisture, while its thirsty roots plunged into the water below. Writers waged an on-going battle as to the virtues of clear versus colored glass for the purpose. And, naturally, as the century progressed, enterprising inventors were always striving to build a better hyacinth glass. Advertisements in bulb catalogs featured simple as well as elaborate models, a favorite being Schmidt's patented variety which consisted of two separating parts, thus insuring that the bulb's roots would never be disturbed when changing the water. The plain glass model of this wonderful invention sold for 25¢, while a fancier version rendered of the finest Bohemian cracked glass could be had for 40¢. Whether Schmidt ever realized a fortune from his novelty is a point of some doubt, for the invention completely disappeared from the market after enjoying a very short flirt with fame. The Victorians remained loyal to their simple, fashionable hour-glass vase.

Later in the century, other contrivances for forcing bulbs became popular and offered further opportunities for practicing Yankee ingenuity. Among the most elaborate gimmicks for accommodating bulbs were forcing forms. A forcing form was a ceramic pot rendered into the shape of a hedgehog, beehive, turtle,

A crocus pot for forcing bulbs from Edward Sprague Rand's *Flowers for the Parlor and Garden*.

Single hyacinths.

A forcing form for crocus from Edward Sprague Rand's
Flowers for the Parlor and Garden.

porcupine, or whatever, with small holes from which the blossoms of crocus,
snowdrops or hyacinths peeked.

There was obviously money to be made in hyacinths. They commanded a
broad, sweeping popularity with Victorians of all economic strata. Hyacinths
were everyman's flower or, in Henry T. Williams' words, they would "smile as
sweetly on the poor man's window as in the most costly conservatory of the
wealthy." And the wealthy seemed perfectly willing to share hyacinth forcing
with the lower classes, while still continuing the tradition themselves.

The hyacinth's adaptability was a major factor in securing its success with all
economic sectors. Hyacinths are incredibly accommodating and forgiving
flowers. In 1873, Henry T. Williams expressed his opinion that hyacinths were
sought "simply because greater variety of color and quantity of bloom can be had
for less trouble and expense than any other."

Whether or not the hyacinth was the easiest flower to grow indoors, people wanted coaching. They also preferred to believe that they had achieved something difficult, and not merely pursued the inevitable. There was a correct method of forcing bulbs, performed by the astute student of horticulture; and then there was the incorrect method, which no one wished to be accused of practicing. If a sense of accomplishment was what early gardeners sought, then accommodating garden writers obligingly elevated the egos of the masses—even if that endeavor entailed spending pages detailing the intricacies of a profoundly simple task.

Of course, every writer harbored a personal opinion on how bulb forcing ought best to be accomplished. Basically, there was a standard procedure upon which individual growers elaborated. *The Ladies' Floral Cabinet* set forth a list of basic rules: Choose a bulb of considerable weight and size—single flowering varieties being more tasteful than doubles. Place the bulb so that the bottom barely touched the rain or pond water in a glass. Change the water regularly to prevent stagnation, and refill the glass when evaporation lowered the water level. These preparations fulfilled, the glass was to be kept in a cool (40–45°F.) cupboard for 6 weeks and then removed by degrees to full light. More light stimulated brighter colors while the buds were forming.

Over the years, the Victorians developed the art of bulb forcing into a science, and their insatiable appetite for information was satisfied by a continual supply of articles proposing a variety of methods aimed at accomplishing the feat. There was nothing dull about those instructions. The Victorians had an enviable gift for invoking quite remarkable analogies in their fervent attempts to instill the basic concepts of indoor plant cultivation while retaining a captive audience. This item appeared in an 1846 issue of the *Transactions of the Massachusetts Horticultural Society*,

> The Scythians are said to have thrown their children into rivers, even although frozen, as soon as they were born; and this practice is applied by 99 people in 100 to their hyacinths. They may depend upon it, that whatever may have been the case with Scythian children, Oriental hyacinths cannot bear it.

Of course, few homes had indoor running water at the time, and hot and cold water was not available until the end of the century. Water for plants had to be heated, which provided the housewife with yet another eagerly endured chore for the benefit of flowers and family morale.

Growing hyacinths in glasses was the easiest method of cultivating the bulbs. However, growing hyacinths in pots with soil was considered to be a more challenging approach to the same end. Most writers dismissed glass forcing summarily after paying the practice all due respect. Henry T. Williams summed up the prevailing ennui, "One or two seasons generally satisfy the enthusiast." And then it was on to mastering more complex growing techniques.

To grow bulbs in pots, a gardener applied the same principles as she enlisted in glass-forcing. The bulbs were potted in fall and then cooled in an outdoor ditch or dark cellar until December when they were brought into the parlor where the family could witness the dramatic development of the flowers. Apparently, the results amply repaid the effort, for the Victorians forced bulbs year after year.

Victorians rapidly mastered the technique of hyacinth forcing in both water and soil. However, a more difficult concept for the 19th Century gardener to grasp was the notion that forced hyacinths were the gift of a single season. Nothing could dissuade them from planting their forced bulbs in the garden when spring arrived. Victorians refused to discard forced bulbs at the end of their season and resign themselves to the fact that they had irreparably weakened the bulb in forcing. Although bulbs were cheap and could easily be repurchased the next autumn, the frugal Victorians simply could not bear to throw a plant away.

Hyacinth sales remained strong throughout the era, regardless of the state of the economy. In times of economic depression, bulbs provided the family with an inexpensive source of pleasure. In better times, customers purchased more costly named varieties. And, to keep the flame of enthusiasm aglow, dealers introduced a continual supply of novel colors and new variations. By the 1880s, hyacinths were available in white, red, rose, light blue, dark blue and yellow, as well as double and single forms of those shades. Long lists of named varieties were included in most catalogs. Dreer's Nursery was finally pressed to exercise some restraint and limit their hyacinth collection to "18 of each of the different classes." Nonetheless, their hyacinth list encompassed two pages of fine print.

Inevitably, other forced bulbs followed the hyacinth into the depths of the parlor. But, Victorians were so effusive and liberal with their praises that it is difficult to discern which of the Dutch bulbs ranked second in popularity. Judging from the number of species and cultivars included in period catalogs, it is safe to assume that narcissus took second place, although they trailed hyacinths by a healthy distance.

In the 19th Century, narcissus certainly did not enjoy a renown in any way resembling their current pinnacle of popularity. At present, the Paper White is the darling of the flower-starved winter gardener. Although Paper Whites have been grown in this country for at least two centuries, they were not the Victorians' favorite narcissus. Instead, the Victorians preferred *Narcissus bulbocodium*, nicknamed Medusa's Trumpet, but endeared to the 19th Century gardener by the more trendy epithet of the Hoop Petticoat Narcissus. Referring to this nickname, *Vick's Monthly* commented disapprovingly that the affixing of colloquial names "and the newest fashions in ladies' apparel are only old and often ridiculous customs revived." Perhaps so, but that popular name was earning the James Vick Seed Company quite a tidy sum in bulb sales. In addition, sales of other daffodil-type narcissus were also brisk. After *N. bulbocodium* came a long list of narcissus suitable for indoor forcing including bicolors, trumpet types, *N.* 'Von Scion', and single as well as double Poeticus varieties.

It was not until the last decade of the century that narcissus attained a popularity that reached fad proportions. It was then that *Narcissus tazetta var.*

The Hoop Petticoat Narcissus.

orientalis, the "Lien Chu Lily" burst upon the scene. The Lien Chu Lily, otherwise known as the Chinese Sacred Lily, looked nothing like a bonafide lily; the nickname was probably bestowed to heighten esteem and increase the bulb's monetary value. That many-flowered narcissus is actually a variety of the modern Paper White, which it closely resembles.

When in bloom, *Narcissus tazetta var. orientalis* is a handsome plant. However, it was the bulb's Oriental connection which secured its fame more solidly than its physical endowments. Few catalogs actually described the flower's appearance except, perhaps, to mention the profusion of blossoms. With typical Victorian magniloquence, Farquhar's catalog made the claim that 97 flowers had expanded simultaneously from a single bulb. We cannot, of course, prove him wrong, and neither could his contemporaries, but we reserve the right to doubt.

Rather than dwelling on its physical virtues, the catalogs invested their print space in describing the Lien Chu Lily's Oriental liaison. Not only were the flowers reported to play an important role in the Chinese New Year celebration; but also, according to Dreer's catalog, Chinese Sacred Lilies could "be seen well-grown in season in the window of every Chinaman who loves flowers." Dreer's solemnly promised that "the bulbs we offer are the large, true variety,

The Lien Chu Lily from Dreer's 1887 catalog.

and not the Paper White." They were an expensive acquisition at 30¢ a piece, a fact which partially justified the use of the nickname "Sacred Lily".

Crocus, Lily of the Valley, Snowdrops and (toward the end of the century) Freesias, were all forced in shallow pots to freshen the dull parlor atmosphere and add a touch of life to the stagnant air indoors. Even *Allium neapolitanum* was recommended for winter forcing as well as for the summer garden.

Tulips were also on the list of forcing bulbs, although they took a position well behind the other Dutch imports. Contemporary writers felt confident in recommending only the Duc Van Tol cultivars for the purpose, explaining that the other hybrids were too tall to be comfortably accommodated in pots. When tulips were utilized, they were most often elements of group plantings surrounded by other imports from Holland. In fact, it was not necessarily the tulip's virtues as a houseplant that won it a place on the parlor windowsill. The tulip entered primarily on the strength of its connection with Tulipomania. Although the fires of the tulip frenzy had long since been extinguished, the flicker of their memory still surrounded the bulbs.

Naturally, forced bulbs were exhibited in a prominent spot in the parlor or sitting room. As one of the home's most valuable possessions, forced bulbs took up a position of importance on the mantelpiece, residing proudly alongside the

Freesias from Dingee & Conard's *Success with Flowers*.

resonant parlor clock, wedged in between a family portrait or two. The spot was chosen for its visibility rather than its suitability. The mantel rarely enjoyed the benefit of the sun's rays. But, direct sunlight is not essential for blossoming bulbs such as hyacinths. While the mantel was not the best possible location for the purpose, it was sufficient to accomplish the deed. Later in the century, as bulbs became more frequent seasonal inhabitants in the room, they gradually found their way to more appropriate locations. They were given a place on the windowsill where the light would promote deeper petal color and more compact growth. Eventually, the Victorian penchant for prodigality took rein and they were incorporated throughout the room. Small bulbs were often pinned to the parlor wallpaper and tucked onto picture frames. No nook or cranny was neglected in the effort to be-flower the room.

Having mastered the techniques of bulb growing with the Dutch varieties, Victorians were eager to hone their skills with other bulbous specimens. Oxalis entered the parlor's realm very early in the era's evolution. In fact, oxalis were mentioned as appropriate houseplants in the *American Flower Garden Directory*, a simple, instructive text written in 1832 by Thomas Hibbert and Robert Buist, a partnership which had purchased McMahon's Nursery in Philadelphia only two years earlier. The book pointed out the pitfalls of growing sun-loving bulbs such as oxalis in an early 19th Century home and warned that there was barely enough light to accomplish the deed. In the chapter entitled "Rooms" and dedicated to the month of November, the authors described oxalis: "The autumn flowering species will now be in bloom, and must be kept in the sun to make them expand freely. The neglect of this is the principle reason that these plants do not flower perfectly in rooms." Later in the era, *Vick's Monthly* provided the telling information that oxalis were most popular in the South, where they enjoyed a better winter sun.

Oxalis were tempting to grow. In appearance, bulbous oxalis look like field clover, although the Victorians rarely, if ever, made the comparison. In blossom, oxalis resemble buttercups. In fact, the most popular yellow *Oxalis cernua* (now *Oxalis pes-caprae*) was known as the Bermuda Buttercup. Other species were available which bloomed in white, pink and magenta.

Other than their demand for sun, oxalis are easy houseplants and undoubtedly provided nearly as much satisfaction as Dutch bulbs; although they did not offer the possibility of staggered blossoming to provide a succession of flowers indoors. The instructions for their cultivation were simple, as one magazine noted, "For house-culture five or six bulbs should be put in a 6 inch pot, and this should be done as early as possible in October or November. In potting, place an inch of drainage at the bottom; then fill the pot half way up with well-decayed manure; the rest of the pot should be filled with fresh, light loam." It was a potent mixture, but oxalis are heavy feeders.

One advantage to growing oxalis rather than Dutch bulbs was their willingness to obligingly perform year after year, which effectively circumvented the nasty duty of discarding bulbs after a single season. As one magazine suggested,

After flowering, when the foliage begins to turn yellow, they should be dried off, and the pots put in some cool, dry place until the coming season, when they should be shaken out and re-potted.

Oxalis were just one representative genus from the great brotherhood of Cape bulbs. Cape bulbs are natives of South Africa, in the region of the Cape of Good Hope; and their exotic point of origin enhanced their mystique. Although oxalis entered the home early in the era, other Cape bulbs were of little significance until the end of the century. As late as 1863, Edward Sprague Rand was bemoaning their lack of popularity in his chapter on Cape bulbs in *Flowers for the Parlor and Garden*,

> They combine in a remarkable degree, the two requisites of easy culture and floral beauty. Yet strange it is, that we seldom see them, except in the greenhouse or conservatory in this country, while in England they are popular plants for home adornment, and grown in both window and garden.

The chapter's title illustration divulged the reason for the less than enthusiastic acceptance of Cape bulbs in North America. Although the chapter heading clearly spelled out the topic as being "Cape Bulbs", the accompanying

This illustration of Holland Bulbs headed Edward Sprague Rand's chapter on "Cape Bulbs".

engraving depicted a huge urn filled to capacity with hyacinths, tulips and crocus. Obviously, people were still preoccupied with Dutch bulbs. The Cape bulbs' fame would not be secured until much later in the next century despite an occasional plea from writers such as Rand for the cultivation of Ixia, Oxalis, Babiana, Haemanthus, Amaryllis, Lachenalia, Sparaxis, Anomatheca (now Lapeirousia), Tritonia, Homeria, and Nerine species.

The Victorian disinterest in Cape bulbs was undoubtedly due to the fact that those bulbs were not yet the subjects of extensive hybridizing. The cultivars available in the 19th Century were basically a collection of selected species which exhibited the rudimentary characteristics that would later be enhanced by plant breeders.

Amaryllis provide an excellent case in point. In the mid-1800s, amaryllis were merely a glimmer in the tradesman's eye. Although everyone involved in the plant business could see their potential, they had yet to catch the public's imagination. Amaryllis were the subject of only an occasional magazine article, and those infrequent manuscripts invariably opened on the downbeat note of bemoaning the plant's lagging popularity. The *Gardener's Monthly* wrote, "This family has seldom received the attention it deserves. We find a few of them here and there, - many of these without a name." The *Gardener's Monthly* could mention only a handful of species, and no hybrids were available at the time. The blossoms were described as a mere 4 in. in diameter—a piddling display by present amaryllis standards. But the plant had possibilities. The author of the article in *Gardener's Monthly* speculated, "I feel satisfied that if gardeners in general were aware of the real worth of these plants, they would become universal and indispensable." The prediction was to be realized. In fact, amaryllis eventually achieved a fame that far surpassed the fondest dreams of any Victorian horticulturist.

The only bulb to compete favorably with Dutch bulbs throughout the entire 19th Century was the Calla Lily, or *Zantedeschia aethiopica* (known at the time as *Calla aethiopica*). Not only did the Calla's popularity compare favorably with the products of Holland, but the Calla eventually transcended all other bulbs in the public's affections. As the era progressed, few homes were without a pot of Callas sprouting their spathe-like inflorescence cloaked dramatically in a pure white sheath.

Calla Lilies are by no means easy plants to grow. Callas are aquatic, and no one was quite sure how to accommodate an aquatic bulb in the parlor. Theories abounded, and a multitude of methods were suggested and tossed about. It was a tricky topic for authors who wished to provide specific and intricately detailed growing instructions. How much water was required? No one was positively sure.

Some writers opted to skirt the issue entirely and address the more aesthetic aspects of Calla culture. Edward Sprague Rand did an excellent job of circumventing the problems inherent in Callas by concentrating on their containers. He advised his readers, "If bloom is particularly desired, the best way is

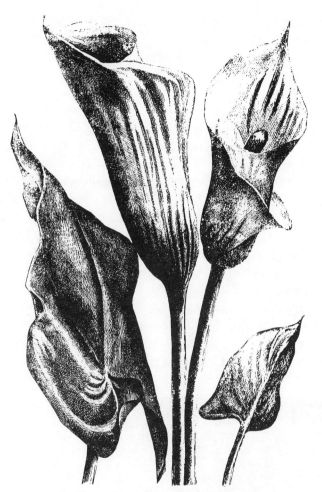

Calla lilies from *The Ladies' Floral Cabinet*.

to plant some 6 or 8 roots in the half of an oil cask. Paint it green, and put on two iron handles."

The Ladies' Floral Cabinet chose to address the issue more directly. The *Cabinet*'s article on Callas published in 1885 opened with the no nonsense introduction, "Opinions differ so widely in the culture of the Calla Lily, I do not wonder that amateur florists are nonplussed to know which way is right." Their answer to the conundrum was to delve into the history of that ancient plant and thus discern its optimal habitat. No doubt, every 19th Century reader was captivated by the fascinating and minutely detailed account of ancient Egyptian seasonal water levels and their effects on the resident Calla,

> If we consult history concerning its native habitat; we shall find that from June 21, the beginning of the summer solstice, the waters of the Nile begin to rise gradually within their banks . . . until the middle of July, when they overflow them. About the 20th of August the valley presents the appearance of a great inland sea, and so continues until the autumnal equinox.

All this data simply proved that Callas required abundant water. However, the article offered no insight into how an indoor gardener might duplicate similar flooding conditions in her home. I entertain visions of innumerable housewives religiously filling aquariums by degrees, beginning the ritual promptly on the morning of June 21st.

Naturally, Callas were an item of deep concentration among enterprising bulb dealers eager to benefit from the rapidly changing affections of the masses. A standard item in every plant catalog was the white "Lily of the Nile" which ranged in price from 10¢ to 50¢ a bulb, and drew an enthusiastic crowd of customers. However, there is always room for embellishment on a popular theme. And so, building on the strength of the Calla Lily's fame, several different variations were introduced to the market by the end of the century including a spotted cultivar and a dwarf Calla affectionately known as 'Little Gem'.

Tradesmen saw a golden opportunity to cash in with the introduction of a novelty item known as the Black Calla. One of the first women to enter the mail-order bulb business, Miss Ella V. Baines, listed the Black Calla in her catalog. From her description, anyone would assume that "The Woman Florist" was promoting a color variant of the sterling-white *Calla aethiopica*. Nothing could be further from the truth. The Black Calla was actually a pleasant euphemism for the fetid-flowered *Amorphophallus*, a plant which was neither beautiful nor

White callas and the "Black Calla" as advertised in Miss Ella V. Baines' 1897 catalog.

benevolent by any stretch of the imagination. Miss Baines billed it with the following glowing description, "Its flowers are enormous, fully a foot in length. The color is clear, coal black." Of course, the size is slightly exaggerated, but overestimation was a besetting problem of the era. She committed a more serious trespass by omitting any mention of the flower's odor—so rank that it precluded the possibility of inhabiting the room while the Black Calla was in bloom. Such negative details (salient or not) were never mentioned in period catalogs, nor did they appear to have a bearing on which plants were recommended for growing indoors. Purveyors of plants sold anything that was new. But, only botanicals that proved their worth in the home survived to become popular houseplants.

We can scarcely leave the subject of bulbs without mentioning the era's most enduring success story—Liliums. Lilies did not wander into the parlor until the era had gathered momentum and indoor gardeners gained confidence in their ability to grow plants. However, those gallant and gaudy trumpets are so typical of the Victorian Era that they became irrevocably associated with the somber and formal front room.

The lily which most often adorned Victorian parlors was "The Beautiful Bermuda Easter Lily" or *Lilium longiflorum var. eximium* (known in the early 19th Century simply as *Lilium harrisii*). The Victorians can be credited with the initiation of the holiday lily tradition which has gathered such momentum over the years that lilies and spring are now virtually synonymous.

Lilies were extremely valuable bulbs. In fact, they were the selling point for cut-rate bulb sets and low-priced offers of mixed bulbs. Lilies were the bait which hooked many indoor gardeners, and the Victorians found them incredibly difficult to resist. Not only did an Easter Lily beam its moral goodness on the household, but it also had strong religious connotations. Although its benefits were fleeting, the Easter Lily was destined to remain among the most desirable houseplants of the era.

Easter Lilies were probably as popular in the 19th Century home as they are in 20th Century abodes. However, it is interesting to note the difference between the Victorian and the modern Easter Lily market. The 19th Century indoor gardener would scarcely entertain the notion of purchasing a fully grown Easter Lily completely budded and ready to burst into bloom. Victorians began their plants from scratch—from the basic bulb. The process was many times more arduous than purchasing a finished specimen, but the rewards were magnified one-thousandfold.

Lilies require more light to thrive than Dutch bulbs, and in that respect they provided the Victorian indoor gardener with yet another challenge. In addition, the indoor gardener also learned the significance of proper potting techniques to support the lilies' tall, weak stems. The subject provided grist for many gardening articles.

Victorians pursued their bulb forcing with an impassioned zeal. The collection grew, it gained additional members and invaded new nooks and crannies of

An advertisement for ''The Beautiful Bermuda Easter Lily'' from *Success with Flowers*.

the parlor. Plants were settling comfortably into the home as contented cohabitants, blessing their surroundings with a benevolent aura.

Amazingly, the houseplant tradition started with bulbs—with a few, squat, ugly bulbs that worked magic when planted. They wove a constant theme throughout the era, developing as the period progressed and evolving as the parlor evolved. With the easily grown Dutch bulbs, indoor gardeners honed their skills until they were sufficiently confident to attempt more challenging specimens such as oxalis, Cape bulbs, Callas and finally Easter Lilies. It was a most fortunate beginning. That starting point was so fortuitous, in fact, that Dutch bulbs still adorn our parlors today.

LIST OF BULBS COMMONLY GROWN INDOORS

Allium
Babiana
Convallaria (Lily of the Valley)
Crocus
Cyclamen
Galanthus (Snowdrops)
Haemanthus
Homeria
Hyacinth
Ixia
Lachenalia
Lapeirousia
Lilium
Muscari
Narcissus
Nerine
Ornithalgum (Pregnant Onion)
Oxalis
Scilla
Sparaxis
Tritonia
Tulipa
Zantedeschia (Calla Lily)

CHAPTER V

THE GARDEN INDOORS

THE VICTORIANS did not pause long to feast upon their bulb victory. The fertile 19th Century imagination was ignited. As soon as people discovered that it was feasible to grow plants within the home, they gave their fancy full rein to toy with the possibilities inherent in that newly adopted indoor sport. And, when the Victorians allowed their imagination to roam on topics horticultural, their thoughts immediately turned toward the treasures in the garden. Those plants had furnished summer months of pleasure outdoors. Why not simply move the flower garden inside the home? The concept caught on with contagious enthusiasm.

Amazingly, the idea worked. The timing was perfect. Although that feat would have proved impossible half a century earlier or later, the environment in the parlor was just right between the 1830s and 1850s to successfully accomplish the deed. Before the popularization of central heating, the home was cold, and the parlor was particularly chilly. At night, the room frequently witnessed temperatures of 45°F. or lower, and frosts were all too common indoors. A few decades later, the march of technology put an abrupt end to the bone chilling parlor temperatures which were so conducive to the well-being of the hardy and half-hardy perennials which first entered from the garden. But, in the 1830s, the climate was just right. Historically, the transplantation of the garden did not occur one moment too soon.

Although perennials received a climatically chilly reception in the parlor, they were warmly welcomed by the gardeners themselves. If familiarity breeds fondness, those garden plants had already nestled into a soft spot in the family's breast. The roses, primroses, violets and carnations of the garden were already old and dear acquaintances to virtually every Victorian gardener. They were among the first plants to impart the secrets of ornamental gardening, tempting gardeners into further and more exotic horticultural pursuits. They were also the ingredients from which Colonial bouquets were fashioned. And, in that capacity, they had already entered the home as cut flowers. But, beyond those practical applications, they were also the stuff of dreams. Surrounded by an awesome accumulation of sentimental, symbolic and romantic connotations, those favorite flowers prompted ladies to delve deeper into horticultural endeavors.

The rose, of course, was of legendary fame. But, other garden favorites were also popular celebrities. Many plants built their reputations primarily on the duration of their relationship with gardeners. In addition, certain garden plants were heavily encrusted with the honors and titles derived from spurious political and social connections. Such honors were primarily afforded to the garden's "old favorites." The more famous a flower became, the more frequently it was chosen as an emblem for political factions or social issues. And thus, its fame or infamy grew. The December 1887 issue of *Harper's New Monthly Magazine* contained this partial roster of notorious garden favorites and their political affiliations:

> The violet of the Napoleon dynasty is even yet worn in France, and at Fontainebleau the apartments of the ex-Empress Josephine are redolent with its exquisite odor. In China and Japan the chrysanthemum has taken the place of honor as the national flower, but one of the latest and strongest party badges is the "pale primrose" of Shakespeare now the ensign of the "Primrose League", an order of Conservatives founded in honor of the late Lord Beaconsfield.

Governments might come and go, heroes might fall in and out of favor but, somehow, despite the political connections which a plant acquired, the public never soured on that flower. To the contrary, such publicity augmented the plant's fame. Any self-respecting lady knew all the old-fashioned flowers intimately. She could, if called upon, deliver a lengthy dissertation describing their personalities, symbolism and preferences in cultivation. Such extensive knowledge became part of the social graces, and horticultural topics were frequently invoked to fill awkward moments in polite conversation.

At a time when women's education was a highly controversial issue, studies devoted to floral matters were on safe neutral territory. Although not greatly respected as a serious scholarly pursuit, the study of the symbolism and care of old-fashioned flowers became a common part of a girl's tutelage, as we can construe from this cartoon printed in *The Ladies' Floral Cabinet*,

> "And so, your daughter is at the academy? How does she get along?"
> "Splendidly; she's studying all the higher branches."
> "Is she studying languages?"
> "Oh yes; she has nearly completed the language of flowers and is now engaged in the language of perfumes. My! What an education that girl will have when she gets through."

But, all fun aside, the Victorians agreed that a thorough understanding of plants and flowers was a crucial component in a young girl's training. And, with this aim in mind, they made every possible attempt to maximize their daughters' interaction with nature. Although spring and summer were replete with innumerable outdoor activities, the autumn and winter months were comparatively empty of recreation prior to the introduction of indoor gardening.

Not only did the domestication of garden plants arrive at a convenient juncture in the home's technological metamorphosis, but it also coincided nicely with an awkward interval in the transition of the feminine role. A woman of the 1830s was faced with the unsavory prospect of spending her winter engaged in out-dated amusements which she had inherited from her Colonial predecessors. Henry Ward Beecher painted a grim portrait of the typical female existence in 1859 as the contemporary heroines floundered in search of diversion,

> Late hours at night, and later morning hours, early application to books, a steady training for accomplishments, viz. embroidery, lace work, painting rice paper, casting wax-flowers . . . these, together with practicings on the piano, or if something extra is meant, a little tum, tum, tumming on the harp, and a little ting-tong on the guitar; reading "ladies' books", crying over novels, writing in albums . . . are the materials, too often, of a fashionable education.

Beecher wisely prescribed plants as an antidote for terminal tedium. Similarly, he harbored high hopes that gardening, both outdoors and in, would prove to be the mental and physical salvation for a population of women who enjoyed chronically failing health and acute bouts of the vapors. Those same plants which quickened the step and brightened the smiles of the young ladies who scampered through the garden outside could accomplish similar feats indoors.

Flowers were responsible for the health and beauty of youth. The color of summer roses somehow managed to appear in the blush on the cheeks of happy daughters who tended the plants. In 1886, *The Ladies' Floral Cabinet* summarized the prevailing faith in botanical cures. They featured a story in which the wise Dr. Stanley was paying a house call on his willowy patient, Alicia Hunter, who lay "pale and languid on the sofa in a furnace-heated room" having "been housed since November with neuralgia and a train of nervous disorders fast settling on permanent disease." His remedy consisted of gardening regularly, "Nothing but a garden will do it. The pills and powder of this medicine-case are no such panacea for bringing the roses to your cheeks or strength and activity to your system."

Of course, under the good doctor's care, the patient revived. And, in order to prolong the garden's curative effects, Alicia sought solace in a seasonal substitute,

> Summer cannot last forever . . . and as the cold chilly days of autumn drew on she could not bear to loose her garden, even for the winter, hence one of the windows in her father's sitting room was dedicated to the purpose . . . Whatever of the plants could be potted and moved to the window-garden were placed there . . .

In addition to restoring the blush of youth, houseplants also proved a comfort in old age. They furnished companionship for invalids whose health had deteriorated to the point that they could no longer seek invigoration from the garden outdoors. In *Window Gardening*, Henry T. Williams described an all too common scene,

> In our country homes; how common to see the plant stand before the window with its dozen or so pots of Geraniums, Primroses, Azaleas &c., while an invalid sister or mother reclines in the easy chair, watching it for hours with delight, unmindful of the snow driving past the pane.

"Life's Eventide" from Margaret Sangster's *Home Life Made Beautiful*.

Although new to Americans, the precedent for introducing hardy plants into rooms had been set, as usual, in Europe. However, unlike other gardening fashions and landscape styles, the practice of cultivating perennials as windowsill pot plants began with the working classes, rather than sifting downward from the upper crust of society.

It all started on the windowsills of laborers who engaged in cottage crafts centuries before Europe industrialized and sent its workers to toil daily in centralized factories far from the home's cozy hearth. At the time, cottagers spent their entire 16 hour work day confined within their homes, weaving, spinning and producing the simple but essential amenities of daily existence. Life was not easy, and did not afford many free moments. But, somehow, they found time to water, groom, pot and admire garden flowers placed on their windowsills for year around companionship. The plants became articles of pride for the cottagers. On an appointed day every year, the indoor gardeners in each hamlet donned shiny top hats and met to exhibit their flowers in "shews", later called "flower feasts". Enterprising inn-keepers hosted the festivities, provided the beverages and awarded the trophies for the best primrose or carnation in "shew".

This was the inspiration which the early Victorians pursued. Still influenced by the unpretentious 1700s, the citizens of the early 1800s wanted little more out of their windowsills than to extend the summer and inhale the beneficence of nature long after its natural season had expired. With this aim in mind, tried-and-true garden plants offered an excellent point of departure.

Although the desire to domesticate old-fashioned flowers was undoubtedly strong early in the century, there was still the small matter of education to resolve. Women were extremely well-versed in the symbolism and social customs surrounding old-fashioned flowers. And, they were quickly becoming equally well-tutored on the plants' preferences outdoors. But, growing hardy plants in the home posed some unique challenges. Here was a new area of expertise to conquer, and the eager indoor gardener warmed to the stimulus. This new task was far more difficult than the simple ritual of forcing bulbs. But, as the complexity of the feat increased, the rewards of success became proportionally sweeter. The first few years of the experiment were filled with daily suspense.

Winter gardening duties commenced just as summer's responsibilities waned. After rescuing garden plants from their summer quarters in autumn, they were potted and transported indoors. The whole project might sound blissfully simple, but it was actually a matter of supreme delicacy. The change in environment from garden to home was a considerable shock to the plant. It was absolutely crucial to minimize the trauma inflicted in the transfer.

It is indicative of the popularity enjoyed by the move to indoor gardening, that a method for digging perennials was developed by none other than the era's favorite clergyman, Henry Ward Beecher. His gardening practices obviously combined the insights and diplomacy developed for handling delicate situations as a preacher. While the perennial was still comfortably situated in its spot in the garden, a pot was selected to receive the specimen. Using the pot as a guide, a circle was drawn around the plant and a spade was thrust down to sever the roots at the perimeter. Thus prepared, the plant was left in the ground for a few days and sheltered from the sun until new root hairs initiated. Then the plant was lifted, potted and brought indoors. The method required some foresight—you could not run out on the afternoon prior to a frosty night and accomplish the deed. But, the process definitely had its advantages. The violence of upheaval was inflicted slowly, affording the victim ample time to recover from the initial shock of root disruption before being forced to adjust to the change in growing environment. All things considered, Beecher had developed an ingenious plan.

Having successfully executed the digging, the next challenge lay in finding a suitable spot to receive the perennial. Bulbs were relatively easy to please compared to the wants of herbaceous plants. According to Henry Ward Beecher, the indoor gardener was faced with two choices when placing his perennials—and neither of them was particularly savory. He set forth the essence of the conundrum in *Plain and Pleasant Talk about Fruits, Flowers and Farming,*

> In our dwellings, one has to make his way between two extremes in the best manner that he can. Without a stove our thin-walled houses are cold as ice-houses, and a frosty night sends dismay among our favorites. Then, on the other hand, if we have a stove, the air is apt to be parched, and unwholesome, fit for salamanders, fat and torpid cats and dozing grandmothers. There is not much choice between an ice-house and an oven.

However, there was little question in Beecher's mind concerning the correct choice when faced with the two extremes. He wrote, "Flowers in small stove rooms can be kept in health with extreme difficulty. The heat forces their growth, or injures the leaves." Obviously, a cool room such as the front parlor, hall, or entry way was preferable to the cozy back parlor or living rooms where the family gathered daily to enjoy each other's company around the radiant warmth of a toasty heat source.

Proper temperatures were not the only problem to confound the novice. Lack of direct sunlight was an equally annoying adversary for anyone attempting to transplant garden plants into rooms. Even if the plants could be cajoled into surviving on a windowsill, perennials did not necessarily perform with the same gusto indoors as they had outside. Henry Ward Beecher kept the expectations of indoor gardeners at ebb with the cautionary words, "The flower stalks will be apt to shoot up taller and weaker than in the garden, and will require rods to support them."

However, the rewards far outweighed the difficulties to be surmounted. A flowering plant remained in blossom much longer on the windowsill than out in a garden. Sheltered from the direct rays of sunlight which quickly spoil a blossom, the flower might extend its moment of glory to twice its normal duration.

Not only was Henry Ward Beecher one of the era's foremost clergymen, he was also an authority on indoor horticulture.

And, shielded from the elements and protected from wind and rain damage, the flower retained its vivid colors throughout its lifespan.

With these advantages firmly fixed in their minds, gardeners were determined to compensate for the inopportune conditions in their homes. They learned to work with what was available. Although windows could not provide the plants with as much light as they enjoyed in the garden, indoor gardeners were advised that a sunny southern window would suffice. They arranged the pots at varying distances from the light source depending upon the individual light requirements of each plant. But still, providing sun-loving plants with ample light often proved to be a point of difficulty, since the sunniest rooms were family rooms, which generally received the heat of a stove. Later in the era, rooms would be designed specifically with plant comfort in mind. In the meantime, if the front parlor had no suitable exposure, the housewife was advised to place the plant in a room with a brighter window and ventilate according to the plants' preferences. Human sensibilities took a secondary role.

Perennials did not always move directly from their summer quarters to a position in the family's midst. They often spent an interim period in the cellar where they were encouraged to rest and gather strength for their winter performance. The Victorians subscribed to the humanitarian notion that all plants must rest for a season during the year. If a perennial blossomed during the summer, either in the parlor or the garden, it was generally given an early autumn respite. However, if an immediate floral performance was needed, the plant was pressed into service first, and then allowed to rest.

Initially, the cellar treatment was recommended for all plants, regardless of their willingness to blossom throughout the year. Apparently, however, many zealous new gardeners took advantage of their plants' accommodating dispositions. Floriferous perennials often did not receive their vacations. Monthly roses and carnations were most frequently over-worked, if we can judge from Edwin Johnson's comment in *Winter Greeneries in the Home,*

> You will not allow yourselves to be misled by the word 'monthly', as if Monthly Roses and Monthly Carnations could go on blooming year in and year out, until they die of old age. Even these vigorous bloomers require, like other plants, some season of comparative rest, and if they do not have it in winter, they must in summer.

After their sojourn in the cellar, the plants were pruned and brought upstairs for display. Since they were being exhibited in a room without the benefit of a stove, frost was a frequent problem. Many of the hybrids which became popular for winter culture indoors could not endure the North American climate outdoors. This was especially true of roses, carnations and Parma Violets. But, even the hardiest plant could be injured by sudden frost to its weak, indoor growth. Most early books and magazines included instructions on first-aid for frozen plants. James Norman Eley offered these remedies in *The American Florist,*

> In case of Plants getting frozen, which they are liable to do in the winter, they should be removed to the kitchen or a place where they can be watered or the leaves washed with cold water . . . As soon as the frost is out of them, they may be placed in the rooms again.

As the winter progressed toward spring, the conditions in the parlor also changed. The light in the room was brighter, and the temperature began to rise. The care of indoor plants had to be modified accordingly. These timely suggestions, offered in *The Ladies' Floral Cabinet,* are as valuable today as they were a century ago,

> With the new year there seems a disposition in plants to increased growth; the days are longer, there is more light and heat to stimulate the tissues, and the sunlight is more magnetic. The long-looked-for flowering buds will begin to appear, in your delight at their appearance be cautious in regard to heat; too much will blast your buds, and with them your hopes. Keep the temperature as low in the house as is consistent with personal comfort . . .

In spring, most houseplants were set outside in the garden. However, once a plant was confined to a pot, many gardeners were loath to release it to freedom again. Potted perennials remained in their containers even during their summer sojourn in the garden.

Most authors suggested that the botanical refugees from the house should continue receiving special attention while in their summer quarters. Having spent winter in a relatively dark home, their growth was soft and spindly. To protect them from the sudden change in light intensity, they were afforded shade.

Meanwhile, they were watered regularly, and the foliage was cleaned periodically, just as they were groomed in the parlor. Repotting, to accommodate the summer growth, was performed halfway through the season. In autumn, before frosts threatened, the plants were again taken up and transported into the parlor to resume their function as houseplants.

Having studied and mastered the process, it was only left to the gardener to select some suitable subjects and commence the project. A truly amazing array of garden plants were suggested for the purpose before gardeners settled into a repertoire of a few favorites. In 1806, *McMahon's American Gardener* mentioned an eclectic collection of appropriate garden plants and bushes including "honeysuckles, African heaths, double flowering dwarf almonds, and cherries, &c. also pots of pinks, carnations, daisies, double Sweet-Williams, rockets, wall and stock-gilly flowers &c." Elsewhere in the same volume, McMahon added "peaches and thorns" to his lengthy roster of suitables.

Eventually, after experimenting broadly, the Victorians settled happily into cultivating a handful of their old-fashioned favorites. Roses, carnations, prim-

Roses provided an inspiration for many young ladies, from Francis Parkman's *The Book of Roses*.

roses and violets led the pack, and their presence eclipsed that of any other garden plants. They already reigned as favorites in the garden, and they eventually became equally popular in the early Victorian home.

After all, who can survive without roses? And who can resist their subtle charms? Almost every garden contained at least one rose, if not a dozen different varieties. And, to judge from the praises bestowed on members of that genus, the love for roses was timeless, as well as universal.

Throughout the romantic Victorian Era, the rose remained paramount. A quick sampling of the poetic out-pourings penned by dewy-eyed young Victorians gives us some indication of the rose's preeminence. For example, Parsons' classic, *The Rose*, published in 1847, includes no fewer than 60 poems dedicated to that genus sandwiched between dry directions on the cultivation of the plant. In view of their universal popularity, there is little wonder that the rose led the train of hardy plants entering the home. The rose's beauty was considered a rare commodity long before the first exotic tropicals appeared on Western shores.

Roses were essentially associated with the garden when the century opened. To ease them onto the windowsill, William Paul's 1848 classic, *The Rose Garden*, devoted a few opening paragraphs to shifting the scene from outdoors into the parlor,

> What advantage is gained by growing Roses in pots? The same question might be asked with equal propriety respecting any class of hardy or half-hardy plants.

While inferring that the question "why?" might be considered rhetorical, Paul was willing to delineate, for those who harbored doubts, many reasons to recommend engaging in the practice of growing roses indoors,

> Some of the delicate and more beautiful kinds have their flowers bruised and spoiled, even in summer, by the winds and rains of our unsettled climate, and many are incapable of enduring the cold of winter.

In addition to negative arguments, Paul also found positive motives to encourage rose cultivation indoors. Not least among the rose's virtues was the "delicious fragrance of the flowers, their richness and beauty, their elegant mode of growth and handsome foliage." Who would not welcome the opportunity to enjoy the rose's qualities at close quarters?

Extolling the rose's endowments undoubtedly went a long way toward endearing the plant into Victorian hearts. However, their suitability as houseplants would be the deciding factor to clinch the argument. As William Paul conceded, "if the Rose is a suitable plant for Pot-Culture, it will undoubtedly continue to gain friends, if not, no praise of ours can essentially serve it." Fortunately, roses stood their ground indoors.

Of the garden's roses, the most popular for indoor cultivation were, naturally, those that required protection from severe winter weather. The roses of the

Orient, and the rapidly expanding ranks of their hybrids were the perennial plants most frequently incorporated into the parlor. June, Perpetual, Provence, Damask, Galic, Moss, Climbing, Austrian, Noisette, and Banksian Roses were all deemed inappropriate for indoor culture, although they were occasionally introduced into the parlor by daring or naive gardeners. Instead, writers suggested patronizing Oriental Roses for indoor cultivation.

China and Tea Roses had arrived in North America around the turn of the century, and they furnished a welcome addition to the ranks of old European roses that blossomed only once a season. The roses of the Orient provided a recurrent display, but their full potential could only be realized when grown indoors.

China and Tea Roses appeared on the American market simultaneously, resulting in widespread confusion about their lineage. Theories were many and usually incorrect, leading most garden writers to circumvent the issue entirely. As a result, it was not until the present century that the breeding lines were untangled. The Tea Roses, which were the prototypes of our contemporary, highly perfected Hybrid Tea Roses, were derived principally from *Rosa odorata*, introduced from China in 1810. More profuse of flower were the China or Bengal Roses, which sprang from *Rosa indica* and *Rosa semperflorens*. Their loyal performance earned them the nickname, "Monthly Roses" or, more optimistically, "Daily Roses". Of the two, China Roses were more common, and more plebeian. Although garden writers may have been hesitant about rose history, they were swift to establish social connotations.

In a rapidly changing social structure, even the roses which a family cultivated provided a statement about their position on the economic ladder. Andrew Jackson Downing, always a social snob, made this observation concerning the distribution of indoor roses,

> The daily China rose . . . cheats the window of the crowded city of its gloom, is the joy of the daughter of the humblest day laborer; the delicate Tea rose, fated to be admired and to languish in the drawing room or the boudoir, wins its place in the affections of the most cultivated and fastidious tastes.

The poorer relatives, China Roses, were sold throughout the city in early spring. Street urchins hawked them on busy city corners and they abounded in the marketplace. The plants were too easily obtained to be particularly elite. However, they were actually superior performers. China Roses are stout growing and more easily managed than the Tea. Yet, according to some rose connoisseurs, they are not as fragrant or equal in beauty. Their chief merit is their abundant bloom. One China Rose may not be as fantastic as a Tea Rose blossom, but the entire display is equally awesome by virtue of profusion alone.

Tea Roses maintained their aloof position by remaining slightly finicky, and thus, not within everyone's grasp. Tea Roses prefer more heat and light than China Roses. And, according to Edward Sprague Rand they are "not as patient under neglect." For the additional attention bestowed upon them, they offered a

A China Rose illustrated in William Paul's *The Rose Garden*.

gardener the greater and more rewarding sense of accomplishment which accompanies having successfully cultivated a challenging subject.

Other roses were occasionally found on the Victorian windowsill. Most notably, Bourbon Roses (*Rosa x borboniana*) were cultivated for their massive blossoms and profuse performance. Originally found on L'Ile de Bourbon, now Reunion, and introduced into France in 1822, Bourbons are hardier than China Roses. However, their most profuse floral display occurs in late autumn and would be lost to early frosts unless they are sequestered indoors. Each Bourbon flower is huge, flat and heavy—they fit perfectly in the torpid front parlor.

By the early 1800s, roses of all sorts were enjoying their heyday. Collections of 600 to 1,000 non-hardy varieties were not uncommon, and nurseries struggled to keep the public equipped with an unending supply of novel cultivars. At times, they were fighting an uphill battle. While striving to increase their rosters of novelties, they often delved into the realms of imagination, or so claimed Robert Buist when he complained that "there are more names than there are roses."

Although roses were undoubtedly receiving more than their fair share of publicity, they would have gotten nowhere, as William Paul pithily explained in *The Rose Garden*, if gardeners were not able to grow them successfully indoors. Fortunately for those who devoted nursery and catalog space to roses, the parlor met the minimal specifications necessary for rose cultivation. The plants flourished. Dingee & Conard, a rose and bulb dealer, described the environment in which roses thrived,

> The conditions most favorable for growing Roses in pots are good rich soil, plenty of sunshine (the early morning sun is best when it can be had), reasonable and regular heat, and moderate moisture; the temperature may range from 40° to 50° at night and 60° to 80° in the daytime.

Beyond those requisites, roses were not particularly difficult to please. In fact, in view of the novelty of the endeavor, most writers preferred to down-play its complexity. For those who had never attempted the cultivation of hardy plants indoors, the comforting words penned by Edward Sprague Rand praising the amenable personality of the China Rose must have sounded very reassuring,

> It will survive almost any treatment, and will live if but a ray of sunlight can reach it. It is the poor man's friend, and clings to him in every vicissitude; yet while possessing adaptability to circumstances in a remarkable degree, no plant will better repay care and attention.

Those words of encouragement probably hooked many a devotee. But most garden writers were swift to define and expound on those golden words: "care and attention".

Roses were not to be embraced lightly. Rose cultivation was a venture to be undertaken with the utmost concentration. As J. N. May, a rose grower from

Summit, New Jersey wrote, "Certainly there is no royal road to success in forcing roses; it is only by hard work, patient and careful watching, night and day, that success can be obtained." Clearly, if a young lady was in search of a hobby that would monopolize all of her time and attention, she could scarcely choose a better pastime than cultivating indoor roses.

Rose chores began before the plants were brought inside for the winter. While resting in the cellar during the fall, roses received regular syringing—writers suggested that the applications should be made no less than twice daily, and preferably three times.

Roses were also pruned (rather ruthlessly) in autumn before beginning their sojourn in the house. The young growth was cut back within inches of the old wood. Then the plant was allowed to grow out at temperatures which were "never allowed to rise above 60°F."

Of course, the main goal in growing roses was the production of flowers. Fine foliage and a shapely habit were secondary objectives. As buds appeared on the plants, sun, heat and water were gradually increased. If several buds crowded together on a stem, only one or two were allowed to remain. These lone flowers would be larger, fuller and more pleasingly formed for having reaped the plant's undivided energies.

Having mastered the basics, many gardeners went on to dabble in more difficult rose-related feats. Rose plants were often coaxed into fanciful shapes as they grew. In the spirit of the era, women were encouraged to develop their hobby into a fine art. Topiary, standard and espaliered indoor roses were quite frequently attempted by ladies who used their plants as a means of self-expression. Most often, roses were shaped into cones. After pruning, the new growth was drawn to the edges of the pot and pinned in placed with hairpins. From that point, the branches were allowed to ascend upward until they met at the cone's tip. More ambitious gardeners tried coaxing their roses into half globes, fans, pyramids and standards.

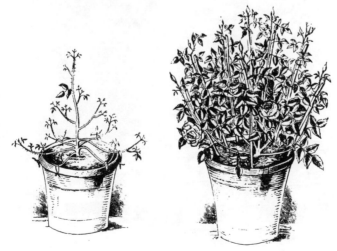

Training a rose into a cone shape from William Paul's *The Rose Garden*.

The goal was always to produce the perfect potted rose, from *McMahon's American Gardener.*

As with all serious art forms, growers developed personal tricks of the trade. Everyone, it seemed, had his or her own method for achieving "the perfect rose". Fortunately many professionals were willing to reveal their "secret formulas" to the public in books and articles. Edward Sprague Rand was particularly generous with his advice. First of all, he felt that a rose's pot size was crucial, "Do not give it too large a pot. Roses will do well in smaller pots, in proportion to their size, than almost any other plant." He also suggested the addition of finely broken bits of charcoal mixed with the soil to impart "the finest brilliancy to the flowers." Along the same vein, William Paul recommended applying camphor water to green the foliage. Many writers suggested stirring the soil continually when watering to insure that moisture did not stand stagnant around the stem. Still more time consuming was *The Household*'s advice to snip off every flower stem religiously as soon as the blossom began to shed its petals, "a pruning process which stimulates the growth of the flower stem."

In spite of the most concentrated and well informed ministrations of the best gardener, a rose is prone to certain problems, especially (as the Victorians soon discovered) when grown indoors. Insects posed a potential threat. Aphids were a particularly vexing pest, and tobacco was recommended as a remedy. Mildew has always been an endemic problem with roses, and it plagued the 19th Century indoor gardener particularly relentlessly due to the fungus' affinity for the damp, stagnant air which commonly prevailed in the parlor. Sulphur was suggested to combat mildew.

Apparently, all the pests, infestations, fuss and bother which accompanied roses were endured cheerfully by the novice gardener who was eager to have one of her favorite flowers on the windowsill.

Deep though it may have been, the romance with the rose was merely a stepping stone to the cultivation of other garden flowers. The same skills and attention which were lavished on roses could also be applied to and practiced on other favorite garden plants. As Francis Parkman wrote in 1866,

> Learn to produce a first-class specimen of the rose grown in a pot, and you will have no difficulty in successfully applying your observations and experience to a vast variety of plants.

No doubt, those words of encouragement were music to the Victorian ear. There were many other old-fashioned garden flowers clamoring for a place on the windowsill, and gardeners were eager to accommodate them.

Carnations took a position of secondary importance in the garden and on the windowsill as well, treading on the rose's heels. In Europe, carnations had slipped in and out of popularity, following the caprices of fashion and the intrigues of politics. Carnations were among that elite group of flowers which were continually entangled in European politics, a fact that greatly heightened their fascination, especially for the by-standers on this side of the ocean. According to an article in an 1846 issue of *The Horticulturist*, the French General, Condé (Louis II de Bourbon, 1621–1687) passed the time during his imprisonment in the Bastille by cultivating a collection of pot-grown carnations. His new hobby may have been derided by some factions of society as a low point in his career, but nevertheless, the symbol held as an emblem of nobility. In fact, during the French Revolution, the aristocracy proudly wore red carnations in their buttonholes as they were marched to the guillotine.

By the beginning of the 19th Century, the carnation had firmly gripped the imagination of gardeners throughout Europe. In Great Britain alone, no fewer than 200 monographs devoted to that genus were published, and hundreds of hybrids were in cultivation. However, by 1824, the carnation's hold on British interest had declined considerably and the upper classes began to look elsewhere for floral amusement. Not unexpectedly, the torch was quickly taken up by the working classes and carnations subsequently became nothing more than "mechanic's flowers".

North Americans typically trailed the fashion trends of their European cousins. And so, just as the carnation's fame faltered in England, the flame was simultaneously kindled in America where it burned strongly until the end of the century.

On this side of the ocean, carnations were popular with all classes of society. The middle class chose from lists of inexpensively priced hybrids offered in mail-order catalogs, whereas wealthier collectors dabbled in horticultural investment. And the stakes of those investments verged on the incredible. In 1897, a new hybrid named 'Mrs. T. W. Lawson' was sold to Mr. Thomas W. Lawson, the great copper magnate, for no less than $30,000. Apparently, it was no coincidence that a shrewd hybridizer chose the millionaire's wife as the plant's namesake. However, Mr. Lawson did not invest foolishly, even when indulging his horticultural fancies. That hybrid was destined to play an important role in the development of the ever-blooming 20th Century cut flower carnation.

The carnations found on early Victorian windowsills were only remotely similar to the frilly cut flower hybrids grown commercially today. In early Victorian magazines and books, they were still referred to as "Pinks", although they were far removed descendants of *Dianthus caryophyllus*, their original wild ancestor which we now call the "Pink".

By the time they reached American windowsills, carnations had undergone countless generations of perfection. Breeding was going strong on all fronts, although hybrids designed specifically for pot culture led the pack. These fell strictly within three groups: Flaked hybrids had stripes of two colors against a white background, Bizarre hybrids possessed irregular stripes of three colors on a plain background, and Picotee hybrids bore small flowers with serrated edges and flecks of color in the petals. Of the trio, Picotee Carnations enjoyed the preponderance of the breeders' attention. By mid-century, yellow, purple, lilac, crimson and white Picotee Carnations were available.   As carnations gained a following, florists labored to render them more suitable for cut flower work. Americans developed the famed strains of Perpetual Carnations from the French Remontant (or Monthly) Carnations. The prototypical Remontant hybrid was introduced from France in 1844, and its resulting hybrids appeared on the American market in 1852. From those plants, American hybridizers created the Perpetuals which increased in number and perfection with the passing years. In fact, the market veritably overflowed with carnations. By 1872, the firm of Dailledouze & Zeller offered no fewer than 54 varieties in the pages of their catalog. Eventually, Perpetuals won glory not only as cut flowers, but as windowsill plants as well.

After delving so thoroughly into the whys and wherefores of indoor roses, there was little that garden writers needed to add in connection with the indoor culture of carnations. *The Horticulturist* warily warned that carnations must "always [be] kept in pots full of the most carefully ordered composts; they are closely watched at all times." But most writers preferred to stress the ease of cultivating indoor carnations, especially as compared to roses.

Although gardening books wished to present carnation culture as blissfully simple, they usually laid heavy stress on the vast difference between merely growing carnations, an undertaking which required no instruction, and cultivating them to the pinnacle of perfection. Naturally, every Victorian sought perfection. And, as the blooming season approached, their attentions increased. The plants were meticulously disbudded until no more than three or four flower buds competed for the plant's energy. Then, as the buds opened, each flower received a "piece of card" attached as a collar behind the petals to prevent them from "turning away". The fully opened flower lay flat, resembling a zinnia.

The blossoming event was choreographed with all the pomp and grandeur of a theatrical exhibition. The plants were set up on tiers, appropriately called "stages", upon which each plant could be displayed to its best advantage. The practice began at the old English "shews", but it was a drama that North Americans eagerly embraced.

Primroses were also exhibited at those "shews". In Europe, primroses had followed a path which closely paralleled that of carnations. The most popular were Auricula Primroses. Those alpine species and hybrids had silver-green leaves dusted by a delicate powder known as "meal". Not only were they cultivated and exhibited with the same care and attention shown carnations, but they were also grown by the same social group—the working classes.

Show Auriculas blossomed in May, simultaneously with the early carnations, and they shared the limelight at "feasts". Although carnations were divided into three strict groups of hybrids, Auriculas enjoyed a greater diversity in their blossom form and pattern. The flowers had zones of color, and hybrids were available displaying bands of green, grey, white, wine, red, and cobalt-blue, as well as countless other shades. Although Auriculas were immensely and deservingly popular in Europe, the fad never really gained momentum on this side of the ocean. Perhaps the strength of the North American sun, which quickly wilts the foliage, was the deciding factor.

In the early years of the Victorian Era, hardy English Primroses, or Cowslips, were frequently lifted from the garden for indoor display. They thrived in the cool, damp and shaded windowsill typical of the early 19th Century parlor. And yet, they did not convey the proper impression of rarity and worldliness necessary to coexist with the other aristocrats in the room. Although Cowslips exuded quantities of country charm, they were not a permanent fixture in the pompous parlor.

No one was greatly surprised when common Cowslips were surpassed by the Oriental *Primula sinensis* (or *chinensis*, as they were often mislabelled). This little primrose seemed to possess all of the social qualifications necessary for a place in the parlor. In addition, it also proved to be a willing performer indoors.

Many period writers who had ignored the pert, hardy English Primroses, and bestowed only a passing word acknowledging the existence of Auricula Primroses, lavished paragraphs of praise on Chinese Primroses. In Henry T. Williams' words, they were infinitely suitable for the windowsill,

> The *Primula Chinensis* is the gem of the collection of window plants. None surpass it in beauty; and for continuous blossom, certainly none can be more desirable. It is one of the best of all plants for the decoration of the drawing room or dining table . . . For 9 months out of 12 they may be made to yield flowers, though most profusely from November to May, and with their colors of red, white, crimson, purple and pink, they form objects of curious ornament.

Primula sinensis from Charles Collins' *Greenhouse and Window Plants*.

Unlike the other highly hybridized garden plants which had wandered into the home, *Primula sinensis* could be propagated from seed. Writers suggested making two sowings, the first in March and the second in early summer, thus insuring that the parlor would never be without that important plant. As the years passed and other exotics entered the parlor, the Chinese Primrose remained popular. In fact, one indication of the respect which the Chinese Primrose commanded is revealed in the entourage of titles which it amassed. By 1886, *The Ladies' Floral Cabinet* had stretched the plant's name into quite a mouthful—*Primula sinensis frimbriata punctata elegantissima*.

Another garden veteran to wander into the early Victorian parlor was the violet. Steeped in romance, symbolism and rural connotations, violets were among the earliest hardy perennials to gain entry indoors. Although they shared the country charm of English Primroses, their status was elevated due to their political connections. They were, of course, Napoleon's favorite blossoms. For that reason alone, they were welcomed into the Victorian parlor.

According to Henry T. Williams' 1873 book, the common dark blue, fragrant violet known as 'The Czar' led the train of popular perennials in the parlor long after other novel violets were introduced. That single-flowered variety was followed by the less hardy, double blue Neapolitan Violet. Gradually, the double violets, known as Parma Violets, took precedence in the parlor and eclipsed the hardier varieties. They retained their popularity well into the 20th Century, not only as houseplants, but as cut flowers as well.

Violets were widely beloved. They were known to the country bumpkin as well as the city socialite. In fact, due in part to their romantic connections, violets were frequently employed as curatives for feminine psychosomatic ailments. In 1888, *The Ladies Home Journal* featured a serial entitled "Miss Athalina's Mind Cure". In that story, a robust older companion by the name of Miss Athalina seeks to restore health to an introspective lass,

> You don't exercise enough Helen Markly. That's half what ails you. Why! great, strong woman ez I am, ef I should set in the house and do nothing all day long, I should soon pine away to a shadder.

Miss Athalina's cure was violets—to be studied regularly. And, hopefully, violets would lure Miss Markly on to further botanical investigations, leaving little time for remorseful conceits. She suggested,

> Don't you see them leaves is nearly smooth? ... some vi'lets' leaves is downy, and some is smoother'n these. See how the leaf's bordered with little round teeth—crenate, Bot'nists call it—and them flowers, to be sure, is double and purple, but all English vi'lets ain't double, and some is blue and some is white ... Don't think of things. Read somethin'. Here, take this Bot'ny and study vi'lets.

Violets enjoyed a reputation equal to the rose, and for that reason alone, gardeners struggled to accommodate them indoors. The fact that it was an uphill battle is recorded by many Victorian writers. When speaking of violets, Ruth Hall wrote in her USDA report of 1863, "They may even be made a window plant, but are not prolific bloomers in this situation as the atmosphere is usually too dry for them."

Miss Hall had a point. Although gardeners continued to attempt the feat, violets were of limited suitability indoors. As the years advanced and technology progressed, the 40–45°F. temperatures which violets require to set buds were not commonly met indoors. Julius Heinrich finally hit upon a possible substitute, he suggested trying pansies instead.

Of course, indoor gardeners did not stick solely to perennials. Annuals from the garden were also brought into the parlor. Eventually, that room played host to a bright array of verbenas, petunias, pyrethrum daisies, wallflowers, and morning glories. Of that list, morning glories might seem to be the least suitable for the purpose. And yet, the Victorians liberally employed those vines in the parlor. Their rambunctious habit was well-suited to the park-like atmosphere which fashionable Victorians strove to create indoors. How could they more efficiently provide the illusion of nature encroaching on the parlor than to drape morning glories behind the sofa or train them to arch luxuriantly over a loveseat, threatening to pounce on the innocent company assembled to sip afternoon tea.

Virtually every plant that was grown in gardens was attempted in the parlor. However, Henry T. Williams noted that gardeners experienced varying degrees of success with domesticated annuals. He wrote,

> Bedding plants like these are not recommended generally for window culture, still window gardeners will have them, and we can only give directions for their culture.

Although the parlor was not entirely suitable to the cultivation of most garden annuals, there was one bedding plant that became an unqualified success. By far the most popular annuals were pelargoniums known to the Victorians, as they are today, as geraniums. If ever there was a success story, it is embodied in that cheerful, broad-umbelled flower.

Pelargoniums were not strangers to the windowsill. They took up a position on the sill in the mid-18th Century, soon after being released from the confines of European hothouses. When they arrived in North America in 1750, they were grown in the garden in summer, but invariably received protection indoors during the winter. Due to the scarcity of available light in the average abode, they were stored for the season. In autumn, the roots were freed of soil and the plants were hung upside down in the cellar to slip into dormancy. It was not until fenestrations were enlarged to allow the entrance of additional light that pelargoniums received sufficient sun to survive on the winter windowsill.

By 1820, all of Europe had fallen head over heels for pelargoniums. At the height of the craze, Robert Sweet published a huge, two volume monograph on the subject illustrated by 500 colored plates. And North America dutifully followed closely behind Europe in the pelargonium fad. By mid-century, inter-

A double flowering pelargonium.

est in pelargoniums was blossoming to such a degree that, in 1854, Robert Buist noted in *American Flower-Garden Directory*,

> Within these few years, the habits and beauties of the plant are improved a hundred fold, and those who are only acquainted with the old sorts would be transported with a view of the dazzling and beauteous colony of new kinds that have been procured by hybridizing those of good habit and character.

Pelargonium breeding moved along at a brisk pace, keeping step with the demand for new cultivars. By 1873, Henry T. Williams was able to entertain his readers with tales of flowers which were the size of a "silver quarter" borne in trusses that measured 6 in. in diameter. No less impressive was the range of colors which breeding had attained. The spectrum was expanded to include white, rose, scarlet, crimson, salmon and striped flowers; while the petal form was improved until it became as round and plump as pansies. The first double flowering hybrids were available in salmon only, although white double flowers followed quickly on their heels.

The pelargonium's growth habit was also a subject of the breeders' concentration. By 1873, the plants no longer suffered from their original straggly stature which was pitifully accentuated on the windowsill. The stems were strengthened and growth was selected for greater compactness.

In addition to the strides that were accomplished with Zonal-leaved Pelargoniums, similar improvements were achieved in the development of both the Scented-leaved and Ivy-leaved Pelargoniums which were equally welcome on the windowsill. A family of dwarf cultivars was born, originally bred to fill bedding displays, but proving more efficacious for parlor display. Fancy-leaved hybrids also came into being for bedding and were available with leaves striped in zones of yellow, burgundy, white and brown. There was no end to the possibilities inherent in pelargoniums, and the public was clamoring for further innovations.

Like most annuals, pelargoniums were essentially plebeian plants, adorning the windowsills of city slums as well as country cottages. However, they were appreciated and admitted into any home, regardless of social rank. Before the days of Gertrude Jekyll's crusade against bedding plants, there was nothing distasteful about a pelargonium. It was only in the early 20th Century that the bright magenta pelargonium fell into disrepute.

At a time when gardening was meant to be "within everyone's reach", the mass appeal of annuals was an important aspect of the new fashion. In fact, the cultivation of annuals indoors was seen as a means for disseminating the love of nature broadly among all classes of society, thus creating a better world. Not everyone had a garden, but everyone had access to a windowsill. And annuals were inexpensive botanical roommates.

In that respect, annuals were an avenue in which classes could reach out to one another. At a time when city conditions were abhorrent and poverty was disgracefully evident, it was obvious that to up-lift one class was to up-lift all levels of society. *Vick's Monthly* described how garden annuals fit into the social scheme,

> Early in spring some kindly disposed persons had collected a little fund and employed a florist of the town to grow several thousand plants of Annuals, such as Cockscombs, Stocks and Balsams, some thousands of young Fuchsias, Pelargoniums, &c. To every one in the Asylum for the Aged, who would engage to care for a plant, according to certain printed rules, and exhibit it at the show to take place on a specified day, a potted plant was given. The same privilege was accorded the members of the Incurable Hospital. One of the most interesting features, however, was the exhibition made by children. To the children of the cottagers who had a patch of ground, a couple dozen plants were given—to others a pot plant . . . Small prizes were offered, and the competition was close and exciting . . .

Every Victorian was effected by the indoor gardening craze, but the middle and lower classes stood to gain the most from the new endeavor. No wonder they embraced the fad with open arms. Obviously, another horticultural victory had been won—the garden had officially entered the average home.

COMMON GARDEN PLANTS ENLISTED INTO THE HOME

Carnations
Clematis
Daisies
Morning Glories
Pansies
Pelargoniums
Petunias
Primroses
Roses
Sweet Williams
Verbenas
Violets
Wallflowers

CHAPTER VI

A STEP INTO THE TROPICS

UP TO THIS POINT, our story has unfolded in the familiar recesses of the middle class American front parlor. However, as the era progressed, that room became less self-contained and increasingly dependent on the input, ideas and technology of the outside world. Those exterior forces effected every aspect of Victorian existence from the minute details of daily life to the broader cultural customs of society. On an even grander scale, the arts and sciences felt the impact of the era's broadened vision of the world. Horticulture was among the many sciences to reap the benefits of foreign influence.

In fact, the next step in the progression of the American botanical scene came from overseas. After successfully growing garden plants indoors, the adventuresome naturally yearned to try their hand with tropicals. Tropicals were the forbidden fruit dangling enticingly just beyond the public's reach, tempting gardeners to pluck and taste their wares. Although the desire to grow tropicals was definitely there, knowledge of those plants and their care had not yet reached a stage which would promote success indoors. North Americans could never have realized their fondest horticultural hopes without the aid of European expertise.

So we turn our attention for a moment from the bosom of the North American front parlor. The scene shifts to Europe where horticulture had become more than a mere hobby, it was a driving preoccupation. We focus on the wealthy landowners who had the power and influence to set trends which would permeate the core of the upper crust of European society, filter downward, and eventually drift across the Atlantic Ocean. Not every man could follow those wealthy citizens' lead in an equally elaborate fashion, but all men would benefit from the time, energy and resources that rich Europeans lavished on their new horticultural infatuation.

In matters horticultural, all eyes were on Europe. While North Americans were puttering around, potting their primroses and gazing through glass vases at the slender white roots of forced bulbs, Europe was forging ahead, always a few steps in advance, paving the paths which North Americans would soon tread. Wealthy Europeans were sponsoring plant collectors, sending those romantic fools on adventures abroad to scour the jungles for rare and beautiful tropical plants. They were patronizing the development of botany and researching the family trees of species which had never been seen before. They were collecting, dissecting, and categorizing quantities of new tropicals. And they were exploring methods of constructing glasshouses to sequester those newly captured botanical novelties which could not survive in northern climates unprotected.

Tropicals were treated with respect, awe and mistrust. Although garden plants had been warmly welcomed into the heart of the home, tropicals were not embraced with the familiarity enjoyed by those tried and true, old-fashioned favorites. Initially, tropicals were viewed as the wild beasts of horticulture. They fascinated everyone. But, like tigers and elephants, they were held at arm's length. Just as the fauna of the tropics was exhibited behind the bars of zoos and provided with special, carefully controlled environments, it seemed logical to assume that tropical flora also required its own specifically designed buildings. Of necessity, those buildings had to be constructed of glass.

Of course, glasshouses were in use long before the advent of the Victorian Era. They came into existence when man first began to lust for fruit long after its natural bearing season had ended. The Romans fashioned transparent structures for the protection of fruit off-season. Their *specularia* were glazed with thin sheets of mica and talc, and were warmed by incredibly sophisticated stove and flue systems. In that way, Tiberius Claudius Nero Caesar (42 B.C.E.–37 A.C.E.) indulged in a daily cucumber throughout the year, courtesy of his *specularium*.

In addition to providing for their Caesar's proclivity for cucumbers, the Romans also experimented with the cultivation of grapes and peaches in their primitive greenhouses, although one observer complained that the resulting fruit tasted no better than turnips. Despite their inferior yield, the use of *specularia* was sufficiently widespread to attract critics. The Roman stoic, Lucius Annaeus Seneca (4 B.C.E.?–65 A.C.E.) observed,

> Do not those live contrary to nature who require a rose in winter and who, by the excitement of hot water and an appropriate modification of heat, force from winter the later blooms of spring?

Seneca was not the only one to voice doubt concerning the propriety of tampering with the season's natural order. Centuries later, Sir Hugh Platt wrote in *The Garden of Eden* published in 1654, that an unfortunately precocious alchemist had "suffered death . . . for the making of a pear to fructify in winter."

Eventually, however, the irresistible temptation to indulge in juicy, sweet citrus won the staunchest critics over to the acceptance of artificial environments for plants. *Orangeries* became popular in the 17th Century. In contrast to the modern definition of a greenhouse, an *orangerie* had only one glass wall, and it was not designed for year around use. Great tubs of citrus, myrtles and heaths resided in protected *orangeries* in winter, and then were carted outside to the garden in spring to enjoy the encouragement of the season's sun. In autumn, those heavy, potted trees were manipulated back into their ornate, glass-sided buildings until the weather moderated again. Naturally, only the nobility could afford to erect and maintain an *orangerie*.

An "English Greenhouse of the 17th Century" from Taft's *Greenhouse Construction*.

Time marched on and the Age of Exploration commenced, sending plant hunters hither and yon plundering the globe for botanical treasures. Their journeys were financed from the pockets of wealthy Europeans who gladly invested additional funds to insure that their newly acquired rare tropicals would survive the "colds and damps" of the Northern European climate. What had been a glimmer of interest in glass structures evolved into a serious study of the technology necessary to heat, light and ventilate hothouses.

All of this research and development was spurred onward by the quantities of rare and valuable plants arriving monthly on European shores. In fact, by the time Charles MacIntosh wrote *The Greenhouse, Hothouse and Stove* in 1838, there was a pressing need for efficient glasshouses. He traced the progression of the mounting interest,

> During the early part of the 18th Century, the cultivation of exotic plants was carried on with great spirit, upwards of 5,000 species being introduced from foreign countries during the period ... The later part of the 18th, and the beginning of the 19th Century, however, has been the great botanical era for which this country will ever be conspicuous. The discovery of Australia, the extension of the British power in India and both the Americas—aided by the patronage of the most wealthy aristocracy of the world, including the sovereign himself, who thought it not beneath his dignity to join his subjects in sending out collectors to all quarters of the globe.

Other garden writers concentrated on popularizing tropical plants and minimizing the association between glass and nobility. The greenhouse's strongest supporter, J. C. Loudon, felt that both kings and commoners would eventually share the new trend toward glass. He saw the passion for hothouses as a natural extension of the all-pervading European love of gardening. In his estimation, one had only to say three magic words—rare, foreign and tender—to gain and hold the sympathies of the ever increasing ranks of amateur European horticulturists.

F. A. Fawkes agreed that the lure of the glasshouse was a manifestation of a natural fatherly emotion. Unable to resist sentimentalizing, even in the pages of a construction manual, *Horticultural Buildings* includes this ode to the developing relationship between man and tender plant,

> To watch in a glass-house the growth of a pretty little helpless plant, to promote its development amidst adverse external circumstances, to shield it from cold, to protect it from the sun's scorching rays, to deliver it from its insect persecutors, to feed it, all these go far to touch in the human mind a mysterious chord of sympathy for the little plant...

Whatever their motivation, for men with money, no expense was too extravagant to invest in furnishing suitable accommodations for those new tropicals which were suddenly placed in their care. They set to work with dogged determination to discern what those transplanted tropicals preferred in their growing environment. And then, they labored to develop the technology necessary to artificially simulate a glass version of that ideal habitat.

J. C. Loudon was among the pioneering researchers to perfect the hothouse. He published several books and presented many papers discussing slopes, building materials, situations and designs. Due in part to his efforts, Europe began to realize impressive advances in the design of glass structures that boasted both sophistication and architectural beauty.

The comfort of tropical plant life was undoubtedly a factor which was always held in view when designing Victorian hothouses. But, utility alone was not the only driving force to guide construction. At a time when only society's upper crust could afford glass, hothouses provided yet another avenue for flaunting the wealth of the age. To fulfill this purpose, the early Victorian glasshouses were built to magnificent proportions. They were erected not only to house tropicals in a grand manner, but also to incite the envy of all on-lookers. Having invested fortunes in plant expeditions, botanical patrons had every intention of exploiting the social fruits of their investments to the utmost.

One notable example of this European phenomenon was Chatsworth, a crystal palace that was ranked foremost among the magnificent glass structures of its day. That awesome edifice was designed by Joseph Paxton for the Duke of Devonshire between 1836–40 and it immediately won international fame for its opulence. Among the North American eyebrows that were raised were those of A. J. Downing, who hastily made the pilgrimage to gaze on that magnificent glass castle. *The Horticulturist* carried a very favorable review of Chatsworth's splendor for its captive American audience,

> It is a glass structure which covers an acre of ground—that is 70 feet high; and that the carriage road is continued directly through it, so that the Duke and his guests can drive through with a coach and four!

If it was fame that the Duke sought, then his glasshouses surely fulfilled their purpose. That wealthy bachelor attracted a great deal of publicity as the press speculated on his motivations and recounted the long roster of his horticultural exploits. Naturally, *The Horticulturist* was one of the many publications to provide their readers with a detailed account of the Duke's credentials and accomplishments,

> He is the President of the London Horticultural Society where he is, among enthusiastic amateurs, the most enthusiastic of them all. He sends botanical collectors to the most distant and unexplored countries, in search of new plants at his own cost. He travels, with his head gardener, all over Europe, to examine the finest conservatories, and returns home to build one larger and loftier than them all.

Chatsworth was not alone in its grandeur. Other immense glass structures were erected as the noble and wealthy vied for prominence in the horticultural sphere. Apparently, even the Duke of Devonshire felt the pressure of competition, for he deemed it necessary to create a further display of horticultural prodigality. In 1850, Chatsworth's head gardener, Joseph Paxton, again put his creative talents to work for the Duke, erecting a glasshouse devoted solely to the cultivation of one plant, *Victoria regia*, a giant Water Lily named for the queen.

The public secured ring-side seats, enjoying every moment of the competition. At first, their knowledge of those tropical indoor gardens was gained solely by word of mouth. But finally, in the 1870s, they were allowed an occasional glimpse into the interior of tropical wonderlands when cities joined the race and erected immense public glass houses, aptly called winter palaces. In fact, the preoccupation with glass was so intense that the British commissioned Joseph Paxton to design the Crystal Palace, an immense glass building which would house the Great Exhibition.

Even in Europe, the general public would have to remain content with their occasional Sunday afternoon visits to glasshouses for many years to come. Hothouses were completely beyond their reach. The price of glass and the difficulties inherent in heating hothouses kept that hobby safely and solely within the territory of very wealthy Europeans until mid-Century. Although glasshouses were increasingly prevalent in the early part of the 19th Century, they were by no means common.

But, interest was escalating. In 1812, the audience seeking a manual on the construction and maintenance of greenhouses was limited to an elite handful, if we can judge from the list of subscribers to John Cushing's *The Exotic Gardener*, published in that year. That volume was circulated by subscription only, and the roster of subscribers was conspicuously placed at the head of the book, reading like a "Who's Who" in British society. The list consisted of 75 names, the majority being titled aristocracy or members of the clergy, and most purchasing more than one copy in their zeal. A similar book, written less than a decade later by J. C. Loudon attracted a much broader and commoner audience.

Although glass castles were within the means of only a chosen few, more

'Inside a Government Conservatory' from Henry T. Williams' *Window Gardening*.

modest glass structures were gradually coming into popular use. In fact, studying the literature of the era can be a confounding experience as the reader attempts to sort out who was in possession of what and when. There was a great deal of confusion accompanying the definition of terms. Glass structures were coming into existence more rapidly than the evolution of the terminology necessary to separate one type from the other.

An "Elegant Conservatory" from Henry T. Williams' *Window Gardening*.

In the early 19th Century, a greenhouse was defined loosely as anything from a movable cold frame to a 100 ft. conservatory. Many early authors used the word indiscriminantly, undoubtedly intentionally attempting to mislead the reader into assuming that they were discussing something much grander than they, in reality, possessed. Later in the century, writers exercised more care by affixing less ambiguous labels to the different types of glass buildings. However, there was always a tendency to upgrade a horticultural structure by calling it a greenhouse even if it was merely a manure hole with a window set on top.

For those who preferred to call a spade by its name and avoid confusion, a cold frame, cold pit or forcing frame was defined as an unheated and often movable glass box constructed to shelter nearly hardy plants from severe frosts. Occasionally, manure was employed to heat the frame, especially in early spring when seedlings for the garden were started under its protective glass. This primitive "greenhouse" was not new in the 19th Century. In fact, its use was common before the Victorian Era opened.

The term greenhouse, when used correctly, referred to a barely heated, permanent glass structure constructed to house tender but stalwart potted plants. The greenhouse was built on a more ambitious scale than a cold frame, and was often partially sunken below ground to retain heat. Most importantly, a man could stand upright inside it.

At first, primitive stoves and manure or peat beds heated those greenhouses, but they provided only sufficient warmth to prevent frost damage on moderately cold nights. Although primitive greenhouses had only one glazed side, the use of glass expanded to include three sides and the roof. Taking their inspiration from the Romans, the earliest greenhouses were erected to shelter tender fruit such as pineapples and grapes.

In comparison, a hothouse or stove was much more elaborate, and required relatively sophisticated technology. That glass structure was devoted to tropicals and was born with the dawn of the Age of Exploration. Ideally, hothouses were heated to 55–65°F. during the winter and were constructed completely of glass with a wooden frame. Initially, they gained their warmth from fires in central furnaces, and later by steam or hot water piping systems. The collection of rare plants that took up residence within those glass walls was potted and arranged proudly on raised benches. This was the glass structure that had captured the European audience and held America in awe. Although unheated greenhouses were erected in growing numbers when the century reached its mid-point, the hothouse was still a rare bird.

A cold frame from Chas. N. Page's *Home Floriculture*.

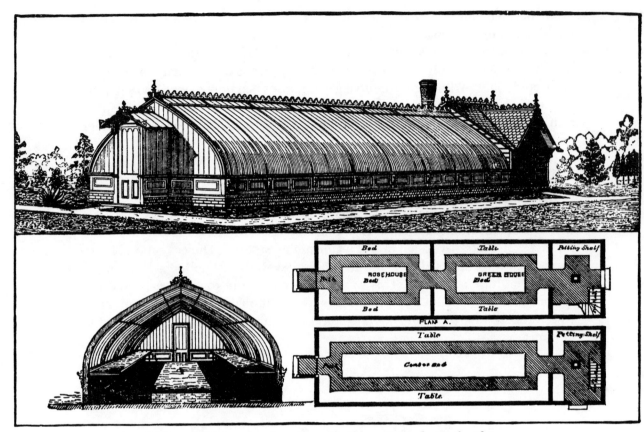

A hothouse with benches from Peter Henderson's *Gardening for Pleasure*.

In Europe, the general public was not only waiting for hothouses to become economically feasible, they were also anxious for an opportunity to cultivate tropicals. Although they were eager to satisfy the overwhelming urge to experience the novel introductions from far off jungles, they were uncomfortable about inviting tropicals into the intimacy of their parlors. And yet, the average Victorian could scarcely afford a suitable glass environment in which to grow those rare plants. Suspense heightened. Everyone was anticipating the moment when they, too, could enjoy the beauty and fascination inherent in a collection of tropical plants.

That moment finally arrived when excise taxes on glass were lifted in 1845. From that date onward, the glass making process developed rapidly, quality was improved and glass became readily available on the market. The public responded with a rush of enthusiasm. Hothouse technology improved, heating systems were upgraded and construction techniques became standardized. All of those fortunate factors could not have befallen a more appreciative and eager public. The Europeans avidly grasped at that new glass status symbol as soon as it came within reach.

An Exhibition Conservatory from *Gardening for Pleasure* by Peter Henderson.

Although the middle class may not have been the audience at which all the splendor of the great glasshouses was directed, the people could not help but be impressed by that show of wealth. Inspired by Chatsworth, Wollaton Hall, Kew Gardens and other grand glasshouses which had been erected, they were determined to create their own personal tropical paradise. Previously, tropical horticulture had been the exclusive pursuit of kings and their cohorts. But, when the common man was given an opportunity to join that divine pursuit, everyone rushed to become lord over his own small, glassed-in tropical domain.

So, the European middle class began erecting glasshouses and filling them with rare botanicals from the tropics. Although every man could not afford his own personal Chatsworth, the appearance of the humblest hothouse on an estate was greeted as a mark of distinction among the up and coming. Glass proved that the owner's tastes were in the right place. Even those who could not quite finance an estate in the suburbs added glasshouses to their in-town homes and thus reaped the benefits of nature while making a statement about their social status.

In answer to the increased demand, prefabricated greenhouses appeared on the European market in mid-century, and were common by the 1880s. A gentleman could simply order the components and they would be delivered to his doorstep, ready for assembly on the spot. With the addition of a gargoyle here, an urn there and some fancy metal work along the ridge, each glasshouse acquired an individual personality. Add a collection of tropicals inside to the external adornments, and every man could enjoy his own instant winter garden.

I do not use the term "winter garden" loosely. In their efforts to capture a tropical atmosphere, Victorians had inaugurated the fashion of planting their exotics in the ground, creating a garden-like scene indoors. Some called this novelty a winter garden, but it was more commonly referred to as a conservatory.

A conservatory was the parlor among glasshouses. Not only was it opulent and

A "Picturesque Conservatory" from *The Ladies' Floral Cabinet*.

grand, but every effort was made to design its interior "tastefully". Whereas hot-houses merely displayed rows of potted plants; in the conservatory, the specimens were planted in beds designed and executed with all the care and planning which outdoor landscapes received. The conservatory was not a building for the display of collections. Although tropicals were the primary components of the scene, the plants themselves were not the main point of concentration. The goal was to create an indoor landscape complete with walks, beds and garden ornaments. As E. A. Maling commented in his chapter on conservatories in *Indoor Plants*, "There is less to be said about the plants themselves under this head than the place in which they grow."

The place was undeniably fantastic. If well designed, a conservatory was a botanical wonderland. Naturally, conservatories quickly became very parlor-like in appearance, while also adopting many of the functions of that room. The conservatory became a floral reception room, a place where visitors could catch a glimpse at the "improved tastes" of the resident family. Visitors might also enjoy a hint of romance in the bowered and plant bedecked conservatory. Unlike the parlor, conservatories possessed the warmth and excitement of the tropics, an atmosphere which young ladies found very advantageous when entertaining prospective suitors. That floral room contained an intimate informality that was completely lacking in the formal front parlor. The conservatory roused the senses. As Charlotte M. Yonge commented in her novel, *The Daisy Chain*, "It is a real bower for a maiden of romance."

The conservatory grew in splendor. That crystal world took wing, riding on the imagination and fantasies dreamt by a generation of romantics. Conservatories provided another creative outlet and a haven of retreat for starry-eyed Victorians. They began to accumulate many of the physical components that the parlor had acquired. In *Country Life*, Morris Copeland described the typical conservatory,

> It should, if possible, be connected with the dwelling and open out of those rooms most frequented by the family. In it may be a fountain basin for fish, aquariums, or birds, busts, statues . . . [it may be] furnished with seats and a table for the convenience of the ladies of the family, should they wish to sit there with work or books, and enjoy the pleasure [of] fragrance and sight which beautiful plants must always give.

This elaborate floral kingdom swept and conquered Europe with its intoxicating personality. Everyone was effected. Everyone wanted a conservatory of their own. By mid-century, most Europeans would readily agree with Benjamin Disraeli's remark, "It is impossible to live without a conservatory."

But romance and entertaining aside, the Victorians were equally enthusiastic about the botanical possibilities inherent in a conservatory. The plants were certainly not overlooked in the rush of emotion that infused the era. The conservatory provided an opportunity for Victorians to view tropicals at a delightfully close but safe distance. Those glass structures offered a taste of the tropics without the inconvenience of travel or the unpleasantness entailed in exploring the jungles. Although Victorians were devoted to their literary diet of adventure stories describing tropical expeditions, the conservatory was as close as the average citizen dared come to experiencing the tropics first hand. *The Ladies' Floral Cabinet* described the sensations that one might encounter when treated to "An Hour in the Tropics",

> To the lovers of tropical wealth in plants and flowers, the prospect of a trip through their own natural domain is most alluring, and doubly so when we can step from our own brisk autumn air into the heavy perfume-laden atmosphere of Borneo or Ceylon, and that without the aid of Aladdin's lamp or enchanted carpet. We have only to enter the portals of some great hot house . . . the tropical world is before us. Palms and orchids are as an East Indian jungle in miniature, without the decided disadvantage of the innumerable creeping things, more or less noxious, that are apt to make a tropic ramble anything but desirable.

With familiarity, the wild beasts of horticulture were domesticated. Tropicals were tamed, potted and exhibited in idyllicly tidy "jungle" scenes. No longer the sole territory of European upper classes, their familiar faces frequented the home grounds in a variety of neighborhoods. Thus the rarified air surrounding exotics slowly dispersed. Tropicals had taken the first step toward their entry into the home.

North Americans were watching this flurry of horticultural activity with baited breath. They observed as Europeans constructed floral castles and immense winter gardens. They sent their foremost horticulturists overseas to gaze and gape at those glass monstrosities, and then called them back home to report on every detail of the splendor. Not a moment in the greenhouse's development escaped the vigilant North American eye—especially at a time when their gaze was always riveted Europeward.

Meanwhile, North Americans were experimenting with glasshouses. Traditionally, James Beekman of New York City is credited with the erection of the first primitive glass-sided building in 1764. But, Geraldine Duclow, a greenhouse historian from Pennsylvania, has recently unearthed evidence suggesting that greenhouses made their debut in America earlier than that date. Her research revealed that 1736 may be a more accurate date for the American "first".

The "First American Greenhouse" according to Taft's *Greenhouse Construction*.

However, the development and availability of glass structures moved along at a snail's pace in North America. In the late 18th Century, Robert Morris, who was considered to be the wealthiest man in the U.S.A. at the time, added glasshouses for forcing pineapples and oranges to "Lemon Hill", his Philadelphia estate which would later become Fairmount Park. Doubtlessly, other very wealthy North Americans living in or near the progressive cities of Boston, New York and Philadelphia followed suit. In fact, the famous botanist, John Bartram, was among the many citizens who longed for a greenhouse. But, like most of his countrymen, he harbored no delusions about his ability to heat such a structure sufficiently to cultivate semi-tropical or tropical plants. Instead, he limited himself to fond hopes of growing a few choice nearly-hardy plants. He wrote in 1760,

> I am going to build a greenhouse. Stone is got, and I hope as soon as harvest is over to begin to build it—to put in some pretty flowering winter shrubs, and other plants for winter's diversion, not to be crowded with orange trees, or those natural to the Torrid Zone, but such as will do, being protected from frost.

Heat was a problem that confounded the efforts of indoor gardeners in the colder regions of this country for a long century after John Bartram made plans for his primitive glasshouse. It was not until 1855, when Frederic A. Lord built his first successful hothouse in the frigid city of Buffalo, that North Americans began to see the glimmer of hope which promised that they, too, might some day participate in the trend toward glass. By the 1870s, Lord was receiving commissions to add glasshouses to many estates in upstate New York, most notably from the wealthy proprietors of mansions along the Hudson River. In fact, business became so brisk that Lord took his son-in-law, William Burnham, into partnership in 1873.

In this case, Americans needed no cajoling from garden writers to coax them into joining the European trend. Few words were wasted enlightening the American public as to the benefits of glass. When the opportunity knocked, the public was ready to answer its call. Finally, the people could respond to paragraphs such as the one featured in an 1870 issue of the New York *Evening Post* which dangled temptation before the public eye,

> Could your readers visit one of these English stoves and see the marvelous beauty of the ferns and foliage plants, or study the indescribable colors and shapes, the blooms of the orchids . . . they would be quite as ready as I am to admit that English gardeners excel us in this direction if in no other. The only wonder is that these classes of flowers have not been more generally cultivated by our florists. Ferns are beginning to be used in Boston, but not to the extent that their beauty demands . . .

Apparently, the *Evening Post* did not realize that there was good reason for the scarcity of orchids and rare tropicals on the market. In the 1870s, North America still trailed far behind Europe in the development of hothouse technology. Most crucially, the quality of glass remained pathetically poor until long after the Civil War paralyzed the nation's economy. In addition, furnaces were not perfected, nor could heating systems circulate heat sufficiently to make hothouses efficient until the 1880s.

To confound the issue, the average man found the price of building a greenhouse in this country prohibitively expensive. As Eben Rexford observed in an 1886 edition of *The Ladies Home Journal*, "a building which affords ample protection against our severe winters cannot be built for a trifling outlay."

Rexford estimated that "a good house of a size to warrant calling it a greenhouse, will cost two or three hundred dollars at least." However, if Mr. Rexford's figures were correct, the cost of building a greenhouse in 1886 had already plummeted drastically from the price quoted in 1860. In that year, Robert Morris Copeland estimated the cost at $800 to $1000, remarking that "such things are out of the question for men whose every moment is spent in struggling for freedom from debt."

If we can believe the words of *The Household*, in the 1870s, when only a chosen few North Americans could afford to entertain the thought of acquiring a hothouse, Europeans were blithely building them onto every shanty with carefree abandon, and investing only a pittance in the project. They reported,

> When we read in the papers that an iron greenhouse; 12 feet long and 10 feet high, can be furnished with glass and all, for 5 pounds ($20), we are not surprised that 5/10ths of all the middle and better classes of houses, with conservatories to each, are going up in London today, and all of them marked "To Let". It seems to be understood that the coming tenant will want his little plant house. Dwellings that only command a rent of $200 have little greenhouses as part of the regular fixtures.

In fact, many years intervened and the end of the century drew nigh before greenhouse construction was perfected in this country. Although Europe was building with glass by leaps and bounds, North Americans were continually frustrated in their efforts to replicate the technology and apply it in the severe climate on this side of the ocean. In 1851, Robert Leuchars gave voice to the frustration being felt by those who had the means, but lacked the technology or instruction to build with glass,

> . . . there appears to be a great want of practical knowledge on these subjects, and though much information may be gleaned from various English works, they are either unobtainable, or the information is inapplicable to the wants of this country.

Finally, guidance came in the third quarter of the century when the florist and nursery businesses were booming and their proprietors could afford to experiment with glass. From the 1870s onward, books began appearing on the subject, written by florists and nurserymen who were eager to succeed with glass, and equally eager for the great American public to taste success in hothouse construction. An increase in home hothouses meant that more plants would be purchased by their customers. Among the most popular of those books written by professionals but aimed primarily at an amateur audience was *Practical Floriculture* written by Peter Henderson in 1878.

Unlike the headstrong optimists who dominated the nursery business in the 19th Century, Mr. Henderson was a humble man, if also a rather gloomy soul. His book painted a dismal portrait of the state of the art of hothouse construction prior to 1878, "There was no fixed system; all was confusion, hardly two of us building alike, and, in my humble opinion, most of us building wrong."

Henderson, who claimed to have "no reason to complain of success in business," laid the blame solely on his greenhouses. He avowed that, during his first 10 years in business "many thousands of dollars were sacrificed in the blunders made in my endeavor to get on the right track." In view of his unfortunate personal experiences, the reader might well wonder why Mr. Henderson had embarked upon writing an authoritative work on the subject. Apparently, having 10 years of blunders behind him, he felt sufficiently secure in his knowledge to share it with his fellow Americans. And the public was appreciative—the book sold very well. Perhaps his most valuable piece of advice, undoubtedly learned first hand was, "Do not listen to what your builders may say, as few of them have experience in such matters."

Mr. Henderson could rejoice on one account, anyway. The quality of glass in North America had improved noticeably after the Civil War. Antebellum glass was wavy and flawed, a trait which frequently caused foliar damage to botanicals due to spot magnification of the sun's rays. The new glass panes admitted more light and were relatively flawless, although complete perfection was a long time in coming.

Undoubtedly, the appearance of improved glass was a welcome advance, but growers still had to grapple with the confounding problem of heating hothouses in a climate that was both severe and unpredictable. In America, as in Europe, the earliest glasshouses received their heat from the warm fumes of hot-beds fed from manure piles. The method was perfected to a science, and proved sufficient to prevent half-hardy plants and semi-tropicals from freezing solidly, although they were undoubtedly touched by light frosts. Many of the early garden writers, including Bernard McMahon, swore by it.

In fact, Mr. McMahon was unwilling to endorse the use of a furnace for heating greenhouses when a suitable device was finally available. Nurserymen have always enjoyed a reputation for stubbornness, and Mr. McMahon was among those who simply refused to change his methods to fit new technology. However, when the time came to defend his idiosyncracies, that old-fashioned gardener voiced a long list of complaints against the new fangled furnaces. He wrote in *McMahon's American Gardener*,

> . . . all is confounded by the introduction of a mettle stove and pipes, which never can be managed so as to give, when necessary that gradual and well regulated heat which will protect the plants without injuring them, and besides, both stove and pipes unavoidably emit in the house a quantity of smoke, which seldom fails to annoy plants.

Undoubtedly, McMahon's complaints possessed some validity. A reliable furnace was essential to the successful cultivation of tropical plants, and the early models were far from trustworthy. With time, they improved. And eventually, for better or worse, central furnaces replaced the manure pile and primitive stoves as a source of heat.

The earliest boiler-heated hothouses sent their warmth flowing throughout the glass range via flues from the furnace in the cellar, a system which originated in 1822. But, most nurserymen concurred with McMahon's charge that the flue system was a dangerous method of heat. Not only was the system potentially harmful to the stock, but according to Mr. Henderson, hundreds of greenhouses caught fire yearly when runaway blazes ignited the adjacent woodwork. On many severely cold nights, the caretaker was given a Hobson's choice between fire and ice. Henderson described one such experience which taught him to bank his furnace with care,

> On one occasion I had in use two houses heated with flues each about 100 feet in length. The chimneys had been made of wood, and they had been safely used for 3 winters, but on the occasion of a severe storm in winter, when our fires were going

full blast, both of them took fire within an hour of each other, though fully 100 feet from the furnace.

Everyone was relieved when hot water systems came into use. With hot water, the danger of fire was minimized, and the plants no longer suffered injury from smoke and gases. However, hot water was an expensive system to install, requiring hefty and not easily manipulated 4 in. pipes. Despite the installation expense, hot water became the system of choice for professionals, although many amateurs preferred to take their chances with flues.

Another alternative appeared later in the century. On and off throughout the era, hothouse proprietors courted the adoption of steam heating systems which entailed more easily managed 2 in. pipe. The system was originally invented by Joseph Hayward in 1820 but, at the time, it enjoyed only a brief moment in the sun. By 1830, hot water systems dominated the scene again. It was not until the mid-1890s that steam finally won supremacy.

At Logee's Greenhouses, our range reaps the benefits of a hot water system. The original 4 in. pipes were installed by a prosperous 19th Century shoemaker who kept the hothouse as a hobby. Although the system undeniably possesses many flaws, it has not failed us since the year that the original greenhouse came into the family in 1892.

In that year, the greenhouse froze solidly while the young proprietors grappled with their first lessons in applied furnace management. There have been many near-misses since that date; and there are times when the furnace seems to have a definite mind of its own, harkening unto moods and humors that are beyond human comprehension or prediction. As *The Floral World* aptly observed in 1867, ". . . boilers will act treacherously, and fires will turn sulky in stoves, as well as in rooms, as housemaids will testify."

After that first long winter, the men who tended the fire in our greenhouses established a regimen that has been followed faithfully over the generations. Robert Buist's instructions for the January maintenance of a house heated to 55–65°F. may have provided the inspiration for our schedule. Certainly, his words are as valid today as they were in 1854 when they appeared in the *American Flower Garden Directory*,

> . . . as soon as the mercury begins to fall in the thermometer, kindle the fire, and sup-
> posing it is anthracite coal, in 20 minutes . . . the heat will operate in the house. If a
> coal fire is kindled about 4:00, it will require addition about 6, and then may be made
> up again about 9 or 10, which will suffice until morning. If the fuel is wood, it must be
> attended to 3 or 4 times during the evening; and, when the mornings are intensely
> cold, a fire may be requisite.

The nightmare that haunted all hothouse owners, both amateur and professional, was the fear of a "freeze up". Nothing could equal the horror experienced upon opening the greenhouse door on a cold mid-winter morning and discovering a scene of total devastation. In an article appropriately entitled "Caught Napping" in *The Floral World*, Shirley Hibberd reveals that, when

"A Village House with a Small Conservatory" from Henry T. Williams' *Window Gardening*.

faced with sub-zero temperatures, the British were as hard-pressed as North Americans to keep their glasshouses from freezing. However, after taking toll of his losses, he offers some very valuable advice on his method for salvaging the bulk of his stock,

When the thermometer sinks below zero, as it did on the night of January 3rd . . . 9/10th of the amateur gardeners (myself among the number) were "caught napping" . . . It required constant attention the whole of the night, I am told by nurserymen, to keep up sufficient heat to exclude the frost, and those that went to bed at 11:00, and bid farewell to their fires by giving a friendly poke and a little more fuel, found on the morrow a very sorry spectacle . . . the plan that I adopted myself . . . was to remove [the frozen plants] at once to a dark cellar, before the sun had time to get around upon the house, and shed its fatal rays upon them. This, of course, is a troublesome operation, and when the cold is so intense that you can scarcely feel the pots in your hands, it is anything but agreeable, but the constant exercise of running up and down stairs . . . soon gets your blood into circulation . . . In this dark abode they are kept for some days, without admitting a particle of light, the temperature being about 35°F.

After reading Hibberd's hair-raising account of a rare cold evening in London, we can fully sympathize with the plight of North American hothouse proprietors who experienced sub-zero nights with bone-chilling regularity. In fact, the expense and inconvenience of heating a freestanding hothouse provided one very appealing motivation for the enthusiastic adoption of dwelling-attached conservatories in North America. A drawing-room greenhouse could be easily heated via a register from the home's main furnace. Or, even more simply, conservatories were often designed to gain heat from the main house by opening a door or window connected to the adjacent parlor or sitting room. Not only was this system economical and fuel efficient, it also had aesthetic benefits.

Heat may have been foremost on the novice's roster of headaches, but he also encountered other problems when learning the specifics of plant maintenance in a greenhouse. Unlike the Europeans, middle class Americans had already invited tropicals into their homes when hothouses became popular in this country. The development of suitable hothouse heating systems and the improvements in glass quality had taken so many years to accomplish that, unable to wait for exotic plants, North Americans accepted tropicals directly into their parlors from the hothouses of Europe. Europe broke the ice and provided the testing ground, while North Americans gladly received their recommendations concerning appropriate plants for the parlor.

So hothouses and conservatories served a different function in this country from their European counterparts. Although a few wealthy North Americans built glasshouses early in the era to acquire tropicals in advance of the coming trend, the masses adopted glasshouses later in the century. Hothouses simply served as an outlet for expanding windowsill collections. Here, the parlor spilled its botanical bounty into the conservatory, whereas, in Europe, glasshouses supplied exhibition plants for the parlor. In an 1886 edition of *The Ladies Home Journal*, Eben Rexford provided an American view of the sequence of the trend,

> The interest in floriculture seems to be increasing, and as those who love flowers and grow them in the windows of the living room become able to afford better conveniences for them, they begin to make inquiries about the cost of a small greenhouse or conservatory. Their experience with flowers convinces them that they must have a room by themselves if one would grow them well, and so fascinating is the work of caring for a few flowering plants that they would like to "branch out" and make a larger collection than it is possible when the only place for them is in the windows of the sitting room or parlor . . .

Although North Americans were not exploring completely virgin territory, they still had a great deal to learn about the art of growing under glass. They may have gained some experience with tropicals in their parlors, but the glass environment shed a completely different light on rare plant cultivation. As always, writers were ready, willing and able to lead the way.

In the Victorians' estimation, the three crucial factors that governed a greenhouse collection's ultimate fate were—cleanliness, ventilation and watering. If

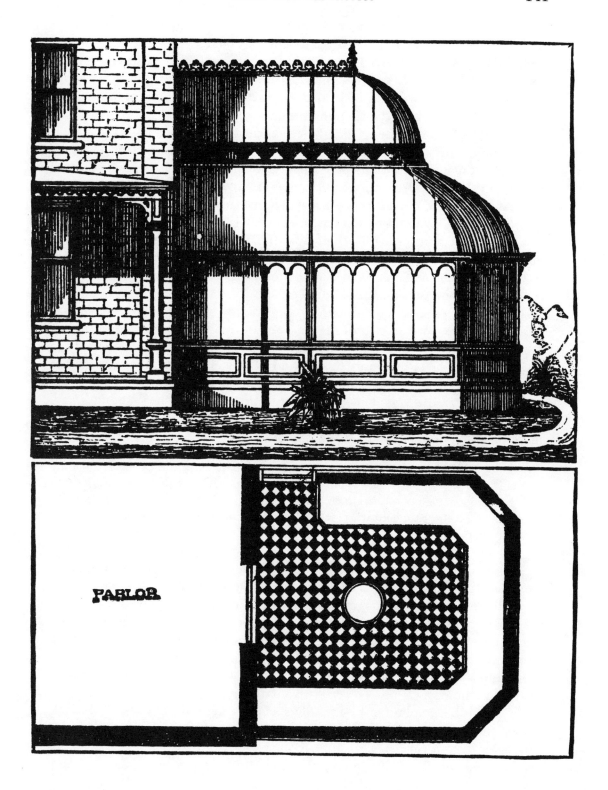

A conservatory attached to the parlor from Peter Henderson's *Gardening for Pleasure*.

the caretaker executed these tasks dexterously and religiously, his venture would undoubtedly succeed, his tropicals would thrive, and his estate would be the envy of his friends and neighbors. One neglectful hour, however, could result in the loss of his entire collection. Naturally, the particulars of these three departments were studied with rapt attention.

Judging from the frequency of articles addressing the topic, it is clear that in the Victorian view, cleanliness was akin to godliness. All aspects of life were guided by this preconception—the home and the garden as well as personal habits and attire all bore evidence to the period's concentration on hygiene and neatness. However, due to the intense and unnatural environment in the greenhouse, that building required constant vigilance to maintain cleanliness. Regardless, it had to be immaculate. Nothing was more heavenly than a tidy, well-kempt greenhouse. But, by the same token, nothing was as hellish as a neglected mass of tropical plants. As F. E. Field commented in *The Greenhouse*, "No dwelling room needs to be sweeter than the greenhouse."

Maintaining a greenhouse in proper order was not a matter to be taken lightly. Acquiring a glass range was only the first step encountered when mounting the social ladder, maintaining that glass kingdom was equally essential to further the ascent. But, the labor necessary to maintain a tropical collection sequestered in those glass structures was formidable. Good plant management began with the arrangement of the specimens when they first entered the building. And, according to Mrs. Loudon, author of *Gardening for Ladies*, that was the department in which most amateurs failed,

> Nothing can look worse than pale sickly greenhouse plants drawn up to an unnatural length and so weak that their stems will not stand upright without the aid of a stick. When greenhouses are crowded with plants, some of which are too far from the light, this must be the case, and when it is, it is quite hopeless to expect either healthy plants or fine flowers.

A tasteful, orderly arrangement of plants was essential. Tall specimens took up the rear, while smaller plants occupied the foreground. Ideally, each plant was given ample space for free air circulation and balanced light. However, the ideal was rarely practiced. As with the parlor, hothouses were filled to brimming with every sort of tropical upon which the gardener could lay hands. Not only had the glasshouse adopted the personality of the parlor, it also acquired the same cluttered ostentation which typically accompanies the display of wealth. Profusion ruled the day.

To establish discipline in the rapidly accumulating undergrowth of the hothouse, the duties incident to plant hygiene were carefully delineated. In his *American Flower Garden Directory*, Robert Buist provided a staunchly regimental schedule of activities, leaving no chore to the vagaries of human nature,

> . . . let all the dead leaves be picked off every day, the dust and other litter swept out of the house, and, when necessary, the house washed, which will be at least once a week.

That the foliage of the plants may always appear fresh, syringe them every morning, when there is the appearance of sun . . . this will in a great measure keep down the insects, and will prove a bane to the red spider.

If the gardener religiously followed this regimen, Buist felt certain that the plants under his care would grow tall and luxuriantly. In fact, he was so confident about the fastidious grower's chances of enjoying overwhelming success, that he felt his next order of business was to optimistically proceed and offer advice on staking. His words on that subject are truly visionary. Unfortunately, too many modern gardeners are guilty of the same errors in staking that the Victorians committed,

Tie up neatly with stakes . . . all the straggly growing plants; let the stakes be proportionate to the plants, and never longer, except they are climbing sorts. Do not tie the branches in bunches, but singly and neatly, imitating nature as much as possible.

From Mr. Buist's reference to "straggly growing plants", we are reminded that, in their zeal, the Victorians were not particularly discriminating when choosing their botanical acquisitions. Whatever explorers collected in the jungle was eagerly welcomed into collections of rare plants at home. The word "tropical" was sufficient to endear a plant to the Victorian heart, regardless of its tendencies to grow wild and wooly, thrusting its gangly arms and legs hither and yon.

As in the parlor, ventilation was an important issue. In Mr. Buist's opinion, two hours of ventilation daily were an absolute necessity, despite the temperature outdoors. It may have been 30°F. outside and snowing, but the ventilators were cranked open religiously at 11:00 AM and shut promptly at 1:00 PM. According to Buist, the breezes thus admitted were of the "utmost importance in drying up damp and clearing off stagnated air, which is a harbor for every corruption."

Watering a hothouse is also a crucial factor in producing healthy, happy plants. However, watering is a skill that each grower must learn by the simple but painful process of trial and error. Undoubtedly, many plants fell victim as indoor gardeners struggled to perfect a regimen which altered with the seasons and the eccentricities of the weather. Winter was a particularly trying season for novice growers. They were caught between the possible damage of drought and the evils of dampness. A plant watered an hour too late in the afternoon might be a mass of fungus-ridden foliage and rotten flowers by daybreak.

Infinitely confounding the watering conundrum, was the fact that the Victorians had no access to running water until the end of the century. However, when homes were finally provided with indoor plumbing, rainwater was still preferred to city water for the cultivation of plants. Rainwater was considered to be softer and richer in minerals than the city's product. So, throughout much of the 19th Century, water for plants was collected in cisterns which were fed, in turn, from roof gutters. During rainy seasons, the system worked marvelously. But, in times of drought, it did not function as effectively. Every green-

Cranking open the ventilators from Taft's *Greenhouse Construction*.

houseman had a tale or two to tell of hauling water in a drought. In fact, their stories began to bear a peculiar resemblance to fish tales as the distance between brook and glasshouse extended in length. However, I do not question for one moment the veracity of Edwin Lonsdale's story written in *The Management of Greenhouses* in 1902,

. . . I have dipped water out of a cistern until same was empty when we had to carry it from a pond 200 ft. away, and in hot, dry weather as soon as we finished watering the plants at one end of the greenhouse we had to begin and go all over them again.

During the winter, drought may not have been a problem, but there was the complication of water temperature to consider. Mr. Buist had these directions to offer those who might be tempted to simply run out to the pump to fetch a pailful of water,

Water, when applied either to the roots or foliage of plants, should be about the medium temperature of the house. Where there are no cisterns, a tank or barrel might be in the house, in which the water could stand for one night or more, as is most suitable. When water is given without being thus aired, it chills the roots, prevents a luxuriant growth, injures the fresh and healthful appearance of the foliage, and too frequently gives to all the plants a sickly hue.

Obviously, the novice had many skills to master. But, somehow, North American gardeners managed to attain proficiency in the greenhouse arts. Glasshouses became increasingly popular as the century wore to an end. Not only were hothouses prevalent, but many different variations on the glass theme were born. Most notably, window greenhouses made their debut in the cities.

In its exterior appearance, a Victorian window greenhouse was very similar to its modern counterpart, although it was constructed wholly of glass. Quite frequently, a glass partition or French doors separated the greenhouse from the body of the room. Inside, the enclosure was often fitted with an aquarium for fish as well as a cage for birds. The Victorians never lost an opportunity to introduce nature into the home.

Another variation on the glass theme appeared on country estates where veranda greenhouses came into vogue. As the name infers, a porch was enclosed in glass with climbing vines sunk deep into holes around the foundation. Potted plants were set in clusters on the patio and hanging baskets swayed gently in the breeze. The benefits and various uses of a veranda greenhouse were extolled by Charles MacIntosh in *The Greenhouse, Hot-House and Stove,*

Such a structure will answer the purpose of an agreeable lounge or promenade, which cannot fail to render them desirable to the valetudinarian at all seasons, and to the young and active in times of rain and bad weather.

MacIntosh also provided instructions for the proper display of plants in a veranda greenhouse, and his suggestions give us some indication of the grandeur as well as the servility of the era. In his estimation, a veranda greenhouse,

. . . should present at all times a perfect whole. The very changing of the plants when going out of flower; or the introduction of such as are coming into bloom, should be conducted early in the morning, or when the family is from home . . . so that no appearance of disorder or confusion may be observed. Of course, in this case we allude to families of distinction and fashion. The more humble, yet not less zealous amateur may take delight in conducting these arrangements personally . . .

A growing number of those zealous amateurs were women. Although it was men who lit the fires, and men who hauled the water, domestic glasshouses became a woman's domain. She gladly allowed men to accomplish the physically laborious tasks which greenhouse maintenance naturally entails, but she quietly and firmly claimed the more pleasant aspects of greenhouse cultivation as her own personal responsibility.

Her conquest was not made overnight. It was a gradual shift of power which began as a campaign to reapportion some greenhouse duties which naturally fell into the female sphere of influence. The ladies contended that men were not well suited to comprehending, and therefore executing, the aesthetic aspects of greenhouse growing. To begin with, the masculine hand was too large and

A veranda conservatory.

clumsy to perform the delicate procedures entailed in tropical plant cultivation. As many Victorian ladies would readily avow, their husbands and hired helpers were all thumbs when it came to plant arrangement and floral design. After all, as *The Ladies' Floral Cabinet* observed, "In matters of taste men are slower to learn than in matters of practice."

So, after conquering the mechanical barricades which surrounded the creation of glasshouses, gentlemen willingly and gallantly allowed women to decorate and oversee the maintenance of plant collections on an amateur level. In most cases, they gave up their glasshouses without a fight, and were perhaps somewhat relieved, as well as proud, that their ingenuity was responsible for creating yet another pastime to keep their wives and daughters safely close to home. In 1829, the British essayist, William Cobbett summarized the sentiments which North American husbands and fathers felt later in the century,

> It is the moral effects naturally attending a greenhouse that I set most value upon. There must be amusement in every family. Children observe and follow their parents in almost everything. How much better during the long and dreary winter for daughters and even sons to assist their mother in a greenhouse than to be seated with her at cards or in the blubberings over a stupid novel or at any other amusement that can be possibly conceived.

Although the glasshouse led to no diminution of the audience for the "stupid novels" of the era, nor any palpable reduction in the rampant card game fad, the contents of glasshouses did preoccupy a large percent of the female population. Glasshouses filled many needs for many women. A greenhouse allowed the lady of the house to play a part in the elevation of her family's social status. It also provided her with responsibilities which were not wholly domestic. Perhaps most importantly, horticultural hobbies often led to study and research.

Hothouses and conservatories filled other feminine needs. Here was another outlet for the female's creative energies. Although women were permitted to join in garden work, they had not yet gained jurisdiction over the maintenance and design of the estate's grounds. And so, the hothouse and conservatory provided women with their first opportunity to experiment with plantings and design. Due to the constantly fluid nature of the hothouse collection, a woman was faced with an ever-changing series of challenges. The conservatory was especially pregnant with possibilities. Although the beds were permanently laid out, the specimens themselves climaxed in 5–6 years from the date of planting, at which time a complete replanting was required.

The hothouse also effected the windowsill garden. With a glasshouse at her disposal, the gardener could arrange her window for continual bloom. Every plant in the window could be in peak condition, rendering the parlor infinitely more attractive than a display which had no recourse to a hothouse. In addition, the greenhouse also provided flowering plants to temporarily adorn rooms which received little light, but might benefit from a dash of color.

So glasshouses proved to be a crucial link in the chain of the windowsill's development. In Europe, they ushered tropical plants into cultivation, providing a special environment for jungle natives before the home could claim conditions suitable to exotics. For wealthy Americans, glasshouses established a European connection, and that link was responsible for the eventual introduction of tropicals into middle class sitting rooms throughout the country. But, perhaps most importantly, glasshouses provided another outlet for horticultural enthusiasm. They allowed gardeners to experiment with exotic plants that were too large or too specialized for the average home.

Over and above their practical contributions to horticultural development, glasshouses were responsible for a subtler, but no less important influence on style and mood. Glasshouses provided the inspiration for windowsill displays. Long before middle class Americans entertained any hope of owning a greenhouse, North Americans began to dedicate their windowsills to imitating the grandeur that existed under glass. For the American Victorian majority, windowsills substituted for hothouses. As a result, North Americans endeavored to design their windowsill collections as if they were miniature hothouses. So, using the crystal palaces of Europe as their inspiration, window gardeners let their imaginations soar. It is little wonder that the verdant display in the parlor eventually attained magnificent proportions.

Pioneers in the Parlor

CHAPTER VII

BLAZING THE PATH

THE DOOR to a new, exotic world was suddenly flung open with the blossoming of the great conservatories in Europe, and the public stood poised on the threshold, waiting to venture into the world of tropicals. Eagerness suffused the era. And yet, physical limitations obstructed the path. It was virtually impossible to provide a tropical environment in the early 19th Century parlor. Instead of rushing into tropicals, those aspiring indoor gardeners were forced to select a few stalwart representatives which they might display in their dark and dank rooms.

The first botanical candidates to slip from greenhouse into parlor were not technically tropicals. They were actually subtropicals. But, they filled all the other requisites admirably, and were therefore eagerly welcomed to share the family's home. Initially, the average household was satisfied with the smallest conquest of a territory formerly available only to the upper crust.

Of course, the public did not stumble upon this convenient substitute independently. They were led patiently every inch of the way by the press. The parlor and its decor were effected by many influences over the years, but none was as significant as the printed word.

Horticultural writers had already discovered that the surest method for attracting an audience was to establish the link between exotic plants and interesting people. And, for the Victorians, wealthy people were the most interesting breed. The middle class was continually striving to catch a glimpse at the ingredients of the rich life. So, writers simply inferred that exotic horticulture was among the upper classes' best kept secrets. To preserve the air of intrigue and maintain an elite position, writers played a carefully balanced double hand. They adroitly juggled both elements of their readership by pandering to the masses but took special pains not to offend the sensibilities of their wealthier patrons.

Never was it suggested that a plant was cultivated in the window due to the want of sufficient funds to construct a crystal palace in its honor. Plants were grown in the parlor to be more closely enjoyed by the family, not because a conservatory was beyond economic reach. This approach flattered the average reader, and it also brought the fantasy of exotics down to a popular level without tarnishing the sparkling tropical image.

Only a certain breed of writer could successfully carry off this illusion and balance the various strata of society. Those who performed the feat adeptly won the affection of the masses as well as the respect of high society. Garden articles were ostensibly concerned with exotic plants. But, in addition to offering insights into the dry facts of tropical horticulture, they were invariably seasoned with social insinuations and graphic descriptions of the grand estates which sequestered tropicals within their confines. One could not help but make the connection linking exotic horticulture with social prominence.

By mid-century, the country abounded with respected horticultural journalists, and their numbers increased with the years. However, few writers performed their roles with the panache of Andrew Jackson Downing. He smugly bore his role of horticultural master of ceremonies with unfaltering confidence. His reserved superiority was undoubtedly the trait which kept him so firmly in command of the public's affections. Throughout his reign, he rarely stooped to recognize the middle class audience which grew to be the overwhelming majority of his readership. Instead, his writing reflected the privileged world of the wealthy.

It seemed as if Downing was omnipresent, he went everywhere and did everything at once. His magazine, *The Horticulturist*, read like a high society gossip column, although the romances reported in the pages of that periodical were strictly between man and flower. He moved in elite circles, dropping into fashionable dwellings at regular intervals to share the latest botanical confidences and inspect the resident plant-corps. Then, amidst glowing superlatives and wild name-dropping, he reported the visit in his journal.

When *The Horticulturist* arrived on the doorstep, the reader could anticipate an evening's sojourn in an enchanted world. Not only were Downing's readers transported to foreign and wealthy estates, but the plants described by his gliding pen acquired a glowing importance. He had an acute sensitivity to any subject which might excite the average mind, and this uncommon talent combined with his penchant for sensationalism to add color to his articles.

Downing and other contemporary writers set the trends. In fact, one of their most important contributions was the formation and definition of a class of botanical aristocrats. Month after month, articles were devoted to the fate of specific photosynthesizing protagonists—their hybrids, newly discovered species, their cultivation, who grew them and the prizes that they captured in exhibition. Thus, a mutual exchange of support evolved between plant and public. If an exotic plant established the proper social connections, it was guaranteed press space as well as an enthusiastic reception throughout the various classes of society.

So, the first subtropical plants to slip from the conservatory into the depths of the anxiously awaiting parlor were botanicals with impeccable social connections. Novelty played second fiddle to nobility. Certain plants had been cultivated since antiquity solely under the munificent and moneyed auspices of the well-born. Such plants as the camellia and citrus were chosen by the Victorians for household cultivation primarily on the basis of their social reputation rather than their physical beauty or suitability for the home environment.

Of course, the average citizen did not fabricate these connections between botany and society independently. Such notions were instilled by the sleek pens wielded by A. J. Downing and his colleagues. Society looked toward hothouses and conservatories with the vague idea that within those horticultural buildings must dwell some likely candidates for windowsill adornment. And, with the help of roving reporters, they found suitable subjects for their parlor. Considering the fact that they chose on the basis of a plant's social status rather than its adaptability, they made some very fortunate selections indeed.

When Downing entered a conservatory or hothouse, he made a running inventory of the botanical company that was kept. Just as other people might prefer certain personality types when choosing their friends, Downing showed a marked affinity for specific plant genera. He harbored a particularly strong affection for camellias.

So, if all was in order, Downing hoped that his eyes would light upon a camellia when he visited a conservatory. Preferably, a collection of camellias should be enjoying his host's hospitality—the more, the merrier. Although a gentleman might successfully grow any number of choice tropicals, A. J. Downing was bound to judge his host's botanical acumen by the state in which he found the camellia collection.

Upon finding those fashionable flowers thriving under his host's auspices, Downing would rush home and take pen in hand. The next issue of his magazine included a tribute to the visit, replete with abundant superlatives and effusive praise. Not only was the number of camellias mentioned, but he also chronicled the particular varieties on exhibition—some were more prestigious than others. Thus, a reputation was won both for the camellia and its cultivator.

Perhaps it was not entirely coincidental that Downing chose to champion a plant which would perform in the average home. Although he never revealed the slightest interest in pandering to "common" tastes, his endorsement was sufficient to set the public off on a full-blown camellia fad. Intentional or not, it was a fortunate point of departure for the future of exotic plants.

Camellias lent an air of aristocracy to their surroundings. Everything about a camellia was regal—its beauty, its demands and its stubborn refusal to oblige except when being slavishly attended. The elegance exhibited in those large formal flowers was unmatched by any blossom hitherto in cultivation. When camellias first reached European shores in the 1700s, they had already undergone centuries of selection and hybridizing in the Orient. As a result, their blossoms far surpassed any other flower grown by the Victorians, with the possible exception of the ever-popular rose.

A camellia in blossom is a poetic sight. I can only explain the lack of verse devoted to the flower by imagining that the Victorians were rendered completely dumb-struck by its beauty. Camellia blossoms unravel their petals in something akin to a carefully choreographed dance, each bloom is an ever-changing piece of art. When fully unfurled, the flower is a study in perfection. If any blossom was capable of up-lifting the morality of the masses, it was surely the camellia.

Added to the camellia's beauty was the element of novelty. *Camellia japonica* was a relatively new figure on the North American scene. It arrived in Europe from China in the 1730s via an East India Company shipment meant to be filled with Tea plants (*Camellia sinensis*). Whether the mistake was intentional or not remains a subject of debate. However, considering the value of the expected cargo, that original immigration of *Camellia japonica* was understandably greeted with something less than complete enthusiasm.

The new plant was named by Carl Linnaeus for an Austrian missionary, Georg Joseph Kamel, who studied and described plants in Manila until his death in 1706. It is questionable whether Kamel ever saw the genus which later took his name. However, the popular Victorian rendition of the botanical introduction describes how Kamel personally escorted a specimen home and presented his namesake to Europe in a lecture reputedly given in the 1730s—a feat which was chronologically impossible. Further, the Jesuit priest supposedly concluded his lecture by ceremoniously handing the revered plant to Lord Petre of Essex, entrusting the specimen into his care. Here we begin to encounter some semblance of truth. Lord Petre did obtain a plant of *Camellia japonica* in 1738, probably from the East India Company's shipment. And, to our knowledge, the first camellia to flower in Europe unfurled in Lord Petre's Essex greenhouse in 1739. Unfortunately, the plant reputedly died soon afterwards due to the overly solicitous attentions of the estate's gardener who provided the camellia with too much warmth. Lord Petre also perished immediately thereafter. From the proximity of the deaths, the melodramatic Victorians assumed that the gentleman died of a broken heart. The theory is possible—but unlikely.

Camellias had established their social connections in the Orient long before setting foot on European soil. Records of *Camellia japonica*'s cultivation date back 1,200 years, and its employment in Oriental gardens probably predates that first written reference. The plant was known in Japan as *Tsubaki*, "the tree with shining leaves", and was worshipped in the Shinto religion as the residence inhabited by gods while in their earthly transfiguration. The tree was similarly revered in China. Although Western Victorians had established no religious connections with camellias, they also worshipped the plant—as they worshipped anything from the Orient.

When Downing began chronicling his travels in the pages of his periodical in 1846, he found camellias thriving in the country's most fashionable greenhouses. Upon its initial arrival in Hoboken, New Jersey in the late 1790s, the camellia immediately piqued North America's botanical interest. That new import obligingly produced a single red flower in its first year of residence under the care of the wealthy collector and railroad magnate, John Stevens. His satisfaction with the plant's performance was clearly evident from the fact that he sent for another specimen post-haste and received a double white variety in July of 1800. That was the auspicious entry of *Camellia j.* 'Alba plena', a hybrid that has retained its popularity for nearly two centuries.

Camellias were disseminated throughout this country with lightning speed. By 1829, the Massachusetts Horticultural Society had already added camellias to their roster of exhibition competitions, offering a premium of $3.00 for the finest camellia flowers in show. In 1822, William Prince's Linnaean Botanical Garden in Flushing, New York listed 17 camellia cultivars in its catalogue. Obviously, the public had both frequent exposure and easy access to that attractive botanical novelty.

So, when Andrew Jackson Downing spoke of camellias in *The Horticulturist*, he was assured of a captivated audience. Plant explorers were also sensitive to the whims of public taste, and duly noted every camellia that they encountered during their travels. Most especially, Robert Fortune, a favorite and often-quoted plant explorer, described his reactions upon meeting huge, 30 foot tall camellia trees while trekking through the Orient. Such eyebrow-raising tales provided sufficient incentive to encourage every gardener in America to run out and throw another bucket of manure tea on the resident camellia.

The home front was also active with camellia-related intrigue. Much to the public's delight, new camellia sports were continually appearing on the market. And, in keeping with the plant's esteemed reputation, novel introductions received appropriately auspicious names. The roster of 19th Century camellias includes varieties named for notables in the worlds of entertainment ('Jenny Lind'), botany ('Robert Fortune' and 'Professor Sargent'), society ('Lady Hume's Blush') and, of course, the nobility of all nations involved with camellia cultivation especially France, Italy, England and Belgium. Marie Antoinette was honored with a camellia as was Napoleon. The Emperor of Russia and a bevy of counts and countesses, dukes and duchesses, lords and ladies were all immortalized with cultivar names. Nor did the list lack documentation of the great technological advances of the century. 'Great Eastern' was named in honor of the first steamship to successfully lay the Atlantic cable. And, naturally, homage was paid to the patron of camellias with the naming of *Camellia j.* 'A. J. Downing'. Prince Albert was commemorated with 'Alberti', while the queen herself—an ardent admirer and collector of the genus—was immortalized with 'Queen Victoria'.

The camellia dubbed 'Queen Victoria' was, in fact, the subject of a notorious money-making scheme. The plant was named by Verschaffelt, a prestigious Belgian nurseryman. As part of a promotional campaign, he offered lottery tickets which entitled the winner to 10 camellia plants and a cutting of 'Queen Victoria'. Over 100 tickets were sold worldwide at an incredible price, earning

Camellia
japonica
'Abbey Wilder'

Camellia
japonica
'H. A. Downing'

Camellia
japonica
'Lucida'

Camellia
japonica
'President Clark'

Camellias were named for the era's celebrities.

Verschaffelt 15,000 francs total—and he still retained possession of the original stock plant of 'Queen Victoria', minus a single cutting.

More than once, camellias were connected with the world of high finance. Marshall P. Wilder, a notable American collector of the genus as well as a pomologist of great repute (we have Mr. Wilder to thank for the Anjou pear, which he introduced in 1844), created two camellia hybrids which were the first to compete favorably with European imports. In the year after Downing began publishing *The Horticulturist*, the Massachusetts Horticultural Society honored the introduction by awarding Wilder first prize and a $3.00 premium. Naturally, the fame of those hybrids spread, and they were soon sold to an American nurseryman who obtained the pair for the tidy sum of $1,000. That owner immediately undertook a whirlwind propagation program, and we next see his name in a British journal. Having departed for Europe, he was selling cuttings overseas for no less than $300. apiece. He made his fortune before returning to America. Such sagas kept camellias fashionable with wealthy patrons, while piquing bourgeois interest in the plants.

Camellias excited the artistic as well as the financial world. The flower was the subject of numerous paintings and the inspiration for the embellishment of many *objets d'art*. In addition, literature and music often made allusion to the flower. By far the most auspicious such mention was made in 1848 when Alexander Dumas *fils* wrote *La Dame aux Camelias*, a novel which fostered an

Marshall P. Wilder, illustration from Bailey's *The Standard Cyclopedia of Horticulture* published by MacMillan.

unfortunate association between the flower and the demimonde. So popular was Dumas' scandalous story that it was soon recast into a play and subsequently set to music in Verdi's opera *La Traviata*.

Although notoriety seemed to enhance the flower in the eyes of its middle class audience, the upper crust would not dream of associating with a plant suffering from a tarnished image. They dropped camellias from their botanical repertoire immediately. Camellias were rising stars on the horticultural horizon from the 1800s until the 1860s, but their glitter faded rapidly when the wealthy caught wind of their shaky reputation. They would never regain that lost ground.

Camellias were still enjoying an impressive following of admirers when they first slipped from the crystal palaces of the wealthy onto the parlor windowsill. Actually, those small trees were entirely suitable for cultivation in the home. They are endowed with the iron constitution necessary to endure the hardships of a dry atmosphere, indirect light and constantly fluctuating temperatures—conditions which were characteristic of the parlor which was to become their home.

The Victorians soon discovered that it was not difficult to keep camellias indoors. However, they also rapidly learned that blossoming camellias constituted a challenge of an entirely different order of magnitude. Here, the aspiring Victorian social climber had a subject on which to test her newly acquired botanical expertise. Anyone could maintain a camellia in reasonable health in her residence, but only those who religiously studied gardening periodicals were privy to the specific routines which would yield blossoms indoors.

The trick to blossoming camellias in the home is to provide just the right combination of light, water and temperature. With the help of the proliferating gardening books and horticultural periodicals, those cultural requirements were revealed to an attentive public. Victorian writers may have been slightly less than accurate when relating historic data, but the experts were extremely thorough when researching and presenting cultural instructions.

No annex of the dwelling could be better suited to camellias than the front parlor. Closed off from the remainder of the home in winter, the temperatures in the parlor were severe and forbidding, a characteristic which readily befit the cold, aloof furnishings which came to inhabit that room. Prior to the widespread adoption of central heat, other infrequently used areas in the dwelling were likewise partitioned off in the winter and left bereft of the fire's benefits. The entry foyer and stairway landings were often unheated. In addition, such spaces were frequently given windows to allow the occupants to glance out at the street or to provide a weary (and often tightly corsetted) stairway climber with the opportunity to stop, rest and enjoy the view before continuing the ascent upward. Those spots were frequently employed for the winter and fall storage of camellias.

The camellia's yearly cycle begins in spring, which is the season to plan for the next year's buds. Naturally, Victorians yearned to have blossoms during the Christmas holidays, and it was toward this end that a growing schedule was devised. To ensure an early blossoming, heat was applied in the spring when growth naturally initiates. Then, during the summer, the plants were carted out-of-doors and grown under the light shade of trees. By September, buds set. It was at this stage that novice growers generally went astray. In order to set buds and hold them, camellias require constantly cool temperatures ranging no higher than 40° to 50°F. at night. Happily, those conditions were readily available in the average front parlor.

Camellias served as botanical "guinea pigs" on which indoor gardeners sharpened skills that would later be practiced on bonafide tropicals. The Victorians were perfectionists, and their methods of houseplant cultivation clearly reflected that propensity. In an era when success was often equated with grandeur, gardeners pursued the goals of impressive specimen size and correspondingly large blossoms with a dogged fervor. In this respect, the average 19th Century indoor gardener was apt to be a more disciplined, patient grower than her modern counterpart. Certainly, Victorians showed greater concern for future attainments rather than bowing to the rewards of immediate gratification.

A primary example of their self-control was evident in the 19th Century practice of disbudding. Small plants were never permitted to blossom until they reached sufficient stature to support both new growth and flower buds. So, with awesome self-control, growers religiously removed the buds from their camellia stock, just as they had thinned the flowers of roses. Every bud was plucked, with the exception of the bud on the tip of each branch which was allowed to swell, gaining the benefit of the branch's entire energy. Whereas modern growers look for quantities of blossoms, quality was of prime importance to the Victorian plantsman. It was an era in which growing plants was elevated to the ranks of craftsmanship, and learning the proper methods was similar to initiation into a revered guild.

Several valuable lessons on indoor plant cultivation were mastered through experimentation with camellias. Perhaps most importantly, the rules of houseplant hygiene were formulated. Victorians expressed a sympathetic concern for the health of their botanical indoor guests. They were especially anxious about the plant's ability to 'breathe'' indoors. This feat was understood as being achieved via the stomata on the leaf's surface.

In their role as the good host, 19th Century gardeners were determined to aid their plant's breathing in every manner possible. One very effective means for facilitating foliar breathing was to keep plant foliage free from dust accumulation. After carefully dusting the bric-a-brac and curios, the housewife also polished the houseplant leaves. The chore became an important part of the weekly cleaning schedule, and the telltale camellia, with its dark, shiny leaves, was a particularly accurate indicator of a lady's impeccable housekeeping.

In addition, camellias were given periodic baths to clean the inevitable accumulation of soot and dust from their leaf surfaces. This hygienic practice served the dual role of assisting the plant's foliar respiratory system while also preventing disease and pest infestations. Therefore, most authors strongly lobbied for the administration of weekly plant baths. The magnitude of this task cannot be fully appreciated unless the reader keeps in mind that most homes lacked the benefit of running water until the latter part of the century. The tepid water necessary to accomplish the feat was only provided after hauling massive buckets to the stove for heating prior to the actual ordeal.

Everyone agreed that over-crowding impeded foliar breathing. Regardless, it is clear from period illustrations that Victorians persisted in exploiting every centimeter of window space to the utmost. Obviously, 19th Century growers allowed their desire for a jungle-like atmosphere to completely override the rules of proper plant culture. The typical windowsill menagerie managed to proliferate into a twining, climbing, tangled mass of foliage and flowers despite the hygienic consequences.

To compensate, free air movement was furnished from an exterior source— fresh air from outdoors was supplied through ventilation. If the temperature outside climbed above 40°F., the windows were flung open to afford one and all with a renewed supply of fresh air. And, when the weather permitted, the entire

The Victorians allowed their desire for a jungle-like atmosphere to completely override the rules of hygienic spacing.

botanical inventory was transported outside to partake of the benevolent breezes, if only for an hour, and then the collection was once again restored to its inside location. The physical proportions of this exercise can only be appreciated when considering the mammoth dimensions which houseplants were encouraged to attain. And, bear in mind that 19th Century plant containers were considerably heavier than our modern, light clays and synthetic plastics. Caring for botanical aristocrats in the home was both time-consuming and arduous. Yet, the chores increasingly fell into the sphere of influence allotted to the "weaker sex".

Actually, camellias are relatively easy plants to cultivate, given their preferred temperatures. All of the fuss and bother of bathing and airing the specimens was, in the camellia's case, performed primarily for the aesthetic purpose of maintaining a neat appearance. In other genera, however, these procedures proved more crucial—especially with plants prone to insect infestations. Although skills were sharpened with camellias, they were tested with more difficult botanical aristocrats such as potted citrus.

Long before camellias arrived in Europe, citrus had established their affiliation with members of the nobility. The romance between European aristocracy and citrus is believed to have commenced in the year 1100 when the crusaders brought the lemon, lime and sour orange to Italy and France. With the advent of the 19th Century, citrus already possessed an established history of care and coddling by members of royalty. Thus, the association was firmly entrenched—citrus was the fruit of kings.

Citrus enhanced this image immeasurably when that fruitful family became the inspiration for the erection of ornate and opulent *orangeries*. The proportions of those buildings are revealed by letters such as the one dated 1620 and quoted in John Hix's *The Glass House* describing a portable wooden structure designed to protect no less than 400 medium-sized citrus trees and 30 smaller specimens between Michaelmas (September 29th) and Easter. Although this was undoubtedly one of the larger early winter gardens, its magnificence was typical of the trend which rendered the *orangerie* and its contained fruit synonymous with wealth. Certainly, the glass structure which cemented that association was the awesome greenhouse at Versailles. Hundreds of citrus trees, sumptuously contained in solid silver pots, were marched in and out of that building seasonally, bearing their summer flowers outdoors on verdant parterres and producing their winter fruit indoors as they basked in the warmth of huge stoves. While the populace survived on the meager remains of last season's harvest, royalty and a chosen few at court dined on the sweet, fresh fruits of the tropics. It was precisely this division between classes which the Victorians hoped to span when inviting citrus into their parlors.

Although the custom of growing citrus in the North American home was popularized in the 19th Century, the practice pre-dated that era. We have records of citrus dwelling in at least one home at Colonial Williamsburg. Lady Skipwith of Williamsburg had an exceptional collection of citrus in her glass-windowed front hallway, and the plants never failed to elicit comments from her guests. Such collections established a precedent which 19th Century gardeners enthusiastically adopted.

When the Victorians embraced a plant, they did so with whole-hearted fervor. Downing made frequent note of the growing affinity for citrus. He wrote, "both the orange and the lemon are such favorites in this country that scarcely a cottage where a flower-pot or tub can be put in requisition is without one or other of these plants." Several decades later, the situation apparently remained the same, for Peter Henderson filched that precise phrase and incorporated it as his own in *Henderson's Handbook of Plants* dated 1881.

Citrus trees lent more than just aesthetic beauty to the parlor, they provided the additional virtue of bearing fruit indoors. This quality immediately took members of that genus out of the female's realm. The management of fruit-bearing plants, either indoors or out, was traditionally the office of the resident bread-winner. The prevailing feeling was that the chore of bringing exotics into fruit was much too complex an issue for the female novice-in-residence to comprehend. However, women were permitted to apprentice and perform the more routine duties of watering, airing and hygienic bathing.

Admittedly, the citrus was a difficult subject for a novice to tackle. In response to the inherent problems involved and the culinary value of the rewards, many magazines thought it wise to devote numerable articles to instructing the masses on the finer points of citrus cultivation. Unlike the typical houseplant article, such manuscripts were written by men for a male audience. Not only were the virtues and vices of each species argued heatedly in those articles, but they often contained illustrated instructions on the fine art of grafting and inarching as well. Composts for fruiting trees were described in unappetizingly colorful detail.

There were several levels of success to master when growing citrus. One could merely keep the specimen alive, which was no small feat considering the plant's nutritional requirements and its attraction for insects. A further level of competence was rewarded by a profusion of headily scented flowers. Then, those snow-white blossoms could be pollinated via insect visitors or through human intervention and thus fruit was set. But the ultimate achievement was the production of ripened fruit, an accomplishment only realized after months of solicitous ministration to the tree and its heavy burden. Understandably, the prideful achievement was not abbreviated by consuming the evidence. Home-grown citrus fruit was traditionally left on the branches and reserved solely for ornamental display.

The Victorian citrus repertoire was limited mainly to oranges and lemons. Although other novelty fruits were introduced, none enjoyed widespread esteem, probably due to insufficient availability. Of those two popular citrus, indoor gardeners developed a preference for the orange, undoubtedly based on the fact that its fruit tenaciously remained on the branches for several seasons.

Although an orange known as 'Havana' reigned supreme in the beginning of the Victorian Era, the Otaheite Orange (Tahiti was formerly known as Otaheite) was the most popular citrus at the era's end. And the Otaheite's general popularity was a good indication of the lack of motivation to produce edible fruit. The Otaheite Orange is a hybrid of *Citrus limon* occasionally called the Lemandarin. It bears sour fruit of poor table quality, but compensates by providing an impressive show. That variety is compact and "parlor sized" in stature, unlike the many ungainly hybrids which are now grown, and the entire bush carries a heavy burden of fruit.

Lemons were frequently found enhancing the parlor decor. The Meyer

A Victorian favorite was the sour orange, *Citrus limon* 'Otaheite'.

Lemon (*Citrus limon* 'Meyer'), a hybrid between the lemon and orange, most often fraternized with the bell-jar clock, mahogany table and polite society at afternoon tea in the parlor. However, the Ponderosa Lemon (*Citrus limon* 'Ponderosa') was more apt to stimulate conversation, and thus, it was occasionally featured in the parlor. That gigantic hybrid between the lemon and citron wielded its hefty, five pound fruits in a corner of the room while attempting to coexist with the other houseplants in quarters which it rapidly rendered uncomfortably cramped.

Those grand trees became heirlooms, especially the novelty varieties. In fact, many an august citrus was proudly passed down through the generations as valuable property of an estate. In our greenhouse, we have a Ponderosa Lemon that was given to the family when its owner grew too weary with age to water and repot the plant. We roughly estimate that our fruit-bearing specimen is upwards of 95 years, and has outlived several generations of caretakers. Not every plant can claim such a long and productive life.

Since those fruit-bearing aristocrats were both widely grown and valuable, much time and effort was spent deliberating about their proper care. In general, citrus prefer conditions similar to camellias, with the addition of strong light during the winter months when buds are set. In fact, camellias provided a cultural standard to which many houseplants were compared. However, citrus posed some further problems rarely encountered with camellias. They are prone to scale and mealy bugs. Fortunately, indoor gardeners were able to control, although not eradicate, these pests by practicing the time-honored remedy of bathing the plants. When baths were employed preventatively, they were administered with both additional zeal and a generous helping of soap.

Although citrus had enjoyed a long and fruitful history in pot culture before entering the home, they do not lend themselves readily to that mode of cultivation. A citrus prefers to sink its roots into the ground. Due to this preference, 19th Century growers were continually coping with chlorotic leaves and flagging plants. Much later, leaf discoloration was recognized as nutritional in origin. Actually, the Victorian remedies revealed a suspicion (but not a conviction) that nutrition might be an underlying factor in chlorosis. In fact, according to Henderson's *Handbook*, the ideal medium for citrus included ¼ bucket of charcoal dust to every bucket of soil. By adding the charcoal, he was effectively providing the plant with additional potassium.

Charcoal was not the only ingredient recommended to bolster citrus soils. Fertilizing indoor citrus became the subject of a heated debate, a topic of immense fascination for 19th Century gardeners. Guano entered the market with much fanfare early in the century, and was sold specifically for the culture of indoor plants. Investors laid heavy bets on the futures of the guano industry. Fortunes were made and lost by men dealing in the importation of bat manure from the caves of Peru and Argentina. A fad ensued. However, it was short-lived and its proportions did not nearly equal the fervor anticipated by speculators.

Although the guano industry did not prove financially profitable, the subject was of sufficient fascination to warrant a great deal of press space. Not surprisingly, citrus was the crop most frequently treated to an experimental dosage of guano, and opposing gardening factions waged an endless battle either extolling or berating the benefits of guano. For the defense, professionals (many of whom were financially entangled in guano deals) insisted that, if properly employed, the fertilizer was capable of working wonders. However, the pages of gardening periodicals were continually sprinkled with letters from irate readers who had lost heirloom citrus trees after applying guano to their soils. Neutral factions pronounced the verdict—guano probably performed an admirable job of raising the nitrogen level in the soil when required, however, an overdose of that munificent manure was capable of producing devastating results.

Of more general acceptance was the use of manure tea, a concoction brewed cheaply and simply in the backyard. The directions for its manufacture adorn every old gardening book: a wooden barrel received a generous helping of well-rotted manure and then was left uncovered to collect rainwater. A few days later, the elixir was drawn off as needed via a spigot from the barrel's bottom.

Propagation was another matter which enjoyed frequent press space. Citrus and camellia plants were expensive commodities. A camellia cutting could be had for a price hovering between $1.00 and $3.00, a figure well in excess of the average family's daily earnings at the time. Understandably, an avid audience interested in learning propagation techniques rapidly developed. Both camellias and citrus could be propagated by cuttings, but most amateurs lacked the facilities to maintain a cutting during the rooting process. In any case, it was believed that citrus propagated by this method were inferior. A cutting might come into flower rapidly, but it would never attain an impressive size - and the average Victorian equated size with success.

Inarching was the favored method of propagation for both citrus and camellias, practiced by professionals and amateurs alike. An inarch involved the fusing of growing plants at a juncture which was stripped of bark, nicked and packed with moss. When roots initiated, the plants were cut apart. Later in the era, other more efficient grafting methods were introduced and eventually completely replaced inarching.

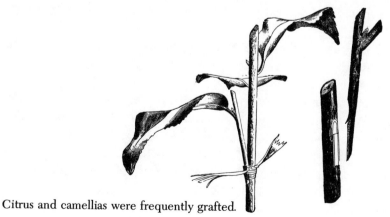

Citrus and camellias were frequently grafted.

Procuring citrus trees from seed provided yet another propagative possibility, although that method proved fruitful only for the extremely patient grower. A seedling eventually produced a suitably stalwart specimen, but a decade might easily elapse before fruit set. Although Victorian gardeners exhibited admirable sufferance when dealing with their sundry botanical projects, they understandably preferred immediate gratification when it was within the realm of possibility.

Camellias and citrus were indisputably the most prevalent protagonists in the parlor. However, other prominent tropicals shared the stage in minor roles. The ambiance in the front parlor was created by the careful balancing of many constituents. Ideally, the room could more accurately be described as a work of art rather than a living space. In the front parlor, the "heavy" objects of culture and wealth such as furniture, musical instruments and paintings were counterpoised against the "lighter" objects of nature. The botanical element in that composition could not be provided by a solitary green representative. To realize the proper balance, an entire botanical chorus was required.

Azaleas often figured as an important voice in the subtropical choir. Hovering around the primadonnas, as if in worship of their dominant splendor, azaleas wandered into the parlor scene early due to their common botanical bond of aristocratic connections.

Any import from the newly botanized Orient was automatically given space in the parlor. Victorians gazed on the objects of the Far East with doting admiration. And, fortunately, the cool-loving botanical inhabitants of Southern Asia responded positively to the assiduous attentions of the Victorians, and to the variable temperatures in the Spartan 19th Century abode.

Azalea indica arrived in Europe from China at the beginning of the 19th Century. By the end of the era, hundreds of hybrids had been developed and established comfortably in Victorian homes and conservatories. A broad spectrum of colors were perfected during the early years, including purple, rose, white, salmon, crimson and violet as well as hybrids with bi-colored blossoms. In fact, 150 years ago, azalea hybrids looked much as they do today. Those tidy little bushes burst forth with an ambitious display of bloom every spring, unfurling their ruffled petals slowly and dramatically until each blossom nearly equalled a camellia flower in size.

But, the rewards of growing Chinese Azaleas were extracted at a cost. The fact that we rarely attempt to cultivate members of that genus in our modern homes is one excellent indication of the difficulty of the deed.

Azalea culture was not fully understood when the plant began its reign of glory in the early 19th Century. However, when the Victorians learned that azaleas require a moderately damp soil and cool roots, especially in the summer, they began to realize success with the plant. Through trial and error, they discovered the tricks of indoor azalea culture. They found that covering the top of the soil with moss in the summer kept the roots cool. Similarly, digging a trench close to the azalea's stem allowed water to penetrate the thick root mass and

Azaleas were often grown indoors.

percolate down to the lower roots. Further, 19th Century gardeners discovered that cool evening temperatures (40°–50°F.) set a profusion of azalea buds, while a dormant period in autumn was necessary for a strong winter specimen. Staggered blossoming could be achieved by gradually bringing a series of azaleas out of storage and marching the pots upstairs from the cellar in slow succession. In that way, the family members could enjoy the longest possible exposure to an azalea's aesthetic and moral qualities.

If plants were invited into the home to provide an up-lifting experience for the human residents, then all senses had to be barraged. Sight and touch had obviously already benefitted from the first botanical entries; and the sense of smell was partially piqued with the parlor-grown bulbs and hardy plants which imparted an aroma of the native woods and fields. But, the Victorians preferred the mysterious fragrances of the tropics. They liked aggressive, romantic, exotic scents which permeated every corner of the home. All of the rooms in the house might benefit from a fragrant plant in their confines but, most importantly, the nose had to be pleased in the parlor.

On the basis of its incredibly sweet aroma, daphne was enlisted as one of the parlor's protagonists. *Daphne odora*, a native of China, enjoyed the esteem accorded all things Oriental. However, the decisive element compelling the Victorian love affair with that rather homely bush was its incredible fragrance. Although it is an excruciatingly difficult plant to cultivate indoors, the Victorians were determined to have daphne flowers within easy inhaling distance.

The daphne which graced the home was *Daphne odora* or, more popularly in Victorian literature, *Daphne odorata*. Just as horticultural history was a matter of vagaries and inconsistencies for the garden writers of the period, the subject of Latin binomials was open to free-wheeling interpretation and rendering. Popular horticultural journalists frequently took the liberty of naming plants as they pleased. An excellent example occurs in Edward Sprague Rand's 1868 volume, *Flowers for the Parlor and Garden*, "Every green-house contains plants of the well-known *Daphne odorata*, sometimes called *D. indica* and vulgarly known as '*Daphne odora*'." Vulgar or not, the latter was botanically correct.

Most months of the year saw the daphne's foliage unadorned by buds. Its shiny, laurel-like leaves looked more akin to an outdoor shrub than an aristocratic and exotic resident of the parlor. But, in spring, umbels of pale pink blossoms opened, providing a feast for both eye and nostril over a prolonged period of time.

The flowers are comely, certainly they are far fairer than the foliage; but their fragrance infinitely enhances their appearance. A daphne in blossom provides a welcome sight for the eye, but an even more stimulating impression on the nose. To smell a daphne in full flower is to take a breath of heaven.

Unlike the other protagonists in the parlor, daphne blossoms were easily evoked. If a daphne survived the winter, spring was sure to find the plant, "wearing right royally its clusters of pearly blossoms," as Henry T. Williams aptly wrote in 1873. But, keeping a daphne alive was a much more complex chore than coaxing bud formation.

Although the parlor provided the bone chilling temperatures which daphnes require both night and day, the plants frequently failed to thrive for want of proper soil. The Victorians were apparently oblivious to the daphne's desire for an acid soil, just as they remained ignorant of all other pH preferences. In addition, a daphne dislikes frequent feeding, while one of the century's favorite indoor sports was bolstering the resident houseplants with copious quantities of fertilizer. Under the circumstances, it is a miracle that the plant survived.

However, the Victorians must have experienced some degree of success when growing daphne indoors, because in-depth pruning instructions accompanied every mention of the plant. We certainly have no modern examples to compare with the 4 ft. house-grown daphnes which Victorians claimed to prune. We can barely keep the plant alive for a prolonged period of time, the notion of the 5 ft., 6 year old specimens which Victorians produced in their parlors is completely beyond modern imagination. Such successes spurred 19th Century growers onward.

So, the foundations for the parlor display were established. The Victorian Era was still in its youth in North America when exotics first entered the home, and the parlor was merely a fledgling institution when subtropicals infiltrated its confines. Over the years, the room grew in strength and definition while still harboring the original horticultural aristocrats as honored occupants. Amazingly, many of those first houseplants have endured, and they remain dwelling quietly alongside the more exotic immigrants which came later.

CHAPTER VIII

FOLIAGE PLANTS:
THE GREENING OF THE HOME

By THE 1870s, the Victorians had completely dismissed any reservations they might have harbored concerning the cultivation of houseplants. Writers no longer prefixed their books with lengthy dissertations enumerating the moral and social motives which might impel their readers to undertake indoor gardening. The cultivation of houseplants had become a well-established venture.

At the same time, the public had grown rather blasé about tropicals. Those "wild beasts" of horticulture were featured in every periodical that crossed the threshold. Tropicals were not yet intimate acquaintances, but they were familiar faces—and familiarity put an end to any doubt that gardeners might harbor about their suitability for the home.

With those issues firmly settled, horticultural trendsetters were left to tackle the burning questions concerning what, where, when and how tropicals would enter the home. The remainder of the era was spent devising a plan for the ways and means of the tropical entry.

At a time when any country preacher could expound long and loud on the moral virtues of houseplants, not many could confidently address the specifics of growing tropicals. Although no one was absolutely certain where they should begin, common sense told them that exotic plants from tropical countries would have to be accommodated in the heated portions of their homes. The sitting room, or back parlor, was the natural choice as a domestic home-away-from-home for the first tropicals.

The sitting room claimed a warmer, more sociable atmosphere than the chilling ambiance which pervaded the front parlor. That room was filled with objects which held nostalgic value for the family, if not actual monetary worth in the eyes of the world outside. Of all the rooms in the home, the sitting room came closest to possessing a relatively cozy atmosphere. Children were free to play in that room, while adults spent their leisure hours communing with their favorite books and magazines or engaged in handiwork. The furniture was relatively comfortable, lacking the excessive ornamentation and stuffy pretension which typified the incumbent furnishings in the front parlor. But, beyond the room's figurative warmth, it also provided a physically warm environment. The back parlor was heated by a stove or furnace by day, and occasionally lit by the glow of a crackling open hearth in the evening. Every aspect of the room was arranged for the family's comfort—as defined in the 19th Century. Of course, houseplants became an integral component of that tranquil scene.

Having resolved the problem of where to begin growing tropicals, there remained the sticky questions of what exactly should be grown, and how it was to be cultivated. The solution to the latter question would come, they were certain, if only the former issue could be disposed.

North Americans had long ago discovered that the answers to most of their horticultural conundrums lay overseas. So, they looked to Europe for guidance. Undoubtedly, they would willingly have followed whatever European fashion dictated. But, unfortunately, when sampling foreign taste, they received a barrage of conflicting opinions. The Dutch were partial to bulbous plants, while the British favored flowering plants, and the French preferred foliage plants. Given the split affinities overseas, North Americans were understandably confused.

Traditionally, they had followed the British lead. However, they hesitated in this instance. Toward mid-century, indoor gardeners experienced problems growing half-hardy flowering plants such as primroses and roses indoors. And they correctly suspected that heat was the culprit. Naturally, they concluded that warmth inhibited blossoms. Given this assumption, 19th Century gardeners rationalized that, if the easy-to-please garden retainers could not thrive in their homes, how could they expect to please finicky tropical flowering plants? Foliage plants seemed to provide a safer route. Therefore, they followed the French lead.

But successful trends rarely begin on a negative note. The ingenious Victorian trendsetters realized that, for the foliage fad to prosper, fancy-leaved plants had to be viewed as superior to flowering species rather than merely as significant and viable alternatives. So, an informal campaign against flowers was launched. Flowers were unnecessary frivolities. They were gaudy rewards sought by unenlightened mortals who required cheap visual compensation for their efforts.

In contrast, foliage plants provided "tasteful" recompense for an indoor gardener's labors. They exhibited a comeliness of form and texture which called forth "higher" emotions in the viewer. Anyone who appreciated the subtle virtues of greenery was obviously functioning on an elevated moral plane.

Foliage plants were not merely pretty. They were grand and noble. Naturally, it followed that gardeners who cultivated beautiful-leaved plants were endowed with those same virtues. In addition, flowerless plants were "chaste", an attribute that was most decidedly to their credit in Victorian eyes. After all, flowers could be considered slightly obscene. As the sexual organs of a plant, they really had no place in the polite parlor. On the other hand, Ruskin and his many prudish admirers need not worry about the morality of young ladies who spent their leisure hours immersed in the study of foliage plants; they would not be corrupted by the slightest hint of sex. Many a prudent Victorian sighed a breath of relief when foliage plants came into vogue.

As soon as everyone fully understood that they were acting out of conviction rather than the absence of alternatives, the next step was to achieve the actual entry. For this move, there were distressingly few precedents to follow in this country, and North American gardeners were not accustomed to exercising their powers of improvisation. Fortunately, the Parisians came to the rescue.

The gay Parisians knew how to entertain. And they liberally engaged tropical foliage plants to decorate their reception halls and banquet rooms. Tropicals filled every corner. Every nook and cranny of their ballrooms held a majestic houseplant or two, creating a festive air. The gregarious, gardening Parisians provided inspiration for North Americans eager to experiment with tropicals.

Unfortunately, the Parisians did not have all the answers. Although their banquet halls were undoubtedly as dark as many North American alcoves, they were not as warmly heated as our living rooms. Their situation was similar, but not identical. We used French indoor gardeners as our role models, and then proceeded with caution.

North Americans wisely decided to start with something simple and familiar to decorate their sitting and living rooms. Rather than plunging directly into tropicals and risking the possibility of double jeopardy by placing unknown plants in a new situation, they first tested the water by introducing a very common foliage plant into the sitting room. Cautiously, gingerly, carefully, lest they break the spell of their success, the Victorians adopted tried-and-true, plain, old, ordinary ivy into the back parlor. It dispelled all of their doubts.

Ivy is nearly indomitable, and it suited their purposes perfectly. Most importantly, that vine grows anywhere quickly and easily. Whatever the back parlor had in store, ivy could certainly survive. Mr. Vick was among those who sang the ivy's praises, writing in *Vick's Monthly Magazine*,

> For indoor decorations, however, we have nothing to equal ivy. It will endure more hardships, flourish under more unfavorable circumstances, and endure darkness, gas and dust better than any plant we think of at present.

In addition to withstanding a multitude of environmental insults, that endurant vine was capable of surviving the vacillating tides of human folly. According to *The Ladies' Floral Cabinet*, "even people naturally thoughtless and lazy may have some enjoyment from an Ivy-Plant when nothing else will grow for them."

But negligence was not the only obstacle in a houseplant's path. Ivies could also endure the momentary transgressions of over-zealous housekeepers. Too much water, too much manure tea, too much ventilation—ivy charitably forgave many sins.

Actually, ivy was the complete antithesis of the aristocratic parlor plants which had previously entered the home. Ivy was a plebeian plant. It grew by leaps and bounds. Anyone could obtain it easily and cheaply, and anyone could maintain it without deep immersion in the study of the horticultural arts. These factors greatly enhanced the ivy's appeal for middle and lower class audiences. Ivy had potential—and the Victorians recognized its hidden qualities.

Ivy also knew its place. Obviously, it was not appropriate for the front parlor. However, the sitting room had a completely different ambiance. In the sitting room, ivy enjoyed a free-for-all, climbing helter skelter all over the walls. With a little ingenuity, and a few strategic wires strung in the right places, a 19th Century gardener could use the plant's kinetic energy to everyone's best advantage. Ivy was encouraged to crawl along the walls. It encased couches in an arbor of greenery, and it curtained windows for subdued privacy. The goal, of course, was to create a park-like scene indoors and to realize the improbable illusion that the sitting room, complete with its Oriental rugs, horsehair sofa and innumerable knick-knacks, had been transported outdoors.

If the Victorians wished to convert the family room into a green jungle, they could not have chosen a better plant than ivy to accomplish the deed. *Hedera helix* hybrids are not tropicals—but the Victorian image of a jungle was not based solely on fact. A room encased with garlands of greenery roaming along the walls was sufficiently close to paradise to suit their taste for the exotic.

When ivy brought the outdoors inside, it invited all of the mystery, romance and inherent goodness of nature to intermingle with the family. It also introduced some new problems into the interior decor. Apparently, 19th Century gardeners were blissfully oblivious to the damage that ivy rootlets might wreak on the plaster and the water stains that might ruin the wallpaper. The Victorians settled back to absorb the moral elevation they were bound to gain by living in very intimate harmony with nature throughout the year.

Not only is ivy a plant for all seasons, it is also a Jack-of-all-trades. Ivy is a master at performing acrobatics, and its uses are limited only by the bounds of human ingenuity. The Victorians stretched their fruitful imaginations to the limit when conjuring up applications for that adaptable vine. Most popular was its employment as camouflage, encasing walls with wandering foliage. In this connection, Annie Hassard could not resist noting the romantic connotations of the vine. In *Floral Decorations*, written in 1876, she suggested that ivy should be,

> . . . employed for trailing around couches, rustic picture-frames . . . and if the frame contains the portrait of some departed friend, Ivy is perhaps the most appropriate of all plants for the purposes here suggested.

She also explained how the feat was accomplished,

> When ivy is grown for wreathing picture-frames, plant it in wedge-shaped zinc receptacles, and hang it on a nail in the wall behind the picture.

Ivy encasing everything in sight including windows and mirrors from *The Home and Farm Manual* by Jonathan Periam.

Other authors also had ingenious ideas. Although not as dewy-eyed as Annie Hassard's advice, J. J. Smith's suggestions in *The Horticulturist* were equally inventive. He pointed out that, as a living partition or portable back drop, ivy was unexcelled. It could quickly and easily,

> form a large screen in a drawing room sufficiently dense to divide conversation parties from each other; or several of them placed around the walls of a room used for dancing, &c., would form elegant ornaments.

Ivy inspired further creative caprices. The plant's willing adaptability lends itself to sculpting fanciful shapes and forms. Hence, ivy became a likely subject for the age-old art of topiary. Formerly, that art had found most of its applications in the garden outdoors, although trained roses frequently adorned the parlor in winter. Ivy provided another avenue for exercising the tonsorial arts inside the home. Vines were fashioned into pyramids and coaxed into globes, they wound their way around every geometric shape known to man. Best of all, anyone could experiment with topiary. Although the art of training plants demands time and skill, it requires little monetary investment. An ivy topiary was a horticultural feather in the cap of any gardener, and it was within everyone's reach, regardless of their position on the socio-economic ladder.

The art of ivy topiary had been elevated to impressive heights by our role models—the gardeners of France. In fact, one of the highlights of the Paris Exhibition in 1876 was a huge ivy trained into a giant 6 ft., single trunked tree with cascading branches 33 ft. in length falling gracefully to the ground from the central stem. The ivy was designed so a threesome might easily fit beneath its curved boughs and enjoy a tryst completely encased in the privacy of a verdant screen. Of course, it was typically Victorian to engineer a design that would accommodate a trio rather than a couple.

Naturally, the Victorians did not confine their employment of such a versatile plant only to the indoor garden. They spread the wealth liberally. A plant with so many innate virtues was bound to procure a position in the landscape design as well as the interior of the home.

To their joy, Victorians found that ivy could endure the polluted and dirty city environment which few other plants would tolerate. It was a discovery that undoubtedly warmed the hearts of any recently urbanized expatriate from the outlying rural farms and towns. To encourage city gardeners, J. J. Smith mentioned some urban uses of ivy, "Even in cities a single ivy plant in a small garden, running over and clinging to old trees or the walls, is a perpetual enjoyment." But if you did not happen to possess either a wall or an old tree, it did not matter. Mr. Smith saw no reason why the enjoyment of ivy should be restrained by such mundane technicalities. He advised, "Where no tree exists, you can bring to the spot most seen from the window a stump ten or twenty feet high, and plant it for the purpose."

Although ivy retained its rich popularity throughout the 19th Century, it also paved the way for more challenging and genuine tropicals. Ivy was followed by a

An ivy screen from Annie Hassard's *Floral Decorations*.

Ivy topiary from Edwin Johnson's *Winter Greeneries at Home*.

train of other, more exotic foliage plants. Ivy furnished the point of departure from which the excesses of the Victorian imagination ran wild. Nothing was done by halves in that century, understatement was an unused virtue. Where a single plant flourished, a dozen or more would surely do better. And so, battalions of foliage plants entered the sanctum of the home.

When the Victorians invited tropicals indoors, they were motivated by concerns other than the mere accumulation of botanical wealth. Their tropical collections were also for study. Finally, they could examine those curious specimens from the far-off jungles close up. They dabbled in botany, contemplating their resident tropicals intently, comparing one plant with another and drawing broad, sweeping generalizations based on limited observations. Any amateur hypothesis was welcome, and few were challenged. Botanical "research" was a casual pastime that was heartily recommended for everyone regardless of educational background.

Safe from exposure to the forbidden realm of gender which flowering plants might introduce, young gardeners could dissect the parts of foliage plants to

Nothing was done by halves in the 19th Century, an illustration from Henry T. Williams' *Window Gardening*.

their heart's content and never once approach the subject of sexuality. The greater the number of foliage species within easy reach, the more intense home botanizing became.

Meanwhile, not everyone was convinced of the importance of scientific study. And those unconvinced family members occasionally objected to the accumulation of plant life encroaching on their personal domain. I speak, of course, of husbands who were not entirely receptive to their wives' and daughters' plans for turning living rooms into jungles. Although men had, at first, supported home horticultural pursuits, they occasionally balked at the increasing preoccupation with that pastime. Sometimes, they voiced their objections.

Fortunately, women could turn to the pages of their *Ladies' Floral Cabinet* for a response to their husbands' qualms. If invoking the name of science failed to sway the powers-that-be into condoning the growing hobby, then the family's novice gardeners were encouraged to call forth the strong argument of utility. Garden writers hastened to explain that a collection of numerous foliage plants had productive advantages. To be specific, *The Ladies' Floral Cabinet* explained that foliage plants actually aided in the discharge of daily housework,

> The highest mission of plants is not merely to please our eyes with color, our mouths with delicious fruits; not only do they do this and more, but they are ever silently but surely eating up what is impure and injurious to ourselves in the atmosphere and in the earth all around our homes; and any dwelling in which plants are well and healthily grown will be more likely to be a clean and healthy house than if plants were not there.

Presumably, this argument always won the case, and permission to increase the quantity of plants throughout the home was not long in forthcoming. So, the next step was seeking worthwhile subjects. Rather than casting blindly about, attempting to independently discover what might or might not be the most suitable foliage plants for their collections, North Americans simply consulted the European fads. In Paris, dracaenas ruled the day.

Dracaenas were novelties on the market. *Henderson's Handbook of Plants* tells us that they were first "brought to notice" in 1820. Henderson continued his paragraph on the genus by describing (with relish) the most extravagant member of the family—*Dracaena draco*, "the celebrated Dragon Tree of Orotavia, in the island of Teneriffe [the largest of the Canary Islands], that was first noticed by Humboldt, who estimated its age at 6,000 years. This tree was several feet high and 79 ft. in circumference at the base." Although *Dracaena draco* may have been the prodigal son of the genus, it obviously would not do for the Victorian home. Instead, *Dracaena terminalis* (now *Cordyline terminalis*) was the genus member most commonly used for conservatory and window cultivation.

Dracaena terminalis was perfect for hot, dry rooms. In addition to being truly stalwart, it was also extremely handsome—a winning combination for any indoor garden. Shirley Hibberd paid the plant a supreme compliment when he

Dracaena terminalis from Lizzie Page Hillhouse's *House Plants and How to Succeed with Them.*

described it as "superb for elegance, and most tropical in outline."

The dracaena began its career by playing the typical role of a greenhouse and conservatory specimen. But, as soon as the plant proved its willingness to endure all that the home might hand out, it was immediately enlisted for windowsill culture. According to Henry T. Williams, the French inaugurated the trend,

> . . . for you may frequently see elegant little *Dracaenas* ornamenting windows there, as they look as well at Christmas as at midsummer, I need hardly suggest how highly suited they are for purposes of this kind. The number of *Dracaenas* cultivated in and around Paris is something enormous . . .

Although novelty may have been responsible for the enthusiastic reception which dracaenas received when first introduced, performance insured that they would maintain the public's affection. Not least among the dracaenas' virtues was their tolerance of gas-lighting, a late century innovation which threatened the lives of many incumbent botanicals. Added to this, there were the combined environmental stresses of a dry atmosphere, insufficient light, and erratic temperatures—all of which dracaenas bore with courage.

To meet the popular demand for this strong-willed plant, the commercial sector was roused into action. In the late 1860s, it was reported that one grower in Versailles was nurturing a crop of 5,000 to 6,000 dracaenas waiting to be sold. By the 1870s, British firms also began investing both greenhouse space and hybridizing time in dracaenas. It proved to be a wise investment, and one which is still bearing fruit.

Eventually, American gardeners felt the repercussions of the foliage industry boom. By the 1880s, 36 varieties of dracaenas, replete with brilliantly colored foliage, were available in our markets. They sold briskly, and the public clamored for more.

Just as camellias provided a model for cultural practices for all subtropicals, so dracaenas were the example to which other foliage plants were likened. Dracaenas are relatively easy plants to please. Their preference for heat fit the prevailing atmosphere in the sitting room perfectly. And, beyond that requirement, all that was necessary for a dracaena's comfort was a ready supply of water to quench its insatiable thirst. Syringing the foliage regularly not only kept it free from dust, but also washed off any insects that might disrupt the plant's happy existence. As it was, few pests were tempted to infringe on dracaenas. The genus is prone only to red spider mites which are readily dispatched with a spray of cold water.

Although dracaenas are among the easiest plants to please, 19th Century writers confounded the issue somewhat by presenting contradictory advice. Readers were commonly left to ponder such enigmatic statements as these words of wisdom offered by Charles Collins in *Greenhouse and Window Plants*,

> If the leaves begin to fall, withhold water for a while—unless you have been keeping the plants too dry; in that case it will be a sign that they need more.

The problem of leaf drop was a frequently addressed issue in horticultural magazines. But, as remedies were tried and failed, the all-forgiving Victorians eventually learned to accept dracaenas as they were—despite the prevailing prudishness concerning naked ankles. In an era when piano legs were modestly covered to conceal their curves, less curvaceous dracaenas were permitted to parade around bare-legged.

Rather than tackling remedies for the perturbing problem of gangly foliage plants, most articles provided instructions for air-layering instead. Air-layering did not cure the unsightly specimen, but it furnished a new, fully foliated replacement to fill its position upon retirement.

According to Henry T. Williams, who was a self-elected expert on foliage plants, Prayer Plants (Marantas) came second in prevalence, following dracaenas by a broad margin. Undoubtedly, their preference for high humidity accounted for their reduced popularity. But, despite their peevish personalities, they were commonly attempted in Victorian homes. Considering the inherent beauty of those plants, we can sympathize with the Victorians for throwing caution to the wind and ignoring the admonitions of experts. A few tattered and browned leaf edges only partially marred the effect of those colorful, intricately patterned leaves.

Calathea zebrina (known in the 19th Century as *Maranta zebrina*) was the most popular member of the Marantaceae grown. Undoubtedly, the species owed its fame to the support and endorsement of the trend-setting French gardeners who promoted it over and above all its relatives. American authors also lent it their support. According to Henry T. Williams, *Calathea zebrina* was,

> . . . the only [Maranta] suitable for steady cultivation in apartments, as all the others succumb to the hot and dry atmosphere inseparably found in the living room.

Modern growers might well wonder how marantas managed to survive the Victorian sitting room. And, most especially, they might marvel at how well *Calathea Zebrina*, the Zebra Plant, fared under those dry, stuffy conditions. The maranta's survival was undoubtedly due to careful ministrations with syringing devices and watering pots by untiring Victorian gardeners.

Much less surprising was the popularity of *Ficus elastica*, the India Rubber Tree. That species held boundless fascination for 19th Century gardeners; and the attraction was not based merely on its physical endowments. The plant was worshipped primarily for its economic value.

Ficus elastica provided a source of natural rubber (or India Rubber) which was later superceded by a superior product obtained from *Hevea brasiliensis*. India rubber quickly became a household word, especially famed for its use in the manufacture of that marvelous new invention which was slipped over shoes to keep them dry despite the vacillations of the weather. That new footwear was particularly popular in Britain for obvious climatic reasons; but, North Americans were equally enthusiastic about those little contrivances which insured dry feet. For this innovation alone, *Ficus elastica* was guaranteed a hero's welcome in every home.

In view of its commercial importance, the ficus' lack of physical virtues was easily forgiven. Although Victorian books were rife with proclamations extolling this or that plant as "unexcelled for beauty", no one ventured to make that claim on behalf of *Ficus elastica*. The best they could muster were euphemisms such as "palm-like" and "endurant" to describe the plant's virtues. Certainly, these were laudable traits in any houseplant, but they compared poorly with the glowing praises that were showered upon other stunning new tropicals.

To be honest, *Ficus elastica* is virtually bereft of physical endowments. Not only is the plant tall, lanky and generally ill-suited to the home, but anyone who has ever attempted to grow a Rubber Tree indoors will readily affirm that the plant persists in the perturbing habit of dropping its leaves frequently. Although we now attribute this problem to lack of root room and suggest repotting the plant into a larger container, in 1895, Charles Collins had a completely different remedy for the problem. In *Greenhouse and Window Gardens*, he suggested that "when you see them doing this, stop watering the roots for a while, but keep the leaves clean." Clearly, according to the prevailing Victorian opinion, there were few maladies which cleanliness would not cure.

Another eccentricity peculiar to *Ficus elastica* was the abundant "milk" which oozed forth whenever the plant was cut or injured. Actually, it was for this trait that the Rubber Tree originally came to commercial and public attention. But, indoor gardeners found the flow of the plant's "life blood" disconcerting. A popular remedy was to slip a hollowed out raw potato over the incision, leaving it in place until the injury healed.

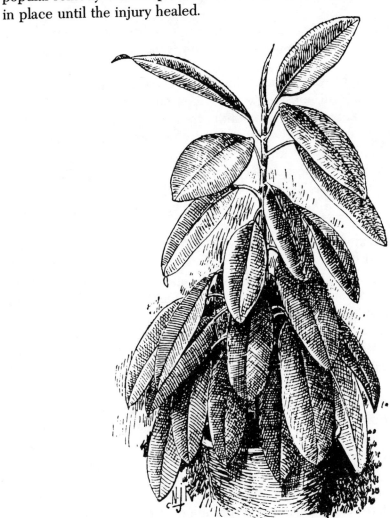

Ficus elastica from *Window and Parlor Gardening* by Jönsson-Rose.

Many Victorians found pandanus, or Screw Pines, to be far more satisfactory specimens than ficus. Screw Pines look something like pineapples with long, strap-like leaves. Not only do most pandanus boast handsome foliage, but *Pandanus utilis* possessed minor economic importance. In its native Mauritius, it was used as a fiber plant to manufacture the sacks in which sugarcane was exported.

Pandanus veitchii, the most popular indoor species, could claim one attribute that was a rare blessing in foliage plants—it branched freely. In addition to this virtue, it was also self-supporting. That is, the plant accommodatingly initiated aerial roots which anchored the stem firmly and acted as props.

All in all, everyone agreed that the Screw Pine's growth habit was a great improvement over the usual foliage fare. Due to this trait, the plant acquired many supporters—one of the strongest being William Robinson. That crotchety Irish bachelor was not in the habit of losing his heart over every plant that came to his notice, but he waxed poetic when describing the pandanus. In his article on pandanus in *The Garden*, Robinson revealed this curious (if also slightly unsavory) bit of information concerning *Pandanus vandermeerschii*,

> ... [it] is a native of Round Island, a small spot in the ocean and a short distance and a dependency of the Mauritius, where however, if report is correct, it is likely to become extinct. A friend of mine who recently visited the place says the little island is overrun with rats, and there being very little food for them they devour everything within their reach and the Pandanus nuts are devoured as soon as they fall.

William Robinson can be described as a late-century version of the effervescent and controversial garden writer, John Claudius Loudon. Like Loudon, Robinson also excelled in the art of capturing and holding an audience, a quality which won the author international acclaim. His formula for sweetening the unpalatably dry facts of plant culture was infallibly effective. In addition to entertaining his readers with awesome (and often inflated) tales of tropical lands, Robinson skillfully supplied graphic descriptions of each plant's native habitat, relating that information to the ideal growing conditions in the home.

Typically, the Victorians treated each tropical as an individual with its own unique personality and needs. Every effort was exerted to make the expatriated plant feel that it was living in a home-away-from-home. Anything short of optimal was considered to be inhumane. Robinson's divulgences on the care of pandanus illustrate how one might play the proper host,

> Screw pines are mostly found growing in swampy places near the sea coast; consequently they require a copious supply of water, and I have often found that a top dressing of sea-weed has a beneficial effect on them...

Most popular foliage plants could boast some major attraction which encouraged the public to seek them out. Ivies grew by leaps and bounds, while dracaenas and marantas claimed colorful leaves. *Ficus elastica* was respected for its economic achievements, whereas, Screw Pines were adopted for their variegated leaves and branching growth habit. What then attracted the Victorians to cultivate the aspidistra? The question remains a mystery.

Aspidistras have long, rather unimpressive, deep green leaves which rise on branchless rhizomes from the soil and unfurl lazily and undramatically. In a word, they are dull plants, being neither exciting nor unusual. To their credit, they do produce very unique flowers. But, alas, the occurrence is infrequent and the blossoms are nearly buried below soil level. We are forced to assume that their immense popularity was based on their fortitude. Aspidistras are both faithful and indestructible. Their common name—Cast Iron Plants—says it all.

Aspidistras were a Victorian institution which tarried long into the 1900s. Undoubtedly, their lengthy reign was partly due to force of habit. In fact, the plant was so firmly imbedded in tradition that it became a symbol of reproach for those who rebelled against their Victorian heritage. For many people, the aspidistra stood for all that was wrong with the Victorians, especially their stifling, prudent and lack-lustre existence. The theme was so strong, in fact, that it found its way into literature. Most notably, the plant set the mood for *An Aspidistra in Babylon*, H. E. Bates' short story about the awakening of adolescence,

> The best description of myself that I can think of is to say that I was dull as one of the many aspidistras that clutter up the rooms, the hallway and even the dining tables of our little boarding house.

Although the 20th Century might not appreciate the aspidistra's reputation for faithful service, that dependability was viewed with relief by Victorians. Actually, the public was grateful for the opportunity to enjoy a little boredom in the rapidly moving Age of Technology. Aspidistras provided a welcome variation from their steady diet of change. As *The Ladies' Floral Cabinet* explained in 1885, "It is so large, so beautiful, and so *established*. It says emphatically 'I am here to stay and no changes of season nor place can make changes in me'."

Although the plain aspidistra rarely had praises showered upon it, the variegated form did receive some deserving compliments on its appearance. The variegated aspidistra (often referred to as the Barbershop Plant) can be called tolerably handsome. The boredom of its long leaves is relieved by abruptly distinct pure white markings which provide sharp contrast. The Barbershop Plant occasionally suffers browning leaf edges if over-watered. But in most cases, it is nearly as cast-iron as the plain species.

Aspidistra was primarily a middle class plant. Wealthy citizens may have grown an aspidistra or two in the poorly lit recesses of their houses where nothing else could be convinced to dwell, but middle class homes were awash with that lack-lustre but faithful friend. Aspidistras were perfect for the aspiring indoor gardener who had neither light, space nor time to devote to any more ambitious horticultural projects.

Less popular, but no less stalwart, was the sansevieria, a plant which hardly excelled the aspidistra in beauty and maintained an equally lethargic growth pace. Sansevieria was known as the Rattlesnake Plant, a common name that was certainly no more endearing than a Cast Iron Plant. It earned its nickname by virtue of the long, sword-like, striped leaves which initiate from the base and grow to be about the length of a rattler, if that reptile ever took a notion to stand bolt upright. Typically, the resident sansevieria was stashed in a dark corner and was then summarily forgotten while the busy lady of the house turned her attention to more pressing matters.

Araucaria araucana was another variation on the verdant theme, with a far more appealing epithet—it was called the Monkey Puzzle Tree. In general, the araucaria was a bit more interesting than either the aspidistra or sansevieria. Although its growth habit and physical endowments were no more worthy of comment, the legends surrounding the plant frequently furnished a topic of conversation. *Araucaria araucana* (known at the time as *A. imbricata*) was the most popular member of the family until late in the century when *A. excelsa*, the Norfolk Island Pine, gained a strong following.

Araucaria excelsa, the Norfolk Island Pine from Lizzie Page Hillhouse's *House Plants and How To Succeed with Them.*

The Monkey Puzzle Tree was introduced from Chile into England in 1795. As was usually the case, that South American plant travelled across the Atlantic to Europe for introduction and trials before returning to this side of the ocean to be grown as a houseplant. No one vaunted the plant for breathtaking beauty, but it was an interesting specimen with strange, sharp-leaved, evergreen-like branches. In fact, the Monkey Puzzle Tree could be called a conversation piece—and anything that would break the monotony of tea-time small talk was always a welcome addition in the home. To begin with, there was the matter of its common name to discuss. Apparently, the Victorians did so with a perfectly straight face, as *The Ladies' Floral Cabinet* unquestionably confirmed,

> Its familiar designation . . . suggests the fact that monkeys cannot climb this tree, a fact singularly favorable to its usefulness to man; for the seeds are as good as chestnuts, and the produce of 20 trees will maintain one person a whole year.

Of course, Monkey Puzzle Trees were not known to yield fruit indoors. Actually, they are painfully slow-growing plants. In their native habitat, they may attain a lofty 150 ft. with fruit at the very top—which explains the monkey's problem. However, in a windowsill environment, an araucaria will seldom grow to more than 4–6 ft. But, the notion of nurturing a tree that was believed to be the staple of the "heathen's" diet was nearly as intriguing to the Victorians as the vision of a horde of monkeys all clamoring in vain to scale the parlor houseplant. The Victorians can be justly accused of many faults, but never lack of imagination.

Rex Begonias were also adept at provoking conversation. With the possible exception of marantas, 19th Century gardeners had never seen such dazzling foliar colors as Rex Begonias boast. Their metallic silver, maroon, green and bronze foliage provided a spark of color in an otherwise dull setting. In addition to the rex's brightly colored leaves, gardeners also discussed the latest hybrids. Soon after the parental rex species, *Begonia rex*, was introduced from India in 1856, an endless array of hybrids entered the market. Breeding maintained a brisk pace throughout the century, keeping begonias in the limelight long after interest in other foliage plants faded. Almost every Victorian parlor harbored a begonia or two somewhere in its confines.

The list of foliage plants clustered in corners, communing with the interior decor is lengthy. Apparently, few indoor gardeners heeded the counsel of *The Ladies' Floral Cabinet* when that magazine pleaded, "Do not grow too many plants; few and good is the watchword, especially for the beginner." The words fell on deaf ears. The Victorians grew as many plants as they could find nooks and crannies to hold, completely oblivious to the admonitions of the tastemakers.

Among the favorite 19th Century foliage plants, one finds a number of species which remain familiar faces in modern homes. Most prevalent are: Aucuba, which is valued for its shiny, broad leaves and robust growth habit. *Cyperus alternifolius*, the Umbrella Plant, still graces many homes. Its long, grass-like

Begonia rex.

foliage is crowned with flat, horizontal, umbrella-like bracts. The Castor Bean Plant, *Ricinus communis*, boasts more than just good looks to recommend it as a housemate. It also claims a commercial connection—Castor oil is derived from its beans. In the 19th Century, the plant was undoubtedly passionately detested by every youngster forced to endure the much-dreaded "daily constitutional". But, adults apparently forgot or forgave their early unpleasant medicinal experience and purchased the plants in great abundance. This broad-leaved beauty was accurately described as "one of the best plants for producing a tropical effect." In that capacity, it was often found in the garden during the summer.

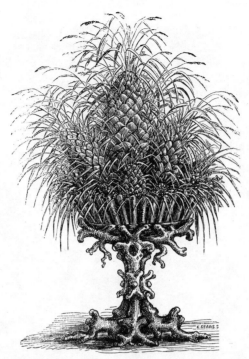

The ultimate foliage plant—Grass.

Another genus which has endured over the years is *Dieffenbachia*. Although the plant was accorded little or no acclaim for its physical attributes, the Victorians were fascinated by its poisonous properties. According to *Henderson's Handbook of Plants*, the dieffenbachia was given its popular name, Dumb Cane, because, "It has the power, when chewed, of swelling the tongue and paralyzing the speech." That claim was apparently based on a story told by Alexander von Humboldt (1769–1859) who originally collected the plant in the tropics. Although the natives warned him of the plant's silencing powers, he was skeptical. Curiosity drove him to sample the plant, and his disbelief was ultimately rewarded by a loss of speech which lasted several days. Given this tale, we can only speculate on the reason why dieffenbachia was also called the Mother-in-Law's Tongue.

Although tropicals were the primadonnas in the sitting room, non-tropical foliage plants also crept into the home, riding the wave of tropical success. The Victorians even went so far as to invite common grass into the home. Grass was employed to bedeck the homes of erstwhile indoor gardeners who were prevented from climbing aboard the bandwagon for economic reasons. Such a houseplant certainly entailed a minimal investment, and yet it definitely brought the outdoors inside. Henry T. Williams described how grass could be "tastefully" displayed,

> . . . far prettier than many a pretentious and costly ornament is a simple bowl of grasses planted in pine cones set in sand, in moss, or common soil.

Obviously, foliage plants had made a successful debut in the home. And, due to their fortitude and adaptability, they attracted a much broader audience than had previously dabbled in the botanical arts. Foliage plants possessed a multitude of diverse virtues and performed many different functions. But most importantly, they paved the way for other, more spectacular tropicals to enter the home.

LIST OF TROPICAL FOLIAGE PLANTS GROWN
CIRCA 1881

Aechmea	Billbergia	Eucalyptus
Agave	Caladium	Ficus
Alocasia	Calathea	Hedera
Aralia	Cissus	Maranta
Araucaria	Coprosma	Mikania
Ardisia	Cordyline	Monstera
Asparagus	Croton	Pandanus
Aspidistra	Cyperus	Philodendron
Aucuba	Dieffenbachia	Pilea
Begonia	Dracaena	Syngonium

Agave from Lizzie Page Hillhouse's *House Plants and How To Succeed with Them*.

CHAPTER IX

THE VICTORIAN FERN AND PALM CRAZE

THE ERA WAS BUSTLING with the excitement of novelty and flushed with the confidence of success. The air was electric with the expectant knowledge that the ficus stationed sedately in the back parlor was only a modest beginning to a blossoming trend. Other tropicals would surely follow. The Victorians sensed that horticulture was bound to march forward just as other sciences stepped briskly along. Dracaenas were only a hint of the Promised Land. Nothing short of the complete conquest of Paradise would satisfy the Victorians.

If you asked the average 19th Century citizen to describe an idyllic scene, he would either invoke images of the hearth and gathered family, or launch into a colorful portrait of a lush tropical jungle with its balmy clime and exotic fruits. Thanks to the upsurge in the output of books and journals coupled with broadened literacy, the average man had a clear vision of a tropical paradise. And that vision was enhanced by occasional weekend visits to public conservatories.

The citizen of the 1870s was well aware of the ingredients of the beatific scene. He knew that the jungle was filled with a tangle of lacy textures from broad, sweeping leaves which formed a confusion of intermingled shapes and forms. He could picture the components of the tropics almost as confidently as he could portray his hearthside tableau. And he wanted nothing more than to merge those two visions of perfection into one, preferably assembled under his own roof. Since exotic plants were an indispensable component of the tropical scene, he naturally wished to recruit a few. Ferns and palms were uniquely suited to play the part.

In Victorian eyes, ferns and palms embodied the epitome of perfection. They stood at the very pinnacle of that great mountain of taste which every Victorian strove to surmount. They possessed every virtue which the 19th Century held dear. In short, they were mysterious, tropical, graceful, tidy, statuesque and chaste. Furthermore, they were plants which anyone could invite into his home with impunity and proudly exhibit amidst the pomp and grandeur of the front parlor. For this virtue alone, they were a step above the great mass of other foliage plants that had already gained entry into the home.

Although the Victorians were undeniably prone to excess, they were not indiscriminating. Ivies, dracaenas, dieffenbachias and the like were not sufficiently aristocratic to warrant admittance into the *sanctum sanctorum* of the front parlor. But ferns and palms were of a very different breed. They elevated the appreciation of foliage to a higher plain. They were art in nature. When contemplating the beauty of ferns or palms, it was not only the color of the foliage that attracted comment; it was the fronds' subtle forms and textures that struck the notice of an observant viewer. Such qualities were only visible to the perceptive eye, and their presence in the home suggested that the inhabitants within possessed a sophistication far above the common lot.

Unlike flowering plants, ferns and palms set off a room to its best advantage. Rather than monopolizing the scene, they blended into the background, providing melodic mood music for the action within. In a room filled with the cacophony of eclectic objects all competing for a dominant role, the foliage of ferny plants spoke with a muted voice, discretely shaping and calming the scene.

Material objects were not the only elements of the parlor to acquire lustre when exhibited against a background of lacy foliage, the human inhabitants of the room also took on a new grace when juxtaposed against fern and palm leaves. Of course, the young ladies of the house took advantage of the complimentary setting to subtly flaunt their wares. Judging from a story entitled "In the Red Room" which appeared in an 1888 issue of *Harper's Monthly Magazine*, the "optical illusion" was very effective. In that story, a young gentleman is faced with the awkward choice between his affection for President Van Buren's daughter and her close friend, a lady by the name of Miss Day. He remained undecided until a visit to the White House revealed Miss Day in a new light, "She was standing against a tall vase of ferns, whose green width and luxuriance formed a fitting background for her charming figure." When viewed from this angle, his choice was easy. He naturally chose the young lady who went well with the ferns.

Of the two celebrities—ferns and palms—ferns took precedence. Not only was the White House bedecked with ferns, but nearly every home in the latter part of the 19th Century harbored a member or two of that great class of plants. Ferns were so popular that their connection with the era became something of a cliché that is still ruthlessly exploited for commercial purposes. However, this is one case in which the magnitude of a trend has not been exaggerated in retrospect. Actually, time has mellowed our sense of the fervor of the Victorian Fern Craze.

The fern infatuation began in Britain, and the first victims to be afflicted by pteridomania were wealthy British gardeners. Not only did those privileged gentlemen possess sufficient land to devote a portion solely to the cultivation of ferns, but they also enjoyed an overabundance of leisure time to spend scouring

Exterior of a fernery from Henry T. Williams' *Window Gardening*.

their woods for intriguing native Pteridophytes to bring back to the resident
fernery. As can well be imagined, the first fern enthusiasts were viewed as
slightly eccentric by those who did not harbor horticultural affinities. Granted,
they were undeniably a "unique breed of men". However, no description of
mine can match that offered by William Scott in *The Florist's Manual* charac-
terizing the typical fern maniac,

> It is not hazardous to say that it is superior minds that have a taste or make a hobby of
> ferns and any other class of plants. Retiring people, and perhaps poor hands at
> swapping horses or even making money, careless in fashion and not up in golf and
> poor in politics, yet superior minds far above the common herd.

As with all nascent fads and gardening styles, the fernery needed strong press
promotion before it could take wing. Fortunately, it found a devoted supporter
in the British garden writer, Shirley Hibberd. Hibberd was something of a politi-
cian, and he was endowed with that rare smooth tongue that typifies the successful advocate. He also had the good fortune of being in the right place at the right
time. In retrospect, it is difficult to disentangle the paradox of whether the fern

fad was created by Hibberd's labors, or Hibberd's fame flowed from the sudden popularity of ferns. One thing is certain, when ferns took flight in the public's fancy, they also found a ready, willing and able mentor in Shirley Hibberd.

The fernery was a logical extension of the newly adopted European Natural Landscape style, and Shirley Hibberd hastened to establish a strong connection between the two. He described the fernery as the "negligence of nature, wild and wide," and that studied disregard of order held a certain fascination for the people of that romantic age. The attraction becomes forgivable, and perhaps understandable when we read Hibberd's description of a typical fern grotto,

> It is truly a garden with gravel walks amidst rocks and waterfalls, and on every hand the ferns present themselves in sheets of delicious verdure or in waving palm-like masses, or in a glorious confusion of brake and lastrea intermingled as if the dryads themselves attended to the planting.

Inevitably, the fernery went under glass. After all, not everyone was a landed gentleman, and those who were not wanted to share in the Natural Landscaping craze. Glassed-in ferneries provided an opportunity to join in the merri-

A city fernery under glass from Shirley Hibberd's *The Fern Garden*.

ment. City gardeners could finally relish the "delicious verdure" of ferns. Since indoor ferneries were darker and cooler than ordinary greenhouses, they were particularly well-suited to urban dwellings which were shaded by nearby buildings or encumbered on every side except the northern exposure.

In time, indoor ferneries became more elaborate, providing a glowing example of the Victorian propensity to pile Ossa upon Pelion. After all, it was the beginning of the Gilded Age. Ferneries grew more and more ornate, while the mood of wildness was enforced with such little contrivances as waterfalls, meandering paths and all manner of exotic fauna. Not to be outdone, Kew Gardens constructed an underground, glassed-in fernery replete with narrow, descending paths and subterranean springs.

The citizenry watched all of this action with rapt attention. But only a privileged handful could afford to add a fernery to their homes, the bulk of the audience did not possess the resources for such an ambitious project. And yet, there was nothing that the multitude desired more fervently than to join in the prevailing mania. Their opportunity arrived with the popularization of the Wardian Case.

The story of the Wardian Case begins in the dirty, sooty town of London. Nathaniel Ward was a dedicated surgeon in that city and, like many of his wealthy contemporaries, he took to the study of nature in his spare time to cope with the pressures of a busy practice in a bustling metropolis. During his years in the practice of medicine and the pursuit of his hobby, Ward learned one fundamental doctrine—although the city could nurture all manner of disease microorganisms, it could not support higher plant life. His profession kept him in the soot, but his hobby could only be pursued by leaving the foul city environment far behind.

Ward dabbled in many of the disciplines of natural history, but he particularly enjoyed entomology. In 1830, that study led him to enclose a Hawk Moth pupa in a large glass bottle fitted with a loose lid. Anticipating the metamorphosis, he checked the cocoon six months later and found that from some moist dirt a sprig of grass and a tiny fern (*Dryopteris filix-mas*) had sprouted and were prospering. This event completely eclipsed the original intent of his entomological experiment.

The observation would probably not have elicited more than passing notice by most observers, but Ward was immediately struck by the possibilities inherent in his discovery. In the past, his efforts to grow ferns in the city had all met with complete failure. But, in his bottle he found the voluntary sporeling and grass sprout thriving contentedly with absolutely no human assistance. The encased plants had survived for half a year solely on the condensation inside the sealed glass. They had not been watered or exposed to the foul London air.

Ward began to experiment with ferns in bottles, choosing more challenging specimens than the easy-to-accommodate native *Dryopteris* to test his glass environment. He found that even rare ferns flourished when shielded from the outdoor miasma. In 1841, Ward published his findings in a paper entitled,

"Growth of Plants in Closely Glazed Cases." The paper's reception was sufficiently encouraging to induce him to continue designing more ambitious miniature greenhouses.

The progress of Ward's inventions was carefully monitored by a fascinated public. By 1851, Ward's Case had gained sufficient renown to warrant a public appearance of the original bottle at the World's Fair. Masses of people filed by the exhibition, peering intently at that wonder of nature which was still thriving in a sealed environment after two long decades. The exhibit could not have elicited more interest if it had featured Rip Van Winkle himself carefully preserved in time.

The era was alive with applications for the new invention. The most important among them from a scientific standpoint was the employment of the Wardian Case as a protective container to transport exotic plants on their maiden voyage from the jungles to Europe. Because the case was air tight, the enclosed plants required no care during transit, and the containers could be left on deck during rough seas. Valuable tropical specimens were no longer at the mercy of bumbling cabin boys who too often forgot their duties or administered to thirsty botanicals with salt water. In a Wardian Case, the plants were watered regularly by the "showers" of condensation, while the case's glass provided ample protection from salt spray.

Thanks to Ward's invention, specimens that were previously too delicate to survive ocean travel arrived at their destinations in vigorous condition. Even the flora of far-off Australia came to London in fine fettle after surviving 8 months at sea with temperatures ranging from 120°F. at the Equator to 40°F. upon arrival in the English Channel. At last, commercial nursery firms could dispatch explorers with the confidence that their investment was likely to yield profitable returns in live plant material. The Wardian Case changed the pace of horticultural exploration.

While the industry was busy putting Ward's glazed case to commercial use, the Victorians were eagerly adopting the case to the needs of their home environment. Ward himself actively endorsed this application to counteract the depressing effects of city life. Not surprisingly, Wardian Cases caught on with astounding swiftness. Everyone seemed eager to own a little glass box capable of accomplishing some pretty impressive feats of fireside legerdemain.

True to their origins, Wardian Cases were usually utilized for the cultivation of ferns, a fact that led to their generic designation simply as fern cases. In this capacity, they provided yet another instance in which invention coincided with the prevailing mood of the times. When the Wardian Case appeared on the scene, Europe was in the throes of a natural history fad. In fact, Nathaniel Ward himself was among the many participants in that new outdoor sport dedicated to collecting nature's objects and bringing them home to the parlor for dissection, observation and display. Ward's Case substantially fanned the fires of the natural history movement and turned its direction toward collecting ferns. Thus, an innocent pastime was gradually transformed into a mania—pteridomania.

When pteridomania reached the general public, natural history excursions suddenly became more frequent and of greater impact on the countryside surrounding London. In their frenzy to fill their fern cabinets, the British citizenry set out to reap the bounty of ferns available in their native woodlands. They converged on forests in hordes. Initially, their endeavors were whole-heartedly encouraged. After all, the people were simply enjoying the benefits of good, healthy exercise while engaged in a wholly laudable pursuit—and all in the name of science. Many contemporary writers saw absolutely no harm in the new hobby, and John Robinson, author of *Ferns in their Homes and Ours*, was among their number. He wrote,

> There is a large class of persons who are so fortunate (or unfortunate, according as they use or abuse the privilege) as to have nothing to do . . . This class must have a hobby, or they will *rust* out. Another class are engrossed by incessant professional work which leaves them every day cross and tried. These should have some hobby, or they will become one-side, crabbed, and *wear* out.

Innocent and beneficial though the hobby may have seemed at first, fern hunting eventually became the scourge of the British countryside. Middle class pteridomaniacs soon proved themselves to be less selective, more zealous and far more numerous than their wealthy counterparts. Their scavenging took its toll on the British meadows and woodlands.

The effects of pteridomania eventually became cause for alarm. Entire fields were dug and their plundered ferns were sold wholesale to dealers in the city. Before anyone realized the extent of the carnage and could call a halt to the exploitation, the countryside was noticeably devastated. Fortunately, thanks to the strong constitution endemic to wild ferns, no pteridophytic species suffered permanent extinction, only a temporary depletion in numbers.

Meanwhile, while all of this action was going forward in Europe, North Americans were blithely concentrating on making their dracaenas and aspidistras comfortable in the parlor. However, as time marched on and the British fern craze spread, North Americans could scarcely escape feeling the reverberations of the epidemic.

North Americans were being inundated by ferny influences. Due to the absence of international copyright laws, articles from British magazines made up a substantial portion of the editorial content of American periodicals. Naturally, ferns were featured in virtually every paper that arrived in the parlor. In addition, a prodigious number of newly published books on the topic were rolling rapidly off the presses. John Robinson, an American fern advocate, could confidently recommend no fewer that ten lexicons, many appearing in multiple volumes, for pteridophytic identification. And he made no mention of the legions of literature penned by eager young ladies who spent their leisure hours compiling illustrated rosters of ferns. Such volumes were rarely published, but there is one in nearly every attic.

In addition to the gravity of the printed word, North Americans were also influenced by the trends in decorative arts. Fern croziers found their way into almost every domestic object that could be carved, painted or etched. The legs of the marble-topped table terminated in stylized wooden fiddleheads, grace-fully gilded fronds encircled the glass in the hall mirror and forest-green croziers swam in the nap of the plush carpet underfoot. Ferns danced along the wallpaper and were etched in the glassed front door. The silver cutlery and china serving dishes also gave testimony to the preoccupation with ferns. At a time when ferns were everywhere, there was absolutely no escaping the mania.

North Americans had little choice but to join the prevailing "insanity", espe-cially if they wished to keep abreast of fashion. However, the American audience chose to follow a slightly different drummer in the matter of fern selection. For the same reasons that had prompted them to ignore the Natural Landscape movement which swept Europe, the pioneering Americans showed little interest in rousting around in woodlands collecting their native species. Instead, North Americans preferred to acquire exotic ferns.

While Britain was tearing its countryside apart in search of Pteridophytes, the American native species went virtually ignored and often undescribed and unclassified. A notable exception was *Lygodium palmatum*, the Climbing Fern. In 1869, that plant provoked the establishment of one of this country's earliest plant protection laws created in response to the ruthless exploitation of Climbing Fern fronds by florists and amateur interior decorators. With that exception, North America turned its attention jungle-ward to continue the romance with exotica.

Ferns were a challenge to grow as houseplants. Early in the fern's career as an indoor plant, gardeners decided that the deed simply could not be done. However, the introduction of fern cabinets offered a ray of hope. North Ameri-cans had been tantalized by reports of the new fern cases for years prior to their appearance on this side of the ocean. When they came here at last, they received a celebrity's welcome. Everyone busied themselves with acquiring, erecting and perfecting fern cases. Although the Wardian Case rage had arrived late on North American shores, it was no less fervent here than it had been in the country of its origin.

In fact, it began to look as if the case itself was destined to completely steal the fern's thunder. On these shores, magazine articles on fern cases appeared in greater numbers than those describing the ferns grown inside. There was some-thing very intriguing about the idea of harboring a fern case in the front parlor. Owning a Wardian Case filled with tropicals was tantamount to keeping one's own private zoo. And, to add to the folly, the daring display was staged in the midst of the soberest of scenes—the front parlor.

The fern case was a device that allowed horticulture to penetrate into the depths of the city. Urban dwellers who were previously deprived of the pleasure of botanical company could now enjoy a micro-rural environment. In *The Fern Garden*, Shirley Hibberd described why "The Fernery at the Fireside" was such

Ferns encased in a dome jar from *Ferns in Their Homes and Ours* by John Robinson.

a compelling notion for anyone forced to reside within city limits. Although he had the great city of London in mind when he penned his words, the description was also apropos to North American metropolises,

> In the heart of the great city where gardens are unknown, and even the graveyards are desecrated by accumulations of filth, the fern case is a boon of priceless value. It is a bit of woodside sealed down with the life of the wood in it, and when unsealed for a moment it gives forth an odour that might delude us into the belief that we had suddenly wafted to some bosky dell where the "nodding violet grows".

Yankee writers were less likely to reminisce on visions of the rural "bosky dell" when urging their audience to join in the fern craze, but their arguments were equally convincing. North American garden writers saw the fern case as a means toward reaching a broader public. Regardless of how hot, dry, and dusty a parlor might be, with a Wardian Case on hand, one could join in the prevailing pteridomania. Even if a young wife was so scatter-brained or prone to attacks of hysteria that she rarely, if ever, remembered that living plants need water— there was still hope. With the aid of that useful new invention, the clumsy, the lovelorn and the hapless could pursue and succeed at a previously elusive hobby. In *Window Gardening*, Henry T. Williams suggested that

> . . . a fern case may be handled with impunity by one in whose hands we would not trust a row of pot plants, and so is within the reach of the careless and forgetful.

Confident that he had attracted the attention of both the adept portion and the bumbling remainder of his audience, Williams clinched the deal by extolling the many labor-saving attributes of that marvelous new invention:

> When once filled they need little or no attention for many weeks; require no unusual care as to watering; can be readily removed from one room to another, are not as quickly affected by changes of temperatures as are plants in the open air of our sitting rooms . . . they afford the only successful means of obviating the effect of the dry heated air of our dwellings. They are reached by no dust, are free from noxious exhalations of coal fires and gas lights, and when a breath of cold air accidently enters the room they are not chilled nor frosted if the thermometer in the room should chance to go below 35°.

It is easy to see why the fern case was so popular. After all, it would be difficult to imagine a better houseguest than one that required no meals, did not gather dust and was never underfoot.

Apparently, the case's mobility was a powerful selling point for the Victorians, and there is little wonder why the lady of the house was so impressed by that particular attribute. After all, she spent a good portion of her waking hours carting heavy pots of plants in and out for airing and baths. Apparently, however, many authors did not have a clue as to why ladies loved the idea of a case with castors that could be rolled from room to room. Shirley Hibberd was among those gentlemen who completely missed the point of adding wheels to the resident fern case; or so it would seem judging from his naive suggestion, "You may take your fern cases with you on your travels."

In truth, Hibberd's idea might well qualify as anyone's worst nightmare. Travelling with your favorite fern case was no easy undertaking. By the time the Wardian Case had reached popular status, it had evolved greatly from the simple glass container which explorers employed. Fern cases were generally about a yard long and 2 ft. wide, ranging in height from a foot for simple cases to a yard or two from top to toe in more elaborate models. The base was made of zinc upon which several pounds of soil were placed and the upper portion was constructed of heavy leaded glass. The price range for one of those novelties ranged from $3 to $25.

Just as everything else in that era was overgrown with befuddled ornamentation, so the fern case naturally followed the same route. Fern cases assumed the most fantastic shapes. They were designed to imitate small scale renditions of temples, pagodas and, of course, Kew Gardens.

Fern cases opened up a new realm of possibilities for indoor gardeners. Just as frail women were greatly admired and affectionately described as "hothouse beauties", so delicate plants were also coveted and coddled for their finickiness. Adiantums, Selaginellas, and Filmy Ferns which could never be grown indoors before suddenly became all the rage. The very fact that those temperamental ferns could not be persuaded to thrive by any other means was impetus enough to send hordes of Victorians scurrying to their local carpenters with plans for building miniature, parlor-sized hothouses.

However, the fern case's incumbents were not necessarily the most beautiful plants known to man. After all, it was an era when rare plants were valued simply because they were unique. In fact, some of the era's favorite Pteridophytes were the obscure Filmy Ferns (*Trichomanes*, *Hymenophyllum*, *Leptopteris*, etc). Those small, moss-like ferns are curious, perhaps, but not sufficiently handsome to warrant all of the woodwork that was undertaken to facilitate their entry into the parlor.

A fern case was generally devoted to the display of many different Pteridophytes, and its arrangement was viewed as a creative canvas on which a lady could express her highly developed "taste". Understandably, gardeners crowded as many botanicals as possible into each expensive case. In addition, cases also became cluttered with a vast array of trinkets. Fossils, shells, minerals and even little statues were not uncommon elements of the resident fern cabinet. Horticultural writers sensed the approach of yet another breach of science, and battled in vain against its infiltration. However, the fight had already been lost, judging from John Robinson's weary comment, "Remember that it is a *fernery*, not a *curiosity-box* of which we are speaking."

Although inanimate objects appeared to be in danger of stealing the show, animal life also occasionally became a part of the fern case scene. Nineteenth

Century gardeners could never be called squeamish if Shirley Hibberd's running account of the fauna in the parlor fern cabinet has any basis in fact,

> Vermin of all kinds occur in fern cases in spite of all precautions; mysterious nibblings of fronds are noticed . . . the marauders may be woodlice, slugs, or larvae of small beetles. Trap them, if possible, by inserting fresh lettuce leaves in the chinks you suspect them to frequent . . . If you can put a few glow worms in a case infested with vermin, there will be a rapid clearance made; toads are good vermin killers, but they do not add to the beauties of the scene, and they are apt to squat on the tender rising fronds of some delicate fern, and do more harm than good.

Although the Wardian Case was certainly the most popular means of displaying ferns, parlor-grown Pteridophytes were not confined solely to the rarified recesses of plant cabinets. After indoor gardeners had gained familiarity and confidence with ferns, they freed the more stalwart incumbent species from their cases. In the open air of the parlor, they enjoyed the greatest success with *Pteris*, *Davallia* (Footed Fern), *Cyrtomium* (Holly Fern), *Platycerium* (Staghorn Fern), *Adiantum* (Maidenhair Fern) and *Nephrolepis* (Sword Fern). In homes that were too dry for ferns, *Lycopodium* was called in to substitute as a close second choice.

Hanging fern baskets offered solace for the liberated ferns. They held specimens that were too large to fit into a case, as well as those which were sufficiently vigorous to survive the front parlor unprotected. Baskets were "rustic" in appearance, a quality that was always welcome in the home. However, "rustic" had acquired a new shade of meaning during the latter part of the 19th Century. It no longer referred solely to the atmosphere and members of the surrounding native woodlands—the jungle was also encompassed in that term. Thus, rustic fern baskets were frequently carved of the jungle's most prized fruit—the coconut. After relishing the coconut's contents, the shell was split in half, filled with moss and packed with cascading ferns which sent croziers dangling gracefully downward.

ARCHED AQUARIUM. TABLE AQUARIUM.

The parlor was filled with fauna as well as flora.

Rosher's Fern Pillar, a "little contrivance" for the exhibition of ferns.

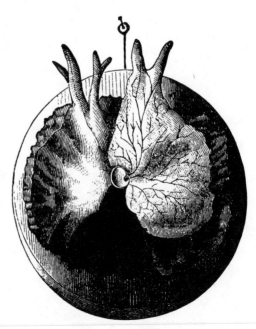

Platycerium grande, the Staghorn Fern.

A Chinese stand featuring a Pteris.

A Maidenhair Fern from Jönsson-Rose's *Ferns in their Homes and Ours*.

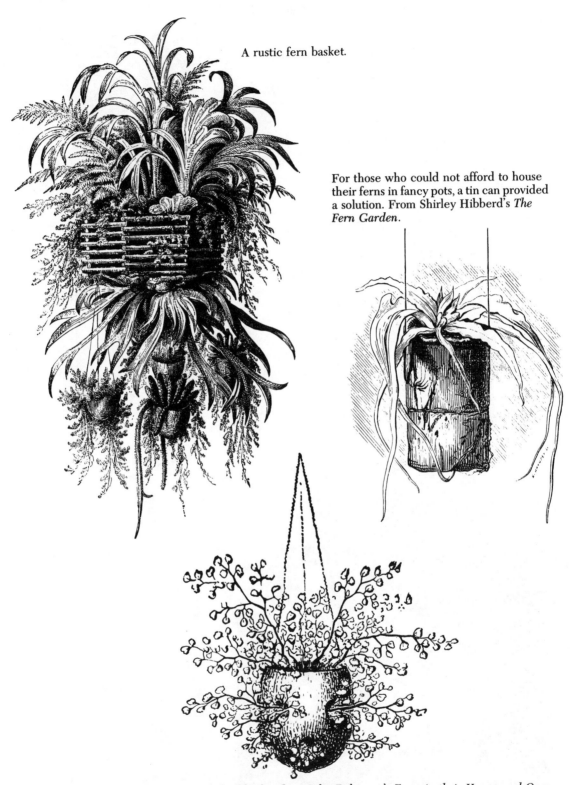

A rustic fern basket.

For those who could not afford to house their ferns in fancy pots, a tin can provided a solution. From Shirley Hibberd's *The Fern Garden*.

Maidenhair ferns in a coconut hull basket from John Robinson's *Ferns in their Homes and Ours*.

Many new ferns entered the recesses of the front parlor in the latter years of the era. However, no fern attained the enduring position acquired by the Boston Fern. Long after the Wardian Case and its Filmy Ferns were forgotten, the Boston Fern lived on as a thriving, photosynthesizing symbol of the Victorian Era. Although the Boston Fern was born just as the century was drawing to a close, the plant established a firm connection with the fashion and decor of the times. The reason for the enduring bond lies in the fact that the Boston Fern was pteridomania's last and loudest hurrah.

It all began in 1894 when Robert Craig & Company of Philadelphia dispatched a shipment of 100 Sword Ferns (*Nephrolepis exaltata*) to a customer in Cambridge, Ma. Upon opening the box, the recipient discovered that one fern had slightly broader, feather-shaped fronds which varied markedly from those of its bedfellows.

When this new breed of Sword Fern was singled out, another very valuable characteristic became evident. The new mutant possessed a growth habit that was distinctly different from the bolt upright posture which Sword Ferns normally assume. The new Nephrolepis cascaded gracefully downward, showering its feathery fronds over the edge of its container. It was the perfect candidate to fill those popular fern baskets which had recently come into vogue.

The new mutant was dubbed *Nephrolepis exaltata* 'Bostoniensis' by the Royal Botanical Society. And the great North American chest swelled with pride at having finally made a significant contribution to the world of indoor horticulture. It was a great moment for both amateur and professional horticulturists in this country.

It was also a great moment for the commercial nursery trade. Boston Ferns became the latest fashion. They sparkled with the irresistible glow of novelty which overshadowed and then dethroned the glittering Wardian Case from its pedestal. That American-born celebrity became so popular that the supply could scarcely keep abreast of the demand. As a testimonial to the fad's magnitude, we have this note in *The Mayflower*, a popular early 20th Century periodical,

> No other fern ever attained such widespread popularity in the cities of the country at large, and the city florist decorators and plant dealers find the demand for it seemingly unending. This is due to two reasons: its distinctive and highly decorative character, and the fact that, like the Sword Fern, it is as easy to grow as a geranium, thriving equally in sun and shade.

The Mayflower's claim for the Boston Fern's reception by the masses was undoubtedly valid, but the analogy between ferns and geraniums was a little far-fetched. In fact, no two plants can be further from each other in cultural preferences than a fern and a geranium. Boston Ferns prefer indirect sun or shade, whereas geraniums will not perform without very good light. And the Boston Fern is actually one of the more challenging Pteridophytes to tackle indoors, even under the best of conditions. As the years brought new technology and more efficient heating systems into the home, the environment was rendered continually warmer, drier and less appropriate for ferns. In *Home Floriculture*, Eben Rexford enumerated the problems inherent in the typical Victorian parlor scene, while offering remedies that are as effective today in our hot, dry abodes as they were a century ago. He suggested that,

> . . . the prevailing dryness of the air in such rooms can be modified to a considerable extent by keeping water constantly evaporating on stoves, registers or radiators . . . If showering is to be done, let it be in the form of a fine spray—a mist, rather—and do not carry it to such an extent that the delicate foliage is heavily saturated.

If 19th Century gardeners had their hands full pleasing the resident Pteridophytes, they could easily find solace in palms. Palms offer all of the benefits of ferns, but require only a fraction of the investment in time and labor.

Palms and ferns were kindred spirits in Victorian eyes. In fact, palms were continually confused with ferns. Even when their identity was correctly established, palms were invariably compared with ferns—they were treated like a pair of close siblings. Ferns and palms belonged in the same places, kept the same company and claimed the same virtues.

Of the list of requisite social graces—good breeding, elegance, chastity and a handsome physique—palms lacked only chastity. But, the absence of that virtue could easily be overlooked in plants, as well as people, if the transgression was handled discretely. And palms were very discrete. The chances of a palm flowering indoors are as remote as the likelihood of an expectant Victorian mother venturing out in public—it simply was not done.

Although palms were entirely proper, they were also one of the era's most romantic plants. There is nothing more exotic than a palm. When the Victorians first laid eyes on palms in the great public gardens, it was definitely love at first sight.

In their specially constructed palm houses, majestic palms rose up in statuesque splendor, their enormous leaves interlacing two stories overhead, just as they did in their native habitat. The jungle-under-glass became a frequent theme for public winter gardens. In fact, every effort was made to imitate the mood, sounds and appearance of the tropics, providing the public with a vicarious jungle experience.

Period writers unanimously agreed that Kew Gardens boasted the most realistically designed palm house of the century. Andrew Jackson Downing was among those who journeyed to Europe to sample the palm house at Kew. He returned with a report that sounded more like footnotes from a tropical expedition than a visit to a British hothouse,

> You open the door, and, but for the glass roof that you see instead of sky above your head, you might believe yourself in the West Indies. Lofty palm trees, thirty or forty feet high, are growing, rooted in the deep soil beneath your feet, with the same vigor and luxuriance as in the West Indies. Huge clusters of golden bananas hang across the walks, and cocoa nut trees, forty-two feet high, wave their tufts of leaves over your head. The foliage of the cinnamon and camphor scents the atmosphere, and rich airplants of South America dazzle the eye with their strange and fanciful blossoms.

A Boston Fern from Lizzie Page Hillhouse's *House Plants and How To Succeed with Them.*

A palm in all its grandeur.

The palm house at Kew was built in 1848, it stood 66 ft. in height, while its cast-iron frame was glazed with no less than 45,000 sq. ft. of glass. Even without the resident palms, it was a structure worthy of comment. The opulence of the proportions and the careful craftsmanship of the iron work all spoke of the importance that the Victorians placed upon their palm collections. Inside that mountain of crystal and iron, a vision of paradise was captured, complete with all of its requisite botanical accouterments. In point of fact, the scene may not have been a completely accurate documentation of the tropics—but accuracy was not its goal. Instead, the palm house was meant to portray utopia—as defined in the 19th Century.

Meanwhile, back on the home front, the public recognized something that they could use in the pompous palm house. The front parlor would definitely benefit from a hint of paradise growing lushly, greenly, and vitally in the corner of the room. Linnaeus had called palms the "Princes of the Vegetable Kingdom". Then they fit perfectly with the other aristocrats in the parlor.

Palms were custom-made for the parlor. Their haughtiness reflected the prevailing mood in that room and carried it one step further. Palms effectively introduce an atmosphere of formality wherever they abide. In this capacity, they languished unobtrusively beside couches at dances, they regaled the table setting at formal dinners, and they loitered solemnly in hotel lobbies. Few places were inappropriate for palms.

Not only were palms suitable for all situations, but they could be grown nearly anywhere, and that fact added immeasurably to their popularity. Although it may have been awe that first inspired the Victorians to bring palms indoors, it was familiarity that rendered them indispensable components of every scene. No one hesitated to exploit that adaptable plant to the hilt. Palms were among the era's most frequently encountered celebrities.

Palms had more than just pretty faces to recommend them as household companions—they were also tough. Underneath that graceful exterior lurked a steel-belted constitution capable of guffing all manner of environmental insults. In fact, the palm's fortitude and subsequent omnipresence can best be likened to the popularity of its modern counterpart, *Ficus benjamina*, the Weeping Fig, a plant that is always called upon to perform impossible missions. And 19th Century magazines such as *The Ladies' Floral Cabinet* attested to the fact that the front parlor never was, and probably never will be an easy place to survive,

> No plants are more easily grown and none are more tenacious to life than the palm, enduring alike dust and the hard knocks that houseplants are apt to receive, the cold from open windows and the unnatural heat from furnaces and from gas.

Although palms may have maintained a steady upper-lip in the face of adversity, their needs could not be neglected entirely. All too often, palms were pressed into situations that were above and beyond the call of duty. Typically, they were relegated to windowless corners to stand sentinel where nothing else would grow. To their credit, they endured this treatment much longer than other plants. However, they could not stand deprivation indefinitely. A far more satisfactory arrangement was to alternate tours of duty, standing the palm in some gloomy corner for a few weeks, and then rejuvenating the plant in a brighter location for a while.

The list of palms that dwelt in conservatories or hothouses was formidable. It includes *Areca*, *Cocos*, *Kentia* (now *Gronophyllum*), *Phoenix*, *Ptychosperma*, *Verschaffeltia*, *Oreodoxa* (now *Roystonea*), *Caryota*, *Chamaerops*, *Livistonia*, *Seaforthia* and *Rhapis* palms. Obviously, the Victorians were not only confronted by a large inventory of unfamiliar botanical faces, but they were also bombarded with a long list of seemingly unpronounceable Latin binomials. *The Ladies' Floral Cabinet* had this comment on the situation,

> The variety of stove palms seems endless, though every grower does not command sufficient space to let them grow. One requires a good deal of extra room to accommodate their names, too, take for example the thief palm, known in polite circles as *Phoenicophorium seychellarrum*. It looks rather like an Aztec swear-word... But to those who say that botanical names are difficult, I respectively submit the following, the genuine name of a Welsh village, given me by a native. Here it is:
>
> Llanfairpwllgyngyllgerchwimpwllgertropllgogertropllgo-gerpwlldisiliogogof.

To relieve amateur growers from the mental exercise and verbal gymnastics inherent in attempting to remember and pronounce the Latin binomials of all those palms, they were assigned common names. Amazingly, even the British, who traditionally excelled in botanical and taxonomical savvy, preferred to address palms by their familiar names. Thus, *Phoenix* was the Date Palm, *Cocos* was the Coconut, *Livistonia* was the Chinese Fan Palm, *Latania* was the Bourbon Palm, *Caryota* was the Fish Tail Palm, etc. It was all delightfully simple.

But not all conservatory species were suitable to the average home. Size alone rendered many of them inappropriate. And it took some experimentation to discern which were the best palms for the job. Those most frequently recommended for parlor decoration were *Cocos*, *Chamaerops*, *Caryota*, *Kentia*, *Phoenix*, and *Seaforthia*. Even when the field was narrowed to these genera, it was still remarkably broad. And the many choices available were a drawing card in the palm's favor. Palms may have been omnipresent, but people continually encountered a variety of species. Diversity is the key to a prolonged romance.

The resident palm took up many positions in the home. It stood guard in the hall, it languished in the parlor and it sat unobtrusively in the study. But, one application which was novel as well as inventive was the palm's employment as a table decoration in lieu of a centerpiece. By the turn of the century, palms (especially *Cocos weddellianum* now known as *Microcoelum weddellianum*) were so frequently found eavesdropping over polite dinner conversation that they came dangerously close to completely dethroning bouquets and fruit bowls in that role.

Mixed palms, illustration from *The Ladies' Floral Cabinet*.

There was an art to the arrangement of palms. Entire chapters of housekeeping books were devoted solely to the fine points of palm placement at dinner parties. The rules of proper etiquette were consulted, of course. Tall palms were preferred for the job because they allowed for easy conversation between parties across the table. Unfortunately, the foliage aloft persisted in the nasty habit of interfering with the chandelier. Very low-growing specimens made way for the smooth flow of conversation and precluded imminent disaster by fire, but their frond size was not nearly as impressive. One rather inventive solution was to fit the dining room table with trap doors into which tall specimens were set while the tops poked out the holes. This brainstorm may have wreaked havoc with the furniture, but it held the obvious advantage of effectively hiding the pot. The idea was so well received that tables were occasionally designed with smaller holes at each place setting to accommodate personal specimens. The fact that palms were welcomed as table partners at every guest's elbow speaks well of their talents for stimulating conversation.

Linnaeus' analogy between palms and princes was certainly apt, especially in view of the palm's frequent appearance at formal occasions, gala dinners and elegant dances. They were the members of the botanical kingdom most often seen in the right places at the right time. If a social climber wished to appear chic, then there was no better place to start than to invite a palm to his next party. In so doing, the host could rest assured that the other guests would be in the best of company.

In fact, judging from the illustrations in period magazines, palms were employed just about everywhere, and ferns were equally omnipresent. The fern craze, with its plant cabinets and tamed exotics, brought tropical horticulture to everyone's notice. And palms carried the notion one step further with their easy-to-accommodate personality and very visible dimensions. Ferns and palms effectively changed the face of the average home.

Palms as table decorations from Henry T. Williams' *Window Gardening*.

By the mid-1880s, indoor gardening had come a long way since the birth of the era. Just as the home and its resident family had grown more sophisticated and worldly, so the indoor garden grew increasingly lush and exotic. Palms swayed in the corners, ferns dangled their fronds from hanging baskets while the family became engrossed in their domestic botanical pursuits and drank in their quota of ambient goodness. Horticulture had taken incredibly broad strides in a short period of time, but it still had a great deal of ground to cover. The greening of the parlor had been accomplished. Now all that was needed was the addition of living color to the scene.

Cycad.

LIST OF FERNS AND PALMS GROWN IN THE VICTORIAN HOME
CIRCA 1881

Ferns
Adiantum
Asplenium
Blechnum
Davallia
Dicksonia
Doodia
Gymnogramma
   (now Pityrogramma)
Hymenophyllum
Lycopodium
Nephrolepis
Platycerium
Polypodium
Selaginella
Woodwardia

Palms
Chamaerops
Chamaedorea
Cocos
Cycads
Phoenicophorium
Phoenix
Rhapis
Seaforthia
   (now Archontophoenix)

CHAPTER X

THE TROPICS BLOSSOM IN THE PARLOR

BY THE END OF THE CENTURY, horticulture was blooming and, finally, North American windowsills were also bursting with flowers. At last, it was not only pansies and morning glories that brightened the window panes—lush exotic tropicals shared the sun's rays. Those tropicals that had remained elusive, lying just beyond the public's grasp throughout the era, came into reach at last.

For nearly a century, the parlor had been preparing for the entry of tropical flowers. Throughout the long wait, the Victorians never allowed their fondest hopes to outpace the logical progression of events. Nothing was pushed aside or hurried along to make way for the next entry upon the scene. Instead, gardeners patiently savored and enjoyed every *fait accompli* which paved the way to their ultimate goal. And yet, all the while, everyone quietly understood that those minor victories were merely precursors to bigger and better things. While the Victorians were ostensibly engrossed in foliage plants and palms, the parlor was actually being prepared to receive tropical bloomers.

When that long-awaited moment finally arrived, the entry of flowering tropicals was nearly anti-climactic. It had been a long time coming. But, the stage had been so carefully set and the gardeners were so meticulously educated that the entry glided along with amazing smoothness. The battle was won without a struggle.

No fanfare was wasted on the introduction of flowering plants into the home. Although other victories were heralded with much ceremony, the final and greatest achievement happened quietly. Flowering tropicals simply followed silently on the heels of exotic foliage plants and were greeted with comparative nonchalance. The absence of commotion is especially noteworthy considering that the Victorians were accustomed to making much ado about everything.

I blame the want of zeal on the inevitability of the event coupled with the previous exposure which flowering tropicals had received. Exotics were no longer strangers. By the end of the century, their faces were nearly as familiar to the average North American as the features of Queen Victoria. The aura of mystery which had once enshrouded tropicals entirely vanished during the latter part of the century.

People read about flowering tropicals, they visited glasshouses full of flowering tropicals and, before they really knew it, they were hosting flowering tropicals in their parlors. The progression was logical, smooth and, in the eyes of every Victorian priding himself on his new-found worldliness, the achievement was completely unremarkable.

What became of the conviction that foliage was more "virtuous" and more "elevated" than frivolous flowers? That pretense vanished as soon as expanded windows admitted more light and furnaces capable of maintaining even temperatures were introduced into the average home. Suddenly, flowers became the highest goal to which a gardener could aspire. Success was now measured in blossoms.

However, before flowering tropicals could successfully make their entry, the parlor had to undergo some changes. Neither the public's lack of education, nor their hesitation to embrace the wild flora of the jungles had actually prevented flowering plants from infiltrating the parlor long before. If it were possible for flowering tropicals to survive in the parlor, they would certainly have entered. In truth, it was the unsuitability of the living room environment which held them at bay.

Nineteenth Century gardeners had clearly learned that the primary requisite for growing tropicals was light. A southern exposure was preferable and large, bright windows were also needed. At first, having acquired experience only with foliage plants and ferns, many indoor gardeners failed to appreciate the importance of full sun for flowering plants. A little education was required to explain the connection between sun and flowers. All too frequently, gardeners with ample windowspace did not grow their bloomers sufficiently close to the glass to reap the benefits of light. In *The Ladies' Home Journal*, Eben Rexford described a rather severe case of horticultural naïveté,

> She went to the cupboard, and from the semi-darkness of its recesses took out her poor slips [plant cuttings] for my inspection.
> "Why, you don't mean to say that you keep them there all the time; do you?" I asked.
> "Yes," was the reply, "The children won't let them alone if I put them in the windows, and they're such little things I didn't suppose it would make much difference where I kept them now. When they get ready to blossom, I shall put them in the window, of course."

While some gardeners continued to grope in the dark, disregarding the opportunities that architectural innovations brought, others took advantage of the appearance of indoor horticulture's greatest boon—the invention of the bay window. Alexander Jackson Davis, a popular New York architect who had once worked with Andrew Jackson Downing, took credit for the introduction of bay windows. Although that type of fenestration was originally adopted to compliment the Gothic Revival style of architecture which Downing and Davis endorsed, the bay window undoubtedly owed its resounding popularity partly to the houseplant fad. The bay alcove jutted out from the body of the floor plan with large, over-sized windows surrounding the annex on three sides, providing the resident botanical collection with bright and balanced light. Plants grown in its confines were far superior to those whose allotment of sun came from a window facing a single exposure.

A bay window from Jonathan Periam's *The Home and Farm Manual*.

In addition to providing abundant light, the bay window was also several degrees cooler than the body of the room. And heat was still an important factor, despite the growing use of central furnaces. However, late century growers grappled with the problems of too much rather than insufficient heat. Actually, it was not the heat itself that wreaked havoc with tropicals. Rather, it was the resulting dryness that did them harm. Since a bay window remained cooler, it was also more humid than the rest of the room, and the plants clustered in that small area also raised the humidity in their immediate vicinity.

For those who had no access to a bay alcove, many corrective measures for the humidity dilemma were proposed, including such innovative inventions as portable greenhouses that looked uncomfortably similar to flying saucers. However, a simpler solution to the problem was suggested in *The Household* which suggested that, "If [the room] must be heated by a furnace, set a pail of water on the register, and at night shut off the heat so that the temperature may fall gradually to about 45° before morning." The remedy is equally effective in modern abodes.

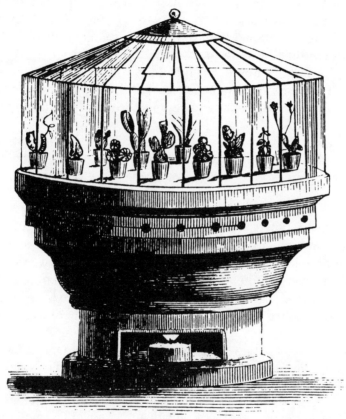

One means of providing humidity to plants was to grow them in portable greenhouses that looked similar to flying saucers.

Meanwhile, as the new technology was being integrated, the parlor and the drawing room were also undergoing personality changes. Most notably, they gained brilliance. The soberness which reigned in mid-century rooms was replaced by a predominance of color. Swirling wallpapers, busy carpets and bright upholstery ruled the day. Red and shocking pink were everywhere. Even Oscar Wilde, whose opinions on interior decor were notoriously conservative, was breathless to adopt color into his living room, as this letter to E. W. Godwin on December 4, 1884 illustrates,

Dear Godwino,

. . . I must see you. I arrive tomorrow (Friday) and will be with you on Saturday morning. I wish you to choose the colors—the red for the drawing-room—as the thing is at a standstill. Is it to be vermilion? is it not? The universe pauses for an answer! Don't keep it waiting!

Flowers were frequently enlisted to brighten the parlor. Not only did their diverse textures and forms add to the prevailing confusion typical of fashionable, late Victorian decor, but they also furnished an inexpensive means of endowing middle class parlors with a splash of color. Tropical flowers were a godsend for those who could not afford to continually refurnish their rooms in obedience to the dictates of fashion. Even the most expensive tropicals hardly approached the cost of a new set of furniture. And yet, as Eben Rexford assured the readers of an 1888 *Ladies Home Journal*, flowers were an entirely tasteful, discrete and appropriate means of keeping abreast of the trends,

With a few good pictures on the walls, some good books on the table, and a window full of flowers, we do not need costly furniture to make a room attractive to persons who appreciate beauty in its truest sense.

For some reason, flower worship was a cult pursued primarily by the ladies of the house, and was generally ill-understood by the incumbent males. As an illustration of this phenomenon, we turn again to poor Otto who we met earlier when he suggested to his sweetheart, Reata, that she take up botany. Here we find Otto still struggling along, trying to comprehend Reata, whose ideas on flowers were just as unfathomable as her reactions to the study of botany,

"You are very fond of flowers, are you not?" remarked Otto at last, more for the sake of hearing her voice again than for any other reason, as he deemed the question superfluous.

"You are very fond of people, are you not?" she answered, after a second's pause, without lifting her eyes, and exactly imitating the tone of his question.

"Of people?" repeated he, slightly taken aback; "why, what has that got to do with my question? Of course I like amiable and agreeable people."

"And I like amiable and agreeable flowers," returned Reata, with such perfect gravity that Otto could not refrain from laughing. "You do not understand me," she said, coloring impatiently; "can't you see that there is as much difference in them as in people, and that it is nonsense to talk of liking or disliking them in a body, or of caring about them at all times? There are some days when I wouldn't have a flower in my room for worlds—they would disturb me; just as one does not always want society. Each flower has got its own character and its own history, just as much as we have; and of course I only select the flowers that are sympathetic to me. Just look at this little pink Cactus, for instance; did you ever see such a silly, vacant expression?"— tearing it to pieces as she spoke—"while its twin-sister here is as intelligent as possible."

Although Reata might have been guilty of some girlish silliness, she was not alone in her sentimental view of flowers. The prevailing affection for flowers was shared by women of all ages, and it was partially responsible for the increase in the blossoms found in the average living room.

Of course, the parlor offered many opportunities for female interaction with flowers long before tropicals entered the scene. In spring, it was adorned with blossoming bulbs; and in winter, camellias added a brief but greatly appreciated hint of color. Primroses, roses and azaleas all took turns brightening the windowsills of cool rooms. However, there was a brief period of horticultural barrenness that occurred when family rooms first began to enjoy the warmth of improved heating systems. Those living rooms which were connected with the newly installed central heating systems were suddenly bereft of color. Camellia buds dropped and primroses simply refused to open. The room's entire inventory of cool-loving, nearly hardy garden flowers was suddenly worthless. Tropical bloomers were the only answer. Fortunately, they were ready to enter the home just as the parlor and drawing room were made environmentally suitable to receive them.

The first flowering "tropicals" to filter into the home were actually natives of the hot, dry deserts of America. Although they were not bonafide jungle specimens, they were the easiest flowering exotics to please in the steamy recesses of the late 19th Century parlor. So, it is not surprising that the Victorians started with cacti and succulents. As long as they are given bright light, cacti can endure the hottest, driest environment on earth—and that was certainly a fairly accurate description of the climate that greeted botanical entrants into the late Victorian parlor.

Cacti were not novelties in the late 19th Century. When cacti first arrived in Europe in the 1830s, they enjoyed a brief but fervent encounter with the public's affections before falling into obscurity. In mid-century, the fad resurfaced on North American shores, but its fires were equally fleeting on this side of the ocean.

It was not until the end of the century that the "Cactus Craze" (as it was dubbed by those not afflicted) reasserted itself. A fascinatingly clear and accurate record of the sequence of events appears in A. Blanc's catalog. Not only were the proprietors of A. Blanc & Co. confessed "Cactus Cranks", but they can be held partly responsible for the spread of the epidemic. Their history of the risings and fallings of cactus hysteria runs thus,

> We read in older publications that about the year 1830, Cacti were eagerly sought and fought for by rich plant amateurs in England . . . The rivalry existing between them caused enormous prices to be paid for the new and rare plants that were occasionally brought over from America—as much as $150. often being paid for single specimens. In the United States a similar state of affairs took place. The craze, however, abated, and for many years not a plantsman handled more than half a dozen varieties . . . It has only been within the last 4 years, since we turned the Cactus culture from a "hobby" into a business, that those very interesting plants have become so exceedingly popular. Little did we dream of such a craze being started again.

Unlike the previous cactus craze, the outbreak in the 1890s infected the middle class rather than confining itself to wealthy collectors. By the latter part of the century, nurseries were prepared to supply a large demand for cacti and, therefore, prices remained within reasonable limits. Nevertheless, those who were truly smitten still experienced trouble keeping their addiction in hand according to this narrative from A. Blanc's pamphlet, *Hints on Cacti*,

> In one case, the wife of a customer complained to us that her husband actually starved himself and his family so that he might buy Cacti. We wrote her that we would send him all the Cacti he desired, free of charge, but even that seemed an objection, as the old gentleman neglected his business to experiment in grafting and propagating.

Although the Victorian fern mania could easily be rationalized as an infatuation with form and texture that was completely consistent with the prevailing classical tastes, the cactus craze was not quite so readily explained. In fact, outsiders were at a loss to comprehend why cacti were so attractive to the public. Try though they might to see it, the cactus' beauty was not immediately apparent. Although Victorian writers could lavish praise on just about any living plant or animal, they were hard-pressed to find complimentary adjectives to employ in connection with cacti. An 1895 *Ladies Home Journal* finally concluded that the cactus craze was among the unfathomable workings of blind love, They wrote,

> The grotesque, rigid, self-willed and seemingly unmanageable plants comprised by the Cactus genera have worked their way into popular favor in a most surprising manner during the past few years.

Although the popular press may have been confounded by the craze, the more sympathetic horticultural journals such as *The Ladies' Floral Cabinet*, could explain it easily. After all, beauty is in the eye of the beholder, and cacti provided any viewer with something completely different to gaze upon,

> Notwithstanding the rough exterior which these plants present, some species are remarkably attractive for their peculiarity of form, while others are noted for the superb beauty of their large showy flowers.

Cacti's grotesque form was actually a strong drawing card in their favor. It was a time when Barnum & Bailey were amassing a fortune from audiences willing to part with a portion of their hard earned wages for the satisfaction of viewing "freaks of nature". Clearly, the idea of housing a botanical freak must have seemed very alluring to some citizens. The commercial trade quickly exploited the trend judging from A. Blanc's glib claim, "We are rather pleased to say . . . we have more new monstrosities than have been known to exist."

In addition to unpredictable growth forms, cacti also possess another characteristic that is generally considered to be a negative attribute, but was seen in a positive light by smitten 19th Century collectors. The spines brandished by many cacti were undoubtedly a drawback for anyone accustomed to enjoying intimate contact with their houseplants. However, the commercial sector effec-

A cactus advertisement.

tively down-played that vice, obscuring it behind the guise of ornamentation and billing it as a virtue. Those anti-social spines were described as pretty plumage in A. Blanc's catalog which bubbled forth with praises for every aspect of cacti. At the same time, the catalog thoughtfully offered suggestions for handling those thorny beauties without suffering puncture wounds.

Although cactus foliage was intriguing, the most popular varieties were those that also featured flowers. The Victorians soon learned that the trick to inciting bud formation was to place cacti outdoors in full sun during the summer. That seasonal sojourn in the garden fortified the plants for their winter residence in the parlor.

The most rewarding blooming cacti are epiphyllums, and they were immensely popular at the time. However, even the irrepressible Victorians had to admit that epiphyllum foliage was not particularly ornamental. Undaunted, they avowed that the huge, dramatic flowers amply compensated growers for enduring the months of nakedness. Further, a collection of epiphyllums could be choreographed to blossom throughout the winter. Thanksgiving, Christmas and Easter Cacti were among the most frequently grown succulents, even though their popularity predated the development of those catchy common names.

An epiphyllum in bloom.

Whereas epiphyllums were famed for their lengthy, profuse blossom display, the closely related cereus cacti were distinguished for their short but dramatic exhibition. The Night-Blooming Cereus enjoyed a mystique all its own. That succulent amassed a contingent of aficionados who were willing to devote a sizable portion of their growing space to the unwieldy, unsightly mass of spines and succulent leaves merely to witness a few spectacular hours of breathtaking floral splendor. Night-Blooming Cereus open only once a year, and the buds do not begin to unfold until about 9:00 PM. Two hours later, when the frilly nest of bizarre petals, filaments and stamens has completed its dramatic unfolding, the fully open flower dangles agape measuring no less than a foot in diameter. There may be a dozen blossoms on a vine, all perfectly synchronized to unfurl simultaneously on that one evening. The visual effect is awesome. And, in addition, the evening also provides olfactory entertainment. Cereus flowers emit an eerie but fragrant aroma.

By daybreak the show is completely over. On the morning after, those once magnificent cereus flowers are as limp and homely as they were stupendous the night before. Naturally, writers could scarcely resist composing long and fervent accounts of the evening's entertainment, and the opening night became a social event for the proud owners of a flowering vine. The nocturnal escapades of the cereus received sufficient publicity to convince gardeners to experiment with other genus members as well. A. Blanc's catalog listed no fewer than 105 different cereus.

Although epiphyllums and cereus were the stars of the display, they shared the stage with other cacti and succulents. *The Garden* recommended sedums, sempervivens, echeverias, and mesembryanthemums as front runners in any cacti collection. *Pereskia aculeata*, a leaf-bearing member of the Cactaceae, was often grown for its blossoms in addition to providing rootstock for grafting thornier succulents.

The cactus craze kept pace with the excesses of the age. Cacti and succulents were collected until the windowsill groaned under the weight of dozens of pots filled with heavy, sandy cactus soil. When gardeners grew tired of merely adding specimens to the collection, they amused themselves by arranging several cacti in shallow dish gardens. When the dish gardens failed to hold their attention, cactus rockeries came into vogue. A cactus rockery was a desert version of a fernery. Amongst carefully and tastefully arranged rocks and gravel, cacti were artistically placed. Of course, the finished scene was meant to look deceptively "natural", and the observer was supposed to entertain the illusion that the Mojave Desert had suddenly migrated to the confines of the family drawing room.

Cacti were of great value as curiosities, but they did not fulfill the need for flowering tropicals in the home. The fact that they were native to North America may have enhanced their interest from a patriotic point of view, but it diminished their status as bonafide exotics. Most Victorians were more interested in exploring the flora from the far corners of the earth rather than pursuing native species. In addition, most cacti blossomed too infrequently for reliable color in the parlor. Nineteenth Century growers would have to search elsewhere for a dependable winter-time floral display.

The Victorians had developed a very specific image of the ideal flowering tropical. That image was first formed and then perpetuated by the flowery descriptions and glorified engravings found in popular magazines. Most importantly, a flowering tropical was expected to look significantly different from the flora grown in the garden. Preferably, the flowers should be bizarre, unique and over-sized. White was not the favorite color. Hot pinks, steamy yellows, oranges and royal purples were much more stimulating. Multi-colored flowers such as fuchsias and clerodendrums were a big hit.

The Victorians found many specimens that met those criteria. Unfortunately, only a handful of the qualifying botanicals found the parlor atmosphere agreeable. Nevertheless, the first tropicals to enter the scene provided the foundations of the flowering indoor display upon which gardeners later elaborated. Before flowering tropicals entered en masse, a few stalwart representatives tested the water in the parlor.

Abutilons, with their abundance of colorful, bell-shaped blossoms, were among the prominent early entrants into the parlor. Their suitability for windowsill culture led to their popular designation as Parlor Maples or Flowering Maples, nicknames which alluded to the abutilon's resemblance to certain members of the *Acer* genus. Not only was the foliage similar to that of a maple, but abutilons had the tendency to acquire a tree-like stature. This character trait might give a modern gardener pause, but the Victorians greeted the Parlor Maples' enthusiastic growth habit as a virtue. Nineteenth Century gardeners put a premium on size. If a plant grew to immense proportions, it was ten times more valuable than a miniature. And, if it could be encouraged to produce masses of flowers in addition to quantities of verdant foliage, then it was definitely destined to become a celebrity.

So, in Victorian eyes, Flowering Maples were very nearly perfect. Not only could they claim some very attractive physical attributes, but they could also boast tropical roots—they originally hailed from South America. Novelty was an equally important factor. Flowering Maples were relative newcomers to the North American horticultural scene—*Abutilon striatum* (now known as *Abutilon pictum*) was introduced as recently as 1837.

Never blind to opportunity, hybridizers quickly developed varieties to blossom in a rainbow of shades including white, rose, yellow, and orange; each (except the white) was etched with darker veins. In addition, the bell-shaped flowers gained size with the aid of the hybridizer's camel's hair brush. By the end of the century, they were inflated versions of the original relatively small blossoms, although they were still only half as large as our modern hybrids.

All of these breeding advances were joyfully greeted by a grateful public. That is, all except one characteristic that 20th Century growers would view as a bonus, but Victorians saw as a defect. In the 1880s, *The Ladies' Floral Cabinet* mourned the reduction of the Flowering Maple's hefty dimensions. Hybridizers had dwarfed their favorite giants,

> Only the other day somebody discovered that the abutilon might, by careful cross-breeding, be made to yield a vast amount of characters and colors. Presto! Now there are dozens of new names and varieties . . . But as the florists multiplied the varieties

Abutilons from Lizzie Page Hillhouse's *House Plants and How to Succeed with Them.*

they forgot the native in-born elegance of the plant, and were content to grow their named varieties in the form of diminutive bushes, which are certainly pretty, but afford no idea of the proper splendor of the plant...

Flowering Maples were grown for many reasons, but paramount among their virtues was their willingness to perform in a variety of temperatures. This trait was put to the test in parlors that might easily climb to 80°F. by day and then dip to a bone-chilling 40°F. during a winter's night. Flowering Maples grew on undaunted. In fact, all that an abutilon really needs is sun, and light was fast becoming a common commodity in living rooms.

Fuchsias were also omnipresent in 19th Century parlors. Originally introduced in the latter part of the 18th Century from South and Central America, fuchsias were immediately snatched up by nurserymen who catered to wealthy hothouse growers. Snob appeal undoubtedly added to the fuchsia's attractions, but the plant could claim several very appealing qualities to add to its charm.

Although most fuchsias are not noted as winter performers, the Victorians found a few cultivars they could coax into winter-time bloom. For the most part, fuchsias did their entertaining during the summer. They preferred the sheltered life, shielded from the sharp rays of North American sunshine. And so, when their windowsill comrades took to the fresh air for the season, they remained alone indoors. Often, their colorful presence on the otherwise vacant sill made a

A trailing fuchsia.

more memorable statement than a window full of less enthusiastic performers.

Fuchsias satisfied all of the requirements to qualify as windowsill celebrities. Their flowers have a very complex and unique structure which immediately caught the public's attention and imagination, while their colors were equally intriguing. In the 19th Century, pinks, salmon, reds, and purples abounded, and hybridizers were continually adding new combinations. At the height of the fuchsia's heyday, no fewer than 1,500 cultivars were available, a figure that has diminished rather than expanded in recent years.

The profusion of flowers on the typical fuchsia was definitely the plant's most valued trait. In fact, when Peter Henderson boasted in *Practical Floriculture* that he had seen a 2 year old plant "1 foot in diameter giving upwards of 100 flowers which are much esteemed for their rare color", he was scarcely exaggerating.

Added to the enhancement of the floral profusion was the fuchsia's tendency to reach large proportions quickly, a virtue that pleased Victorian gardeners immensely and led to an unofficial competition to cultivate record-breaking specimens. *The Ladies' Floral Cabinet* reported that one fuchsia grown in Southern Ireland had attained the hefty girth of 90 ft. in diameter. The fuchsia's rapid growth rate, coupled with its strong stem proved extremely useful to gardeners who practiced the art of topiary, especially those who enjoyed training their houseplants into standards (tree form).

Like fuchsias, passion flowers had also been in cultivation since the 18th Century when they were introduced from South America. And, similarly, they retained their mystique throughout the years. Those large, complex and bizarrely unique passion flowers were immensely popular as houseplants in the North, although their prevalence as wildflowers in the South limited their fan club solely to those gardeners above the Mason-Dixon Line. In fact, Southern gardeners took great delight in reminding their Northern brethren that those same "exotics" that received constant attention on the windowsills upcountry were weeds in more temperate regions of this continent. Along that vein, a correspondent to *The Ladies' Floral Cabinet* from South Carolina wrote in the 1880s,

> I was in my delightful old kitchen-garden this after-noon watching my two gardeners mowing—not hay, but veritable passion vines,—and gathering with their hands great clusters of the exquisite fragrant, beautiful flowers with quaint flower buds undeveloped, and wondered what our northern flower-lovers would say and think to see two strong men, whose scythes with every sway bring down hundreds of these flowers so prized and nursed there, with each step they are crushed under regardless feet, and the hot summer air is filled with a delicious perfume.

But, the taunts from down South did nothing to dampen the fires of Northern affection. The passiflora's innate tendency to wander and grow rampantly was employed to best advantage on 19th Century sills where it was encouraged to roam with carefree abandon around the window casing. Frequently, passion flower vines substituted for curtains, catching the sunrays and turning them into flowers.

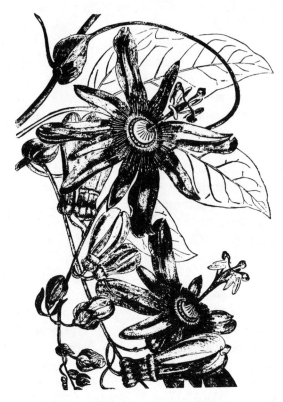

The Red Passion Flower, *Passiflora racemosa* from *The Ladies Floral Cabinet*.

Although passion flowers are not intensely fragrant, their aroma was a trait that was always mentioned when describing the vine. Fragrance was one of the most important virtues a flower could boast. In fact, the possession of a pleasant aroma amply compensated for a lack of color. At least one fragrant specimen was an essential ingredient on any windowsill.

When gardeners had room for only one fragrant plant, they usually opted for a jasmine. Jasmine ranked at the very top of the list of windowsill-grown olfactory delights. And they have not yielded that prominent position even in modern times. Few floral fragrances can compare to that of the jasmine.

Most jasmine hail from the Orient or thereabouts, and that attribute alone won them instant acclaim from the horticultural crowd. In addition, their fragrance infinitely compounded the power of their exotic attraction. Jasmine entered the indoor garden early, taking a position right alongside the rose as a floral favorite. And, like the rose, their popularity not only infected gardeners, it also inspired writers. There is nothing like the romantic perfume of jasmine to excite the pens of poets - whether ancient, Victorian or modern. Many a starry-eyed amateur lyrist practiced her iambic pentameter while gazing at, and inhaling the essence of the resident jasmine.

Not all jasmine are fragrant. And the repertoire of fragrant jasmine available to the home gardener was somewhat limited prior to the 1880s. Until that time, *Jasminum grandiflorum*, often known as the Catalonian Jessamine or the Poet's Jessamine, served as the sole jasmine to reside in the average home. The fact that *J. grandiflorum* was grown commercially in French perfume fields immeasurably enhanced its attraction, although its vining growth habit rendered it a little unwieldy on a windowsill. Toward the end of the century a more manageable bush-type jasmine, *Jasminum sambac*, acquired a place in the parlor. And, later still, the fully double variety, *Jasminum sambac flore pleno* (now known as *Jasminum sambac* 'Grand Duke of Tuscany') made its dramatic entry on the domestic scene. 'Grand Duke' may have been a mass of flailing arms and legs, but it possessed the most exotic perfume known to man, and that trait alone was reason enough to recommend it for a position in the parlor.

Other fragrant flowers added olfactory enjoyment to the windowsill bouquet. Heliotrope, introduced in 1757, was among the earliest flowering tropicals to enter the average home. Although heliotrope was prone to a hoard of insects (most particularly white flies and aphids), its vanilla-scented, purple flowers compensated for the problems inherent in maintaining the plant indoors. By mid-century, no fewer than 10 varieties were commonly grown, including a white hybrid, whereas today there are scarcely 4 heliotropes in cultivation; and they are currently only available through specialty greenhouses.

Gardenias were very popular, and their musky, overpowering perfume was perfectly suited to Victorian taste. *Gardenia jasminoides*, the common Gardenia, often took a post in the parlor. In addition, a species known as *Gardenia citriodora* was a frequent resident on the windowsill due to its stoic tolerance of a wide range of light and temperature conditions. The plant was lost and apparently forgotten until quite recently when it resurfaced as a novel discovery amid much fanfare. It is now known as *Mitriostigma axillare*, nicknamed the African Gardenia.

Stephanotis was another fragrant favorite. That rambunctious vine was originally cultivated as a conservatory plant. But, as soon as its fragrance reached the nostrils of the public, it was destined to enter the home. In the 19th Century, the florist trade had not yet discovered that its snow-white, trumpet-shaped flowers could be employed as cut flowers. The idea of promoting Stephanotis for bridal bouquets remained an aspect of the flower for future generations to exploit.

But fragrance was not the only virtue that Victorians valued in flowering plants; bright colors and unique petal shapes were also esteemed. As flowering plants became more common in the parlor and their importance in the family's daily life increased, indoor gardeners began to search the ranks of conservatory plants in an attempt to enlist other suitable subjects for the home windowsill.

By late century, the average gardener was well versed in the physical attributes of the rarest plants, thanks to her visits to botanical gardens and the information that she gleaned from magazines. Through that wonderful mode of communication, she was fully cognizant of who was growing what—when, where and how. Her knowledge of rare and obscure exotics was truly phenomenal. Magazines were filled with descriptions of such intriguing but unattainable wonders as the Nepenthes that drowned insects mercilessly in its cup-like foliage; and *Victoria regia,* a huge Waterlily whose gigantic ribbed pads could support the weight of a child. In fact, the rarest plants in the world were discussed calmly at afternoon tea with the same nonchalance that once was reserved only for native violets and primroses.

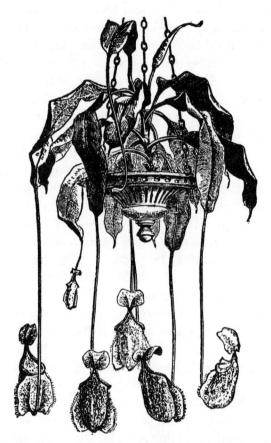

A Nepenthes, certainly one of the era's more bizarre botanical celebrities. Illustration from Lizzie Page Hillhouse's *House Plants and How to Succeed with Them.*

Magazines brought news of rarities that no one would ever consider inviting into their home, but they also described novelties which held promise as potential botanical roommates. From the day that a new species was discovered until it was propagated, hybridized and available at flower shops, horticultural magazines kept the public abreast of its progress. The coverage was so extensive that novel tropicals were already old acquaintances by the time they entered the parlor. With all of that publicity, plant shops could rest assured of an avid audience for any new introduction they might offer.

The confidence of amateurs was also at a high point. Although window gardens relied on tried-and-true performers like heliotropes, the Victorians eagerly experimented and often succeeded with such esoteric exotics as allamandas, begonias, bougainvilleas, clerodendrums, hibiscus, bouvardias, Reinwardtia and daturas, to mention only a handful of their exploits.

Orchids were common on the windowsill. In the 19th Century, no one thought twice about acquiring an orchid for the parlor. And there really was no reason for hesitation when orchids were available at the incredibly low prices which prevailed at the time. A. Blanc's late century catalog listed *Laelia*, *Odontoglossum*, *Epidendrum*, *Oncidium*, *Brassia* and *Brassavola* at prices that would make a modern collector weep. Their advertisement read, "These plants, being somewhat out of our line, will be disposed of at the low price of 50¢ each . . . large clumps at a higher price. Twelve varieties for $5."

In fact, the typical late 19th Century Victorian windowsill might provide reason for envy on many accounts. In addition to the obvious fact that plant collecting was a less expensive hobby than it is today, there were also more plants readily available to the amateur collector. The market was literally glutted with opportunity.

Nineteenth Century gardeners commonly grew many subjects that are not readily available in modern plant shops. Few modern growers have ever encountered mandevillas, Iochroma, Hibbertia, Diosma or the bevy of other flowering botanicals that were popularly grown a century ago. Unfortunately, many of the species, sports and cultivars that were commonplace during the Victorian Era have been completely lost to cultivation. And, in many cases, commercial growers can be held responsible for the loss of important plant material as they eliminate varieties in an effort to stream-line their inventory. There are far too many examples of this tragic state of affairs. But, one particularly lamentable case is that of bouvardias. Those prolific bloomers and valuable cut flowers were once favorite windowsill plants, although they are difficult to find on the market today. George Nicholson's *The Illustrated Dictionary of Gardening* published between 1886–1889 lists 9 bouvardia hybrids including 'Alfred Neuner' featuring double white flowers slightly tinged with rose and 'Pres. Garfield' displaying double rich red-pink flowers in addition to many mouthwatering shades of single hybrids. At present, our selection of bouvardias is limited to white or rose-pink. Each horticultural loss is a tragedy when we consider that the quirk of nature that produced certain cultivars is unlikely to occur twice.

However, if it is possible to have too many plants at your disposal, then the Victorians definitely had a surfeit of tropical plant material with which to play. They were bombarded. And the over-abundance of botanicals in turn led to further alterations in indoor gardening practices.

As all of this novel plant material appeared in the parlor, changes were underway to facilitate plant care. Cultural practices were radically modified. When indoor horticulture was still in its infancy, many rules and procedures were propounded which had a good basis in theory, but were not absolutely essential to the health of houseplants. Later in the era, the art of indoor horticulture was refined, as it is still being amended. The end of the century witnessed the battle of new cultural ideas conflicting with old dictums. Confusion was inevitable as growers readjusted and settled into a more familiar relationship with their photosynthesizing housemates.

One common notion which did not die easily was the belief that all plants need a dormant period. Actually, flowering tropicals fare poorly when subjected to a period of cold temperatures and low light. Even so, gardeners were not eager to over-tax tender botanicals. Finally, however, this cherished tenet succumbed to a newer and better understanding. Rather than banishing botanicals to the basement in the fall, flowering tropicals were kept in warm rooms throughout the indoor growing season.

In the same way, chores that were previously deemed essential were eliminated in the interest of saving precious time and thus helping the busy housewife cope with an ever-increasing collection of tropicals. Commercial nurseries were particularly eager to stream-line houseplant chores and make the hobby available to a broader and busier public. Dingee & Conard decided to begin by eliminating one of the most time-consuming houseplant related duties—syringing the collection,

> It is no light task to comply with the oft-repeated advice to "syringe plants daily". The housewife who has a good many plants and who does all of her own work cannot find time to syringe her plants daily. She need not on that account deny herself the pleasure of cultivating house plants because they do not really *need* to be syringed daily.

And so the collection expanded. No longer fettered by the fear and hesitation that had once restrained their relationship with tropicals and freed from monotonous, time-consuming chores that shackled the early houseplant pioneers, gardeners could explore the vast array of botanical material which was finally available to them.

A bouquet of bouvardias from Lizzie Page Hillhouse's *House Plants and How to Succeed with Them*.

LIST OF FLOWERING TROPICALS GROWN ON LATE CENTURY WINDOWSILLS
CIRCA 1881

°° = The most popular flowering houseplants.
° = Commonly described in 19th Century magazines and houseplant books.

°° Abutilon
Acalypha
Achimenes
Aeschynanthus
Agapanthus
° Allamanda
Aloysia
Alstroemeria
Amaryllis
Anthurium
Aphelandra
Aristilochia
Asarina (known then as Maurandya)
°° Azalea
Barleria
Beaumontia
°° Begonia
Bougainvillea
°° Bouvardia
Brassavola

Brassia
° Browallia
° Brugmansia
° Calceolaria
°° Camellia
Cantua
°° Cereus
Cestrum
Choisya
Chorizema (known then as Chorozema)
Chrysanthemum
°° Citrus
°° Clerodendrum (known then as Clerodendron)
Clivia
Coelogyne
Coffea
Columnea
Cuphea
Cyanotis
Cymbidium

Chrysanthemums were primarily grown in the greenhouse, although flowering mums occasionally adorned the windowsill. Illustration from Cause & Bissell's 1892 catalog.

°° Daphne
Datura
Dendrobium
Dendrochilum
Dichorisandra (known then as Dichorizandra)
Dicliptera
Dionea (known then as Dionaea)
Diosma
Drymonia
Episcia
Eucharis
° Gardenia
Grevillea
°° Heliotropium
° Hermannia (known then as Mahernia)
Hibbertia
°° Hibiscus
°° Hoya
°° Impatiens
Ixora
°° Jasminum
Justicia
Laelia
Leonotis
Lopezia
Lycaste
°° Mandevilla (known then as Dipladenia)
Manettia
Miltonia
° Mimulus
Musa
Murraya
Nematanthus
Nepenthes
° Nerium
° Olea
Odontoglossum
Oncidium
° Oxalis
°° Passiflora
°° Pelargonium
° Pentas
Peperomia
Petrea
Phalaenopsis
° Piqueria (known then as Stevia)
° Pittosporum
° Plumbago
Punica
Quisqualis
Rondeletia
° Russellia
Ruellia
Salvia

Scutellaria
° Skimmia
Solandra
Sollya
° Sparmannia
Stanhopea
°° Stephanotis
Strelitzia
Streptocarpus
Stylidium
Swainsonia
Tabernaemontana
Tecoma
Thunbergia
Torenia
°° Tropaeolum
Velthemia
°° Verbena
Weigela

Double and single daturas.

A QUICK GLIMPSE AT SOME FLOWERING FAVORITES

Allamanda—A Brazilian native introduced in 1846, this robust vine was a favorite in bay windows where it received the benefits of abundant light. No fewer than 5 varieties of *A. cathartica* were in cultivation, the most popular being *A. cathartica var. Williamsii* with its huge, 3–4 in. gaping, canary-yellow, trumpet-like flowers.

Begonia—The Victorians were ardent begonia enthusiasts, and their favorite group was *Begonia* rex-cultorum which was hybridized until nearly every color in the rainbow was represented in the ornamental foliage. Every period catalog lists at least a dozen different varieties including hybrids with curly foliage, maple-shaped leaves and silver foliage. The more floriferous Angel Wing begonias and Rhizomatous begonias were also frequently grown. One of the era's most popular hybrids was *B. erythrophylla*, the Beefsteak Begonia, which found its way onto every farmhouse windowsill and retained its popularity well into the 20th Century. It is still commonly sold at garden centers.

Browallia—Gardeners still value this cheerful plant for its bright, sky-blue, star-shaped flowers. We now grow it in the garden as well as on sunny windowsills, as did the Victorians. It was first introduced from South America in 1798.

Brugmansia—Together with the closely related daturas, brugmansias satisfied the Victorian desire for hefty specimens. Known as Angels' Trumpets, mature brugmansias easily reach 10–12 ft., and the bushes were often allowed to attain their full stature outdoors in summer. In the fall, those tree-like tropicals were severely pruned and brought indoors for parlor decoration. In the 19th Century, *B. suaveolens*, with its large, dangling, ghostly white trumpets provided quite an impressive and unique display.

Brugmansias were extremely impressive potted plants.

Calceolaria—Known as the Slipperwort or Pocketbook Plant, *Calceolaria* was a vastly different, and relatively unimpressive plant before it was enhanced by European breeders at the end of the 19th Century. In North America, most Victorian gardeners had access only to the canary-yellow species with its small but profuse pouch-like flowers. And, just as modern growers must battle insects when cultivating the Pocketbook Plant, the Victorians complained that white fly harbored a strong affinity for that blossoming annual. Pocketbook Plants are ephemeral performers, they rarely live longer than a single season.

Clerodendrum—The Glory Bower, *C. thomsoniae*, was the most popular clerodendrum in 1881, as it is today, but in the 19th Century it was known as *C. balfouri*. There is little wonder why that plant achieved such all-encompassing fame. Its large, balloon-like, white bracts and red flowers are reminiscent of garden grown Bleeding Hearts. It puts on a magnificent display throughout the year if grown in a warm and sunny spot. Clerodendrums can endure a season of dormancy. Therefore, gardeners who wanted their flowers for summer gardens, but had no suitable spot for a warmth-loving vine in winter, stored their clerodendrums in the cellar.

Clivia—Although Clivias are often associated with the Victorian Era, they were rarely found in the average 19th Century home. According to the 1947 edition of Bailey's *Standard Cyclopedia of Horticulture*, "Clivias make excellent house plants, but, like amaryllis, are too costly to be very popular." In 1828, *Clivia nobilis* was introduced from the Cape of Good Hope. Although that species is not as magnificent as the modern *C. miniata* hybrids, its winter-time umbels of drooping, pale pink blossoms tipped with bright green made an impressive show. *Clivia miniata* was discovered in Natal soon after mid-century. However, in 1890, it had not yet appeared in *Henderson's Handbook of Plants*. Few indoor gardening books made reference to either clivia.

Hibiscus—The double pink *Hibiscus rosa sinensis* was highly valued for its huge, profuse blossoms. Hibiscus have all of the traits that the Victorians valued—including brightly colored flowers, ample size and ease of cultivation.

Hermannia—Introduced in the early 1900s, hermannia is a native of the Cape of Good Hope with floriferous blossoms in late winter. The cheerful, yellow flowers emit an anise-like fragrance which earned hermannia the nickname of Honey Bells. *Hermannia verticillata* was identified in Victorian texts as *Mahernia odorata*, although several authors admitted that they were aware that the plant's correct name was hermannia. Interestingly, a red and yellow cultivar was extremely popular in 1881, although it is no longer in cultivation. Honey Bells are ideal for cool rooms or sunporches where temperatures dip down to 50°F. at night.

Mandevilla—The fragrant *Mandevilla suaveolens* (now known as *M. laxa*) was introduced in 1837 and was frequently grown for its luminous, white, trumpet-shaped flowers. The pink flowering *M. amabilis* (known then as *Dipladenia amoena*), which is now very popular as a houseplant, was occasionally grown in Victorian times, but its cultivation was primarily confined to the humid environment of hothouses. At present, *M. amabilis* 'Alice DuPont' is deservingly popular for its 4 in. wide, glowing pink trumpets which brighten windowsills both summer and winter. It prefers warm, 60–65°F. nighttime temperatures.

Mimulus—The Monkey Flower (*M. luteus*), with its reddish orange blossoms, was a frequent resident on the sunny windowsill. Vying with *M. luteus* for fame was the Musk Plant, *M. moschatus*, a yellow-flowering, North American native.

Nepenthes—The Victorians were always enthusiastic about any freak of nature, and nepenthes, or the Pitcher Plants, as they were commonly called, furnished bizarre subjects on which to lavish affection. Those wierd and difficult to cultivate insectivores were grown in elaborate hanging pots with their ant-catching pitchers dangling ominously over the sides. The first nepenthes was introduced in 1820. However, several new introductions arrived on North American shores in the 1870s.

Nerium—Despite its poisonous properties, the oleander was an indoor favorite. Double and single varieties were in cultivation, although the color range was limited to pink or white. Interestingly, according to Peter Henderson, "a striped variety, with marks exactly like those of a Carnation" was available to collectors willing to pay the price for a novelty.

Olea—Although it rarely, if ever, blossoms indoors, and is not a particularly handsome plant, the Olive (*Olea europea*) was grown in 19th Century window gardens primarily for its economic value and its Biblical associations. After all, the Victorians were great admirers of anything with a Romantic theme. Much more floriferous and equally, if not more, popular was the Sweet Olive, *Osmanthus fragrans* (grown in the 19th Century as *Olea fragrans*) which added delightfully fragrant flowers to its virtues. Not only is it easy to please, but the Sweet Olive will grow in any east, west or south window and thrives at a broad range of nighttime temperatures spanning 45–65°F.

Pentas—Introduced from South Africa in 1842, pentas was a very deserving windowsill celebrity. In fact, it is unfortunate that pentas are not widely grown today. *Pentas lanceolata* (grown in the 19th Century as *P. carnea*) has profuse, star-shaped flowers which appear continually in large umbels. The Victorians knew only the "flesh colored" species, but we now have pink, red, white and lavender hybrids. They thrive easily in a sunny window.

Piqueria—Destined to become an important cut flower for the florist trade, Stevia (as it was called in the 19th Century) was grown as a filler for bouquets. It performed the duties that are now relegated to Baby's Breath, providing a white foil to accent more expensive and more colorful flowers. Not only are the sprays of tiny flowers profuse and long-lasting, but they add aroma to any nosegay. At present, there is a grassroots effort afoot to revive the domestic cultivation of piqueria to combat the expense of flying cut flowers in from the tropics during the winter.

Pittosporum—First introduced in 1789, we can safely assume that Peter Henderson was speaking of *P. tobira* when he described a forest-green pittosporum accented by intensely fragrant, cream-colored flowers. Pittosporum remains a very popular indoor plant especially suitable for cool locations. Also to its credit, it can be grown as a foliage plant in the darkest corner of a shadowy Victorian front parlor.

Plumbago—The Victorians grew all of the plumbagos that are popular today, including the white, blue and red varieties. In addition, all of those profuse blooming, rambunctious vines were also important florist flowers in the early 20th Century. At present, they are enjoying a second flirt with fame—plumbagos are often found in modern outdoor gardens planted in tubs for summer performance. For that purpose, the powder blue variety provides a rare color to accent the greens and whites of an old-fashioned Victorian planting.

Russellia—Although the Fountain Plant is not widely grown on modern windowsills, the Victorians were very fond of that red flowering hanging basket plant introduced in 1812. Today we know it as *R. equisetiformis*, a name that refers to its physical similarity to *Equisetum*, or Horsetails. But in the 19th Century, the plant was known as *R. Juncea*. In the tropics, the Fountain Plant is popular for edging gardens and borders.

Skimmia—We grow this evergreen as a garden shrub south of Zone 6, but the Victorians often invited *Skimmia japonica* indoors along with *Daphne odora* to add fragrance to their winter windowsill. Introduced in 1845, this native of Japan owed its popularity partly to its Oriental connection. Unfortunately, it is not appropriate for the average home due to its preference for very cool nighttime temperatures.

Sparmannia—The Indoor Linden is a large and robust tropical that rapidly becomes too sizable for the average home, but that fact did not dampen the Victorian enthusiasm for the plant. Introduced from the Cape of Good Hope in 1790, *Sparmannia africana* was often grown indoors in Europe, and the custom eventually crossed the ocean to North America.

Tropaeolum—Nasturtiums were among the windowsill's most popular hanging basket plants. Despite their tendency to attract red spider mites, nasturtiums were omnipresent in Victorian homes, especially after hybridizing escalated in 1830. With the encouragement of breeders, who enhanced the colors and added splashed petals to the basic yellow species, their fame continued to grow and has only recently dwindled. Nasturtiums prefer a sunny window and must be groomed continually to remove the spent foliage. Although they are no longer common basket plants, they are frequently found in summer window boxes.

Of Mites and Men

CHAPTER XI

AN OUNCE OF PREVENTION AND A POUND OF CURE

In 1897, Lizzie Page Hillhouse began her book, *Houseplants and How to Succeed with Them*, by quoting Virgil, "Having suffered, I know how to help those who are in distress." And, true to her claim, she ministered to the needs of struggling amateur horticulturists. In the pages of that volume, sprinkled among the tempting descriptions of exotic plants, the reader could find remedies for the many problems that inevitably arise when entertaining tropicals in the home.

On the surface, all looked calm and tranquil in the parlor. Buds sat ready to burst, tendrilled vines clamored up window frames and vegetation overflowed everywhere. But that peaceable kingdom was not realized without a struggle. Shortly after the first houseplant set foot in the parlor, the first plant pest also took up residence in the home. The ensuing life and death foray was the initial scrimmage in what became a never ending battle between humans and houseplant pests.

Somewhere in the recesses of every Victorian window gardener's abode was a closet jammed full of syringes, insect smokers, leaf sponges and insecticidal preparations. Bags of tobacco, unslaked lime and arsenic, bottles of whale oil and fir tree oil stood ready to be marshalled. The gentle housewife suddenly found herself in full command of a bloody battle between luscious vegetation and its ruthless predators.

Of course, the fight between people and pests is as old as civilization itself. The medieval housewife was repeatedly called upon to keep moths out of the linens and weevils out of the grain. But never before had women encountered plant pests in the intimate recesses of the parlor. That particular problem was traditionally confined to the exterior of the home. Although plant-eating insects may have wreaked havoc with the season's crop and the family's food supply, they did not cross the threshold into traditional female territory. An insect in the garden was a nasty nuisance, certainly, but its removal was a man's job. Furthermore, it was usually eradicated by a natural enemy, or an act of God, or both. However, it was an entirely different matter when an insect set up housekeeping among the front parlor's horticultural collection. Not only was its presence difficult to ignore, but its disposal fell wholly on the shoulders of the person who had invited the infested plant into the house. In such an artificial environment, no natural enemy was likely to come to the aid of the afflicted parties. So began the science and practice of applying insecticides and fungicides indoors.

Insects are an inherent problem whenever and wherever plants are cultivated. They are a problem in the vegetable garden, in the flower garden, and even in the forest and meadow. Inevitably, they were present in the windowsill garden. However, the romantic Victorians did not spend a great deal of time discussing the darker side of horticulture. If all was not perfect in paradise, it was not immediately evident from the horticultural literature of the 19th Century. An occasional author mentioned insects in passing, but they rarely dwelt on the matter. For the most part, writers adhered to the old precept, "If you can't say anything nice, don't say anything at all."

Faced with the absence of written evidence, we can only surmise that the Victorians devoted a great deal of time and effort to their battle against bugs. Judging from old photographs and engravings of salubrious botanicals wending their way around the parlor, it is safe to assume that 19th Century gardeners were generally victorious in their eradication efforts. Although the methods and devices of pest control were definitely not part of polite tea-time conversation, they were evidently a part of daily life. And, while insecticides maintained a low profile, they nonetheless developed increased sophistication and effectiveness as the Victorian Era progressed.

At first, the means of pest control was primitive. Vigilance was the key to success, as Robert Buist intimated in the 1854 edition of his *American Garden Directory*, "Man cannot be too frequently guarded against his foes . . . and no profession has more than that of the Horticulturist."

In those early years, the primary means of insect destruction was "the thumb and finger, properly applied" to remove all offending wildlife from the resident botanicals. Lacking adequate methods for halting a full-blown infestation, gardeners were advised to nip the problem while it was still only a minor annoyance. Cleanliness was the answer to a host of ills, and it was the best preventive medicine garden writers could suggest. As Henry T. Williams pointed out in *Window Gardening*, "If plants were as carefully washed and tended as many pet animals are, there would be no need for any remedies against insects."

Good grooming was essential. All dead leaves, faded flowers or yellowing foliage had to be removed from the premises immediately. Filth bred bugs.

Weekly baths played a major role in achieving cleanliness. Applying the "healing waters" was one of the most frequently prescribed methods of insect prevention and control. Plant bathing was practiced throughout the century, even after other methods of insect control were developed. And, as the era progressed, the variations on the plant bath theme became increasingly ingenious. Plants were dipped in ice cold or hot (120–130°F) water; they were sponged and sprinkled. In fact, the daily syringings and twice weekly bathings constituted more attention to hygiene than most non-photosynthesizing members of the family received.

Plant syringing became a favorite indoor sport; and a syringe was as necessary to the household's upkeep as a mop or broom. A rigorous spray with cold water not only dislodged dust from the leaf's surface, it also washed away insect eggs and mature pests. Syringes appeared in all shapes and sizes. The least expensive model was the "Elastic Plant Sprinkler" which could be had in 1887 for the modest price of $1.50 postpaid. A fancier, larger, easier to use, but also more expensive brass syringe was popular with conservatory owners who had more space to cover and more money to invest in the undertaking. Large mobile pump sprayers were called into action for syringing full-sized greenhouses.

A metal pump sprayer.

This engraving shows how the daily syringing was properly applied. The water should cleanse the under surface of the leaf where insects often hide. Illustration from *Home Floriculture* by Chas. N. Page.

Many years elapsed before anything more potent than water was used on houseplants. Early in the game, gardeners had discovered that their patients were often killed in the process of being cured. Even water (especially icy cold or hot water) could damage a plant, and applying poisons was a much trickier business. No one was completely confident about the particulars of application and dilution. Professionals often confessed to confusion about eradication procedures, and amateur indoor gardeners were infinitely more baffled and therefore more cautious in their battle against bugs.

In the early part of the century, indoor gardeners were confined to employing concoctions of diluted wood ash and unslaked lime to repel insects. The combination was left to sit for a period of time—everyone had a favorite recipe that governed the dilution, the waiting period and the application procedure. Then, it was either watered into the soil, syringed on the leaves or the plant was unceremoniously dunked into the lime/ash brew. Afterwards, the leaves were rewashed or the soil was drenched with clear water to remove the poison.

Variations on the basic lime/ash theme were recommended for whatever ailed your plants. Outdoor and indoor gardeners alike relied on those two all-purpose insecticides. For example, Charles Dudley Warner tried heaping wood ash around his plants in the vegetable garden to confound the resident predators. The plan may have worked, but was the victory worth the consequences? He voiced his doubts in *My Summer in the Garden*,

> Speaking of those yellow squash bugs, I think I disheartened them by covering the plants so deep with soot and wood-ashes that they could not find them; and I am in doubt if I shall ever see the plants again.

Nicotine, or tobacco smoke, became an increasingly common weapon of combat in the bug battle. The use of tobacco for insect control undoubtedly began in greenhouses where the task of fumigation was performed by professional gardeners. However, as amateurs "caught wind" of that effective cure, it was used in conservatories and even for window garden collections. Finally, the ladies had found a constructive employment for one of their husband's worst habits.

By the end of the century, "smoking" became part of the regular maintenance routine. In the greenhouse, gardeners set fire to little piles of coals and tobacco stems placed in the gravel walkways, encouraging them to smolder and fill the structure with fumes. Modern tobacco "bombs" contain saltpeter to keep the fumes puffing without human assistance. But early greenhousemen had to constantly tend their fires to keep the coals glowing and the smoke pouring out. The chore was not handled with a great deal of consideration for personal safety. In fact, daredevil antics often accompanied fumigation. Andrew Jackson Downing described a procedure that was so common, it became par for the course for greenhouse assistants. Alternatives were slow in coming.

> I have often had occasion to observe, that during the process of smoking glass-houses, for the purpose of killing green fly, the men who perform this duty remain in the

Fumigation was usually performed in the great outdoors rather than smoking up the living quarters.

house to keep, as they say, the coals glowing; and they blow away [the smoke] with bellows, or what is more convenient, with their own wind-pipes. Having filled the house with smoke, they retire half suffocated.

Eventually, some progressive greenhouses were fitted with special portholes which could be closed when not in use, but were opened and hooked to smoking devices weekly so that caretakers could remain safely outside while fumigating. However, the typical greenhouse did not contain this revolutionary feature.

For smaller jobs, or spot fumigating, a special bellows fitted with a tin tobacco box was usually employed. These devices were quite common and were not used with protective respirators. However, most homeowners were wise enough to confine their bellowing chores to the great outdoors rather than smoking up their living quarters.

During the winter, there were fewer alternatives available to windowsill growers. Some window gardeners requisitioned a closet or a closed barrel for fumigating indoor plants. More commonly, the offending plant was taken outside and smoked on a mild day. Of course, tobacco was most effective when the plant was forced to bask in its vapors for a few minutes rather than simply allowing the fumes to dissipate into the surrounding air. For example, half an hour was the recommended exposure for eradicating aphids. To facilitate the operation, the Victorians fashioned a bevy of ingenious fumigating tents. Some gardeners constructed special wire frames which they covered with muslin. More resourceful amateurs recycled household materials for the purpose. Broken parasols were requisitioned and, surprisingly, even old hoop skirt petticoats were occasionally called into service to keep smoke hovering around houseplants.

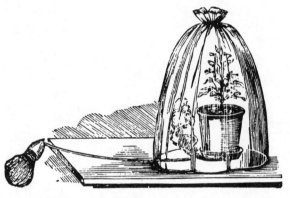

A fumigating tent.

Tobacco was employed primarily for the control of aphids, which were generally referred to as "green flies" in period books. Although aphids are the most frequently encountered indoor plant pest, they are relatively easy to conquer compared to other houseplant foes. Fortunately, they are also among the easiest foes to identify. It takes very little imagination to connect that evil-looking, little sucking insect with the havoc that it wreaks on the resident botanicals.

More elusive and better camouflaged insects were not quite so easily detected, especially by the novice grower. Scale looks like an innocent brown bump on the plant's stem, mealy bugs look more like cotton balls than destructive adversaries and red spider mites are so tiny that they are hardly visible at all. For identification purposes, the newly popularized microscope was invaluable. That magnifying tool put everything into its proper perspective, revealing minute malefactors that appeared to be merely specks of dirt to the naked eye. Many authors urged their readers to invest in one of those tools and "examine anything having a suspicious appearance." In *Gardening for Ladies*, Mrs. Loudon went one step further and suggested that "entomology should . . . be studied by everyone who loves flowers."

Despite the newly available tools, entomology was a novel science for most Victorians, and they had a great deal of trouble correctly identifying the sources of their pest problems. The most difficult concept for a 19th Century novice to grasp was how a microscopic insect could possibly cause such visible and drastic devastation. Even professionals had difficulty connecting the red spider mite with its symptoms as Peter Henderson attested in *Practical Horticulture*. Henderson discovered a greenhouse riddled with red spider and angrily ordered the house's manager to dispatch the insects posthaste. Undoubtedly, he had a spraying regime in mind, but his manager assumed that the problem called for more drastic measures,

> John was on all occasions rather demonstrative, but one morning he came rushing towards me, his face radiant with triumph, with his hat off, but clasped in his hands, in a careful manner, evidently having something of no common value within it. Before I had time to inquire what was the cause of his excitement, he yelled out. "I've got him! bedad! I've got him at last!"
>
> "What have you got?" I inquired, expecting to see something in the way of a rat or mouse.
>
> "Arrah, the big divil himself, the blaggard that has been doin' us all the mischief, the *Reed Sphider*!" and opening his hat, a villainous Tarantula-looking fellow ran out, bigger than a thousand red spiders . . .

Relentless insects such as red spider mites require more elaborate control measures than merely soapy water or tobacco smoke. Those tiny mites are not phased by fumigation with tobacco and cannot readily be destroyed with "thumb and finger". An early remedy was simply to maintain an atmosphere that was distasteful to the insect. To this end, the leaves were sprayed with cold water and the environment was kept moist—red spiders prefer a hot, dry climate. This worked wonders as preventative medicine, but it did nothing to destroy an already extant population. Henry T. Williams had two rather unique ideas for eradicating the microscopic mite. He suggested boiling 1 qt. of quassia chips in 3 pts. of water until 2 qts. of the brew had evaporated. The infested specimens were then dipped in the decoction. Or, if sufficient helping hands could be enlisted, the red pepper cure might be put into effect,

> It should be dusted upon with a pepper castor, holding the plant bottom side upwards, while another person dusts on the pepper. Of course, you must take care not to let it fall in any quantity upon the soil of the pot, lest it should injure the roots.

More daring, but also more effective for killing tough insects, was the use of sulphur. Of course, this remedy could only be used in greenhouses. Respirators had yet to be invented, and therefore direct application was out of the question. However, as early as 1840, Samuel Hereman, who wrote *Blight on Flowers* (assisted by an anonymous "nobleman's gardener") reported that a system of washing the exterior of the greenhouse flues with sulphur had been developed. The system worked wonderfully until the heating season began,

> ... this answered very well until fire was lighted in the flues, the sulphur then ignited, and the destruction of vegetable as well as animal life was the consequence.

Five years later, James N. Eley announced in *The American Florist* that a slightly safer system of setting pans of sulphur on a warm (but not hot) section of the flue was being practiced by professional nurserymen. But, for obvious reasons, sulphur was not used in the home.

Mealy bugs are more easily identified than red spider mites, but their tenacious character rendered them an equally pernicious foe. Although most insects show a preference for certain families of plants, mealy bugs are indiscriminate. Nearly everything that grows looks appetizing to a mealy bug. They are the bane of any window gardener's existence. Naturally, as the windowsill collection expanded, so did the mealy bug malice while gardeners desperately sought solutions.

Mealy bugs responded to soap and water as well as applications of tobacco water, although they were not affected by fumigation. *Success with Flowers* suggested that its readers try a kerosene and alcohol dip, and the cure was extremely effective. In fact, it proved so efficacious that ethanol alcohol is still frequently employed as a mealy bug remedy. The poison is usually applied by touching an alcohol soaked cotton swab to the offending insect. Equally popular in the 19th Century, but no longer appropriate today was the practice of applying whale-oil soap dissolved in water.

Scale paid no heed to either dense tobacco fumes or whale-oil applications. And scale was a serious problem, especially on the thick-leaved foliage plants such as oleander, palms, ficus and ferns that were so fashionable in mid-century. Growers had a tendency to simply ignore that lethargic insect which did no immediately apparent damage to its host. However, that seemingly innocuous bump on the stem eventually took its toll.

To save the resident botanical in distress from a protracted and painful demise by scale, several different concoctions were recommended. In fact, by mid-century, a great deal of research had already been conducted by professionals eager to rid their greenhouse-grown pineapple crops of that destructive foe. However, although nurserymen had explored methods of scale control, most of their remedies were only practical under glass.

Originally, scale was removed by filling a greenhouse with steam at 110°F. temperatures. Not only was the procedure difficult, but a grower also risked heat damage to his crop, especially if the sun was shining while steaming.

Chemical concoctions were often summoned to aid in the battle against scale. Desperate nurserymen literally emptied the contents of their medicine cabinets and tool boxes into the greenhouse. Samuel Hereman's book, *Blight on Flowers*, written in 1840, proposed several favorite formulas developed by the period's best growers. The roster read something like an heirloom cookbook complete with Nicol's, Griffin's, Millar's, M'Murtie's and Baldwin's favorite recipes. However, the ingredients were anything but appetizing; they included turpentine, camphor, nux vomica, rat poison, train oil and stable urine.

With the popularization of houseplants, the gentle housewife joined in the battle against scale. That insect has an affinity for dark, poorly ventilated situations, and so it found the front parlor entirely to its liking. However, something a little simpler (and more savory) than M'Murtie's recipe was called for in the parlor. Applications of sweet oil or soapy water were the most common remedies. Soluble fir-tree oil, the prototype of our modern Cedaflora, was just beginning its reign of popularity. Although that novel remedy was highly recommended for scale, 19th Century writers always added a cautionary note suggesting that the oil be applied only in the evenings and washed off 10 minutes after application.

Thrips were occasionally troublesome on shady, cramped windowsills. As always, the experts advised curing the cause before treating the symptoms. The obvious solution was to provide better spacing and more light as a precautionary measure. To dispatch an already extant infestation of thrips, gardeners called a concoction of tobacco water mixed with soot and lime into service.

Although worms do no direct damage to a plant, they persist in the nasty habit of heaving the soil from its container. Hand-picking was suggested as the most efficient means of removing offending worms from the premises. A more serious concern was wire worms, which were dissuaded by burying potato slices in the soil.

Slugs always have been, and probably will forever remain the bane of every gardener's existence throughout the ages. The earliest treatment recorded was documented in the 14th Century when Arabian gardeners scattered ashes to discourage that grotesque and noxious intruder. The Victorians came up with a few new maneuvers in the age-old battle against slugs. *The Ladies' Floral Cabinet* suggested spreading little heaps of bran on slate pieces placed around the slug's hunting grounds to attract the pests. Every morning the proceeding evening's collection of captured slugs was removed by simply sweeping the beasts off into salt water. Not only did this method obviate the necessity of handling those slimy malefactors, but it also eased the gardener's conscience. *The Ladies' Cabinet* assured its readers that "death was instantaneous."

The bran on slate trick was but one of many ingenious schemes engineered to foil slugs. Some gardeners tried scattering turnips around their plants to attract the pests. More effective was the scheme of placing elevated inverted pots around the garden. Slugs tended to gravitate toward the dark, damp, moist environment under the pot and adhere to the clay sides. Every morning, the traps were checked and the evening's catch was disposed of. The inverted pot idea was only one of many slug attracting devices. In fact, in the latter years of the century, there were nearly as many slug snares suggested in the pages of gardening books and periodicals as there were mouse traps illustrated in household manuals.

Gardeners complained long and loud about the despicable slug. And one of the slug's greatest and most vociferous adversaries was Celia Thaxter, an ardent indoor and outdoor gardener on the Isles of Shoals off Portsmouth, NH. She expounded on gardening and its many pleasures and pitfalls in *An Island Garden* published in 1894. Unlike most of her contemporary female garden writers, she did not waste many words idly romanticizing about her flowers. Instead, she addressed practical issues. As can be easily imagined, she was continually combatting slugs in her damp seaside garden, and her ultimate solution was to import a predator,

> In the thickest of my fight with slugs someone said to me "Everything has its enemy; the enemy of the slug is the toad. Why don't you import toads?" I snatched the hope held out to me, and immediately wrote to a friend on the continent, "In the name of the Prophet, Toads!" At once a force of only too willing boys was set about the work of catching every toad within reach.

Celia Thaxter went on to describe her glee at the receipt of the new pets and her fascination with their physical beauty. But beauty is in the eyes of the beholder, and few of her fellow gardeners were equally enthusiastic about the prospects of adopting a regiment of toads to patrol the premises. However, when faced with the choice between slug or toad, the amphibian was the lesser of the two evils. *The Mayflower* stressed that those happy, horny hunters were the best natural enemies for a long list of other odious foes,

> Should you have a greenhouse or conservatory try to keep toads in it, for they will keep your place clean of woodlice, cockroaches, slugs, in fact, every insect which is troublesome to your plants. I have at least a dozen toads in our private greenhouses . . . They keep in their holes in day time, therefore you cannot see much of them, but when it gets dark their work begins.

In addition to utilizing all of their available resources in the fight against bugs, new and exotic remedies were continually being imported. Quassia chips, from the South American *Quassia amara*, were often used as an insecticide. More elusive, was the popular Persian Insect Powder which appeared on the market in mid-century. Its ingredients remained a carefully guarded secret for many years. Finally, scientists solved the mystery of the active ingredient, and publicly divulged that it was pyrethrum from the tropical daisy. However, for most of the century, North Americans could not manage to procure seeds of the plant. The powder was produced in Caucasia, and the natives were sufficiently wise to the ways of the Western world to know that if they parted with seeds of their daisy, the country's main source of revenue would quickly vanish. After a series of bogus shipments, an entomologist from the U.S. Dept. of Agriculture finally succeeded in imported the seeds of the pyrethrum daisy in the 1880s.

While we are addressing the painful topic of pest problems, it is also interesting to note that certain insects did not plague 19th Century indoor gardeners.

Although the greenhouse whitefly is one of our most hated and virulent pests, it was never mentioned in 19th Century books. Whitefly was first recorded in this country in 1870, but it apparently took time to circulate and become a force to be reckoned with. Cyclamen mite, which wreaks havoc with impatiens and many other plants that were grown on the 19th Century windowsill, did not enter North America until 1898. Although the Victorians may have cursed the newly encountered problems of indoor gardening, they could be thankful for many small blessings.

Not only did the Victorians have a new realm of insects with which to contend, they also had to grapple with the baffling problems of plant disease. When the era began, scientists had only a very primitive understanding of the pathology of plant disease, while the cures for plant ailments were a complete mystery. Little was known about diseases in farm crops that had been cultivated for centuries. And, of course, the new problems of houseplant ailments were but another facet of a barely explored science. However, there was a strong desire to remedy the prevailing ignorance. Everyone, scientists and laymen alike, joined in a united effort to find causes and seek cures. In fact, in 1837, the Pennsylvania Horticultural Society offered a $500. reward to anyone who submitted an effective remedy for pear blight. The entries included schemes for hanging iron in trees, binding trunks with brimstone-soaked rags and driving nails into the trunk. Although the Pennsylvania Horticultural Society may have found the submissions entertaining, they found none worthy of the $500. prize.

Fortunately, indoor gardeners did not have to contend with anything as tricky as pear blight. The worst of their problems was merely mildew. Even so, mildew was grievously misunderstood until mid-century. According to Mrs. Loudon, writing in *Gardening for Ladies* in 1849,

> The cause [of mildew] was long unknown; and some supposed it to be produced by unhealthy winds, and others that it was the work of insects, it is now, however, satisfactorily proved to be a parasitic plant or Fungus growing on the leaves.

Although scientists were beginning to understand mildew, they were far from discovering a cure at the time when *Gardening for Ladies* was published. Mrs. Loudon could only feebly suggest the removal and burning of all affected parts. Much later in the era, in 1885, Bordeaux Powder was developed. That copper based fungicide was first used on grapevines. In fact, Bordeaux Powder owed its development to the fact that someone observed that extraordinarily healthy and virtually mildew-free grapevines grew in the region immediately surrounding a copper factory. Bordeaux Powder remained the primary fungicide in use until recently when it was superseded by Benomyl for the control of mildew.

Although the Victorians were on shaky ground in their knowledge of disease pathology, nonetheless, they knew how to handle a sick or weak plant. In fact, their nursing skills far surpass those of many modern growers, despite our expanded repertoire of chemicals. James N. Eley, writing in 1845, suggested a procedure for the care of invalid botanicals that reveals a keen sympathy for the suffering plant, and an equally astute insight into the conditions that harbor disease,

> When a plant appears sickly, it should be taken out of the pot and the roots examined, and all that are decayed should be cut off, and the plant repotted in fresh soil and kept a little moist, but not too wet, and if not much injured, it will soon recover.

In *Winter Greeneries in the Home*, Edwin Johnson was quick to point out that most houseplants do not die of either disease or insects, they perish of misunderstanding. He explained, "In general it is the result of either disagreement between the plant and the place or of neglect . . ." He presented a roster of the most frequent blunders—too much water, too much or too little sunshine, too low a temperature or sudden fluctuations in temperature, lack of nutrients, and over-potting were the most common causes contributing to the untimely demise of resident botanicals. Although Johnson's list was blissfully straightforward, the challenge to the reader lay in correctly identifying which of those seven trans-

A healthy plant is a happy plant according to this advertisement.

gressions she had committed. As with all aspects of gardening, the task was easier said than done.

Gardeners shared other knowledge in addition to insecticidal formulas and suggestions for disease prevention. Every gardener had his or her own private trick-of-the-trade for growing better houseplants than those dwelling on the windowsill next door. Many of the era's most effective secret formulas undoubtedly died with the lady of the house and never passed her lips. But, fortunately, a few family "recipes" have come down to us over the years.

The Victorians had a genius for using common, ordinary household goods in the window garden. According to *The Household*, charcoal put brilliancy into the colors of dahlias, roses and petunias; while carbonate of soda reddened pink hyacinths. Ammonia (10 oz. to 1 g. of water) produced strong growth and encouraged prolific flowers. Egg shells scattered on top of the soil strengthened a potted plant. In addition, casein was often painted on glass for shading houseplants in summer.

Pots for houseplants were the subject of an on-going debate. Victorians grew their houseplants in an incredibly diverse collection of eclectic containers, and they were continually arguing over which was the best for the purpose. Depending upon the family's income and taste, the household's botanical collection resided in anything from broken tea cups, jam dishes, basins, tin cans, rustic hollowed logs, wooden barrels (preferably pine or hemlock but definitely not spruce), china, terra-cotta, to empty coconut hulls.

The use of glazed versus unglazed pottery was an issue of much contention in the 19th Century. One faction felt that glazing added necessary beauty to plain, unadorned clay; while another strongly insisted that glazing inhibited the root's access to oxygen. Testimonials for and against glazing flew back and forth, clashing in gardening periodicals. *Vick's Monthly* finally laid the matter to rest in 1884 when they reported that the *Journal of Horticulture* had conducted an experiment which proved conclusively that plants potted in glazed pottery thrived as well as those in porous containers. Even so, most Victorians preferred plain, unglazed clay pots which they set inside highly ornamental jardinieres (also known as cache pots). Those outer containers were a pleasure to behold, often boasting inspirational scenes such as cupids flitting about, babies happily playing or classically attired maidens dancing in a ring around the periphery. They also served the very practical purpose of protecting the roots from drying out too frequently or scorching in bright light. Toward this end, sphagnum moss was often tucked into the space between the cache pot and the plant's clay container.

Crocking was always used when potting. In fact, the practice of crocking pots has only recently fallen into disuse. The Victorians made a science of carefully crocking the bottoms of their containers with broken bits of old pots, sandstone or charcoal to facilitate proper drainage. Andrew Jackson Downing suggested a complex formula consisting of 1 concave pot shard placed over the drainage hole, followed by a layer of bean-sized crockery and finally topped by a layer of

Jardinieres were extremely ornamental, but they also performed a useful purpose. Illustration from *The Window Flower Garden* by Julius J. Heinrich.

pea-sized bits of pottery carefully placed in each container before the potting medium was added.

When potting a plant, the Victorians were firm believers in the theory that every species prefers a custom-made soil to be mixed individually for its edification. Fuchsias were grown in one type of medium, while pelargoniums were given another. Basically, the medium was composed of different ratios of soil, manure, sand, moss and leaf mold. Interestingly, 19th Century gardeners ridiculed the use of bone meal as a fertilizer instead of manure. However, fertilizer in the form of cow or horse manure tea was applied regularly and generously.

Fashionable gardeners fertilized with guano. The gardeners in this country were first introduced to that miraculous manure at the August 1830 Agricultural Exhibition of the Massachusetts Horticultural Society. Although the vegetables on display did not excite much interest that year, a large crowd of spectators continually amassed around a pile of dung collected in Peru by Capt. Smith of Quincy, Mass. Capt. Smith reported that the Spaniards called their wonderful fertilizer "guano". Before the end of the season, guano was the talk of the town, and the fad eventually seized the entire country. Many gardeners swore by the stuff. Others remained skeptical, especially Henry Ward Beecher who wrote in 1859,

> The guano fever sent hundreds of ships a-dung-hunting all over the earth; and lucky were they who espied a precious heap of excrement. How little did the penguins and seagulls of the Pacific imagine, that their unconscious observance of the laws of nature was one day to figure so largely on the British exchange, and to raise such a bustle in chemical laboratories.

Despite the individual opinions concerning that expensive form of fertilizer, the fact that bat dung became such an enthralling topic spoke well for the prevailing interest in horticulture. The guano mania was definitely another example of the fervor that surrounded the cultivation of plants.

All things considered, the first indoor gardeners did a remarkable job of maintaining their ground against the inroads of houseplant pests and diseases while also setting the pace for future generations. Their means of pest control might have been primitive, and their understanding of disease may have been shaky, but nevertheless, they won their battles by sheer perseverance. And, most importantly, the attention and concern that those matters received testified to the fact that the Victorian Era was the houseplant's heyday.

CHAPTER XII

THE BUSINESS OF HOUSEPLANTS

TOGETHER WITH THE PROGRESSION of increasingly spectacular plants infiltrating the front parlor marched a growing band of plantsmen serving the burgeoning horticultural interest. The era was dominated by colorful human personalities as well as bright botanicals. Explorers captured exotics in the wild and came jubilantly scurrying home to introduce their treasures to "civilization." Monarchs financed excursions and societies held exhibitions of the booty. Writers wrote and housewives read. Committed gardeners, horticulturists and botanists were instrumental at every step along the way.

Perhaps the most important people incident to the horticultural renaissance were the seedsmen and purveyors of rare plants. Whether compelled by pure, unselfish devotion or driven by undiluted financial greed, those men and women took the leap into the commercial realm. For better or for worse, they invested their time, wealth and expertise in a growing field. And their efforts did not go unrewarded—the timing was right and the public was receptive. In that atmosphere, horticultural enterprises could hardly fail.

By mid-century, it seemed as though everyone had horticulture on their mind—the country was teeming with horticulturists. As a new science, it opened a vast array of fascinating fields beckoning enterprising young people to enter. In addition to the wealthy patrons who dabbled in horticulture, the profession swelled with a growing body of trained botanists, pomologists, educators and scholars. With all of that interest afoot, there was an obvious potential for economic exploitation. Few men could ignore the golden opportunity to fuse fortune and fancy. And so, at some point in their careers, most 19th Century horticulturists tried their hands at selling plants to the public. Many found the venture to be immensely profitable.

The first purveyors of plants plied their trade primarily with overseas customers. Throughout the 17th and 18th Centuries, botanists abroad had a much greater interest in collecting North American flora than we had in cultivating the fruits of our own native forests and meadows. While North Americans were busy battling the elements on the home front, European horticulturists were leisurely admiring the botanical products of the New World.

Not only did they admire our flora, they were also willing to pay well for it. North American native plants figured as important commodities of foreign trade. Collectors such as John Bartram managed to finance his expeditions by sending off the botanical bounty from our forests to eager recipients in Europe. And, in return, the grateful plant collectors of Europe politely exchanged some of the botanical novelties available in their country.

At first, the general public showed little interest in the redistribution of botanical wealth. But, a few ardent souls were sufficiently curious about exotic plants to prompt the creation of two North American botanical gardens in the early 1700s. John Bartram opened his collection to Philadelphians in 1728, and Robert Prince established the Linnaean Botanical Garden in Flushing, NY in 1730.

Horticulture was a youthful science in North America at the time, and the country was not yet awake to its economic potential. The first botanical gardens were founded simply as display areas, with no ulterior motive other than per-haps an underlying desire to gain acceptance and publicity. Initially, Bartram and Prince were undoubtedly guided by their consuming devotion to horticul-ture rather than any design to augment their wealth. However, Robert Prince was blessed with a long line of horticulturally astute sons, grandsons and great-grandsons who systematically converted his exhibition grounds into a large and successful business.

By the time William Prince II (1766–1842) took charge of his father's botanical collection, the public was beginning to evince an interest in horticul-ture. In fact, they were so keen about the specimens in his collection that the logical next step was to propagate and sell rare plant material. Soon, the Linnaean Garden became a thriving business which flourished through the generations until its liquidation in 1849.

In contrast to Bartram and Prince who had slowly eased into business, David Landreth was the first North American to open an establishment totally dedi-cated to the sale of horticultural goods. Soon after arriving from England, Landreth settled comfortably in Philadelphia and, in 1784, established a seed nursery. Business was good and his sons were interested. The family eventually bought another 30 acres of land devoted to producing ornamental crops, providing the residents of Philadelphia with a ready supply of camellias (his catalog eventually listed 25 varieties) as well as rhododendrons, hyacinths, citrus and such rarities as bananas and the Bird of Paradise (*Strelitzia reginae*).

When one man discovers a lucrative new business, other enterprising gentlemen are bound to follow suit. David Landreth was succeeded by a string of other successful seedsmen who opened shop in Philadelphia including John Mackejohn in 1792, William Leeson in 1794 and Bernard McMahon who started business in 1800. The contagion spread to other cities. Most notably,

Grant Thorburn set up shop in New York City in 1802.

Thorburn is a glowing example of the inherent color associated with the early seedsmen. That feisty little Scotsman landed on American shores in the late 1700s. He stood a mere 4 ft. 10 in. from head to toe, but nevertheless, he packed that tiny frame full of energy, ingenuity, a flaming religious passion and a confessed weak spot for pretty women. Apparently, he found all of those character traits valuable in his future horticultural endeavors.

We are fortunate to have a first hand account of Grant Thorburn's rocky horticultural career immortalized in his autobiography, *Life and Writings of Grant Thorburn*, written in 1852 shortly before he celebrated his 80th birthday. At that ripe old age, his memory remained as clear as a bell, and the book begins with a vivid account of his youthful arrival in bustling New York City. He brought to this

Grant Thorburn at the ripe old age of 79.

country skills and training as a wrought-nail worker and he followed that trade until the grocery business beckoned. It was then that horticulture entered his life. He wrote,

> About this time the ladies in New York were beginning to show their taste for flowers; and it was customary to sell the empty flower-pots in the grocery stores ...

Not only did he carry a ready supply of pots in his grocery store, but he went one step further and painted the pots green. His female patrons clamored for the unique product. The new item increased business, kept his store bustling with comely feminine customers and also opened his eyes to the commercial prospects of horticulture. With awakened interest, he happened to spot a new, exotic plant at a pedlar's stall while shopping one day in the city. Considering the enthusiastic reception that his other horticultural products had received, he could scarcely pass it by. Years later, he described that fortuitous meeting,

> One day ... I observed a man, for the first time, selling Flower-plants in the Fly Market ... As I carelessly passed along, I took a leaf, and rubbing it between finger and thumb, asked him what was the name of it. He answered, a rose geranium. This, as far as I can recollect, was the first time that I ever heard that there was a geranium in the world; as before I had no taste for ... plants. I looked a few minutes at the plant ... and thought it would look well if removed into one of my green flower pots, to stand on my counter and draw attention ... Next day, someone fancied and pur-chased plant and pot. Next day I went when the market was nearly over, judging the man would sell cheaper, rather than have the trouble of carrying them over the river, as he lived in Brooklyn ... Accordingly, I purchased 2 plants; and having sold them ... I continued to go at the close of the market, and always bargained for the unsold plants. And the man finding me a useful customer, would assist me to carry them home, and show me how to shift the plants out of his pots and put them into green pots.

So began what became a thriving plant shop, which eventually evolved into a seed business as well. Thorburn described the process of the transformation,

> The thing being a novelty, began to draw attention; people carrying their country friends to see the curiosities of the city, would stop in to see my plants. In some of these visits the strangers would express a wish to have some of these plants, but having so far to go, could not carry them. Then they would ask if I had no such seed of such plants ...

Apparently, there were no suppliers of seed in the city at the time, so Thorburn was left to his own devices. Not being an experienced grower, he com-missioned his friend from the Fly Market to stay at home and produce seed which he contracted to buy wholesale at the season's end.

The project went well and Thorburn eventually increased his stock to include new ornamental plants from Europe. Those novelties proved to be important items in his store, drawing customers from throughout the area. All went well until the 1808 trade embargo put an abrupt end to his European supply. Undaunted, Thorburn bought land and began farming. But, apparently, the little Scotsman was not as lucky in farming as he had been as a salesman. His crops failed, he went bankrupt and spent the next few years in debtor's prison. Fortunately, he was a resilient man, and the experience did not sour his taste for horticulture. Upon his release from prison, he immediately started a second seed store. Again, he labored to build a thriving business which his son eventually inherited.

Despite his diminutive size, Grant Thorburn became a formidable figure on the horticultural scene. He found that his adopted country was prime soil for cultivating the seedsman's trade. In fact, having tested the waters, he was sufficiently confident of the potential for horticultural growth in North America to recommend the occupation to his friends overseas. Apparently unconcerned about competition, he placed an advertisement in a London paper to recruit British gardeners. He had learned a thing or two about the formula for success in the New World, and he generously passed this knowledge on to his colleagues. In his opinion, a seedsman would prosper "if he has sons grown up, or of the age of 18 or 20 years, he might hire a piece of land near the city, and commence raising greenhouse plants for sale. I have known some do very well in this way, and among them is your worthy friend, Thomas Hogg."

To be sure, Thomas Hogg was another success story. He emigrated to North America in 1820, bought a parcel of land and started a florist business only 2 years after arriving. The business flourished and the next generation continued the tradition. Eventually, Thomas Hogg, Jr. became one of the nation's eminent plant hunters, travelling to the Orient and Europe as well as Central and South America to collect plants for the family business.

Hogg's was a common scenario. Countless other gardeners, especially from Britain, Ireland, Scotland and Germany came to this country in the early 1800s and found the going favorable for anyone knowledgeable about plants. There were fortunes to be made. And, not infrequently, fame also attended the proprietors of successful horticultural firms.

In this country, there was a strong feeling of comradeship among nurserymen and seedsmen. The *esprit de corps* within the trade was unusually strong, and this sense of mutual admiration earned horticulturists broad respect. Seedsmen became local celebrities and were often quoted in town papers—their petty arguments and competitive accusations were news of the most intriguing kind. Everyone waited on their words of wisdom and harkened to their advice and opinions.

A little fame goes a long way. Egos became inflated. When seedsmen heard their words quoted throughout the town, they naturally sought a broader audience. Simultaneously, the new advances in communication brought the entire country within earshot. Nineteenth Century horticulturists quickly realized that the most efficient way into the Victorian gardener's home and heart was through magazines. So they set their pens to work authoring articles, publishing and editing plant periodicals and generally rendering their names household words.

The articles that those nurserymen authored were not only filled with practical advice, they were also amazingly easy to read. Many 19th Century horticulturists were extremely articulate and readily able to convey their affection for plants in print. Their articles were heavily laced with romantic visions, with tragedy and comedy. Article after article rolled off the press, each devoted to describing the attributes of a certain plant and each overflowing with superlatives and sentimentality. But, beyond affirming the innocuous concepts of Beauty and Goodness, nurserymen had the business savvy to turn public interest toward products that were plentiful on the market. Their writing was essentially self-serving. On the surface, they were a generation of sticky sentimentalists mooning over pretty flowers. However, a closer look reveals that many were shrewd and resourceful salesmen, in addition to being ardent plant devotees.

James Vick, a popular garden writer as well as the owner of Vick's Seed Company in Rochester, NY and the publisher of *Vick's Monthly Magazine*.

But, not all those fascinating men were drumbeaters. Some horticulturists were undoubtedly wallflowers. For example, Henry A. Dreer, a bulb merchant and seedsmen was described as a man "of modest temperament and frail constitution, who confined himself to business rather closely. He was liberal in public matters, but always kept out of political life." However, Dreer was the exception rather than the rule. To compensate for a few ho-hum horticulturists, the era abounded with other seedsmen who possessed vividly colorful personalities.

A glowing example was William Cobbett, described as "a powerful author, whose porcupine quill, dipped in republican gall, has shook the monarch's throne." Cobbett was one of the few gardeners who did not migrate by choice— his political boisterousness forced him into exile in this country. During his stay here, Cobbett wrote *The American Gardener*, described by his contemporaries as "one of the spiciest books in the whole history of American horticulture." In addition, he opened a seed business and, true to character, he put as much spirit into the distribution of rutabagas as he had poured into wreaking havoc with the British authorities. Not surprisingly, he found a receptive audience of argumentative agriculturalists here. While in exile, he crossed his "porcupine quill" with a group of men who addressed rutabagas with an ardent zeal. Crowds would collect at the Fly Market to witness the spirited Thorburn/Cobbett exchange on the virtues of one vegetable variety over the other. The New York *Evening Post* kept city residents abreast of the score.

All of these characters, both colorful and otherwise, had a rapidly increasing repertoire of botanical material to propel their work forward. Not only did the 19th Century witness the influx of foreign-born and educated horticulturists, but rare plant material regularly arrived from Europe as well. Many immigrants retained ties with gardeners back home who exchanged new tropicals. In fact, the international market was awash with novel species. Seedsmen in this country need do nothing more than wait and receive the goods with open arms. There was no need of spending time and money breeding new varieties.

Throughout most of the century, hybridizing was not energetically pursued in this country. And that situation only began to change after the bulk of tropical botanicals had been plucked from the jungles, introduced, tested and distributed. Hybridizers finally stepped in toward the end of the century to take up the slack left by collectors. Most notably, Americans made substantial additions to the ranks of carnations, chrysanthemums and camellias. In fact, one of the era's preeminent hybridizers, Marshall Pinkney Wilder, who introduced the valuable *Camellia japonica* 'Wilderii', had a reputation for arriving at posh parties replete with a camel's hair brush tucked in his coat pocket "and was always hybridizing plants."

Marshall Wilder was one of the many early North American breeders who undertook hybridizing as a hobby. As fortune would have it, he managed to realize a windfall profit for his efforts. But, he was the exception rather than the rule. Most hybridizing hobbyists worked for the pleasure of creation and experienced little pecuniary gain from their projects. However, the century could boast a handful of professional breeders who labored as "freelancers" for the trade, supplementing their income by dabbling in botanical genetics. A notable example was Mrs. Theodasia Shepherd who left her Midwest home together with her lawyer husband in 1873 to seek their fortune as pioneers in California.

Upon arriving on the West Coast, Attorney Shepherd found that his legal services were rarely called upon. To make ends meet, Mrs. Shepherd earned commissions supplying Peter Henderson's mail-order business with new hybrids of shrubby begonias, tea roses, cosmos, nasturtiums and petunias.

Although North Americans made a substantial contribution to the ranks of a few genera, the bulk of the era's novelties came from abroad where plant breeding was more spirited. In particular, French horticulturists were continually breeding houseplants, and they enjoyed a reputation for introducing some extremely impressive hybrids. Dozens of new pelargoniums and begonias bearing the names of the French aristocracy were featured yearly in North American catalogs. Naturally, there was a steady stream of American nurserymen making pilgrimages to Europe in search of the latest creations.

With all of those new hybrids coming from various sources in this country and abroad, it soon became necessary to establish trial gardens for their testing. At first, this chore was performed in a casual fashion. Well-known gardeners simply received new plant material which they tried out for a year or so while jotting down their impressions. Even large concerns such as W. Atlee Burpee initially had nothing more scientific for their trial grounds than a vacant lot adjacent to a Doylestown, PA residence where Dillwyn E. Darlington sat, gazing out at the gardens, and making note of his favorite flowers from 1883 to 1888. In that year, Burpee acquired a farm specifically dedicated to establishing a trial garden, and they hired Mr. Darlington to officially preside over the experimental grounds.

As hybridizing increased, so did the offerings in trade catalogs. Miss Ella V. Baines, the famed woman florist, advertised no fewer than 20 pelargoniums, 15 hibiscus, 57 chrysanthemums, 7 abutilons, 50 coleus, 88 ever-blooming roses, 12 begonias and 20 fuchsias in her 1898 catalog. Hybrids dominated the list.

Miss Baines' catalog was primarily for mail-order customers, and hers was one of the many newly established nurseries that conducted business through the postal service. With the development of faster, more reliable mail delivery came the appearance of nurseries devoted to shipping living plants. Like so many other 19th Century innovations, mail-order businesses evolved from a unique understanding of the plant buying public.

Being shrewd and discerning businessmen (and women), 19th Century plant purveyors quickly discovered that the best place to make a sale was in the intimacy of the parlor. The Shakers employed this sales approach early in the game, sending their representatives out knocking on doors, peddling their seeds face to face. It did not take long before someone realized that a much more efficient method of reaching the masses was through the mails. Mail-order nurseries sprang up everywhere, and with them a growing catalog industry blossomed. It was a most successful approach.

Mail-order was a realm in which anyone could succeed, regardless of sex. Given a little capital, some good business sense and a touch of old-fashioned luck, a mail-order firm was bound to thrive in that receptive climate. Miss Ella V. Baines was among those who saw the opportunity, although she did not enter the field lightly. She wrote in her 1898 catalog,

> When I started in the floral business 2 years ago, I confess it was with fear and trembling. It was a new field in the commercial world for women to enter. Every one said, "don't", but I did, and I am happy to say that my business success has been assured from the very start.

Mail-order catalogs were not born or perfected overnight. They evolved slowly, beginning as simple lists of plants set in nearly microscopic type and only later blossomed into lavish, colorful magazine-like folders. Undoubtedly, their metamorphosis was due to the ingenuity of individual seedsmen. In *The Standard Cyclopedia of Horticulture*, L. H. Bailey described how one of the earliest catalogs was born. In 1862, a German Quaker named Alfred Conard teamed up with Charles Dingee to sell roses. The business prospered, prompting the partners to hire an experienced propagator in 1869. Soon, they found that a surplus was sitting in the field with no wholesale outlet. That was when their catalog began,

> With rare foresight Mr. Conard conceived of the idea of disposing of it at retail through the mails. The company issued at first a very modest catalogue. It was skillfully prepared, and offered bedding plants, shrubbery, bulbs, seeds and the like, in addition to their attractive list of roses.

Mr. Conard was a perceptive businessman. Not only had he learned that diversity was the secret to success, but he had a feeling for graphic lay-out and design. And he was not alone in his talents, other horticulturists also displayed a natural affinity for good taste and fine artwork which was incorporated into their catalogs. In fact, many of the 19th Century catalogs make modern brochures appear pale and bland in comparison. Their grammar was impeccable, their illustrations were clear, if not always strictly accurate, and nearly every genus was depicted with a picture. Horticultural catalogs were among the first commercial publications to employ color (for example, Miss Baines' catalog added color in 1900), and they remained at the forefront of printing technology throughout the era.

However, any student of business will tell you that the first step toward selling a product is accomplished by exciting interest in the company's brochure. Toward the middle of the century, nurserymen began running advertisements promoting their catalogs in periodicals such as *The Horticulturist* and *The Ladies' Floral Cabinet*. Even magazines owned and published by nurseries generally included competitor's ads.

In addition, 19th Century businessmen were well aware that a commercial reputation is also circulated by word of mouth. Miss Baines began her catalog by making this appeal to members of her own sex, "Buy your Flowers of a Woman." She also asked her patrons to pass the knowledge along, "If you keep sending me your orders and speak a good word about my plants to your friends, I am sure that my success will be permanent."

Robert Buist's mail-order business was brisk.

Other seedsmen found more aggressive means of spreading their reputation. OK Seeds of Watsontown, PA employed a particularly ingenious tactic to promote their wares. Unlike most contemporary catalogs, the cover of the OK Seed brochure did not boast bright, colorful illustrations or a fancy logo. Instead, it was adorned simply with a 5 stanza poem which began,

> Would you have flowers in place of weeds?
> Give to your gardens "OK Seeds"
> Your fields will blossom as the rose
> If "OK Seeds" the farmer sows.

Although the Victorians were ardent lyrists, the verse was meant to be more than merely a cute piece of poetry. Inside the catalog this advertisement appeared,

> To any boy or girl under 10 years of age, who commits the 5 verses of poetry on the cover of this catalogue to memory, and sends us 12 cents in postage stamps to pay packing and postage, we will send Free of all charges 10 Packets of Beautiful Flower Seeds ... and we would request as a special favor that you will recite or sing this little song to your friends.

OK Seeds was not the only company that resorted to gimmickry to gain their clientele. As more plant purveyors turned to mail order, catalogs became more competitive. Obviously, their elaborate formats turned many heads and recruited new indoor gardeners. However, additional sales promotions also excited business. Premiums of magazine subscriptions, free postage offers, extra plants and group rates for clubs were just a few of the many sophisticated marketing tactics that were universally employed.

The home gardener was the focus of all this sophisticated hype, and she duly responded. Every Victorian home with an attic full of old treasures has a box of catalogs tucked away somewhere. They are dog-eared and much thumbed through, while comments are invariably scattered in the margins. They furnished the grist for many a winter evening's contemplation by the hearthside.

The colorful pictures and the tantalizing descriptions in those catalogs made houseplants irresistible. Who could peruse such a brochure without purchasing some hyacinths, a sapphire blue heliotrope and a heavenly scented Confederate Jasmine? People who had never entered a greenhouse or dreamt that dracaenas existed were suddenly introduced to tropical flora in living color. Windowsills in rural towns became just as blossom bedecked as those in the big city. Due to the efforts of a few devoted men and women, rare tropicals were truly within the reach of every man at last.

Improved steam transportation delivered catalogs, seeds and living plants throughout the country.

A plant resplendant parlor windowsill from Edward Sprague Rand's *Flowers for the Parlor and Garden*.

CHAPTER XIII

HORTICULTURE CHANGES THE HOME

MEANWHILE IN THE FRONT PARLOR, the belljar clock still resounded against the woodwork and the gilding still glittered salubriously from every nook and cranny. And yet, by the end of the century, a visit to the family parlor was no longer an experience to be dreaded. Although the parlor remained a maze of tangled furniture, draped fabric and bric-a-brac, tropical plants now added a little levity to the scene, softening the room's stern mien.

Thanks to the resident houseplants, the window shades were thrown open and sizable windows let light stream merrily in. Ventilation cleared the stuffiness and the bustle of plant-related chores relieved the boredom of a previously soporific annex. Finally, architecture was answering to horticulture, and an appreciative array of houseplants produced an informality in the home decor that period tastemakers had failed to achieve by invoking either cajolery or ridicule.

The parlor's metamorphosis was greeted with a collective sigh of relief. No one really wanted to be a stranger in their own sitting room. But the horticultural renaissance had a more marked effect on the era than the mere alteration of the parlor's interior decor. Directly or indirectly, houseplants changed the Victorian world.

Just as many seemingly random occurrences had combined to smooth the entry of houseplants into the home, involvement with houseplants touched off changes in other areas of Victorian society. Hundreds of reverberations, both subtle and momentous, followed in the wake of the horticultural renaissance. As the 19th Century drew to a close, the life of the average North American was vastly different from what it had been 50 years before. And many of the changes that intervened could be traced directly or indirectly to horticulture.

Although the effects of horticulture were felt by Victorians of both sexes throughout the country, in all walks of life, the world of middle class women was most drastically altered as a result of horticultural ventures. It was women who

273

most often commandeered the parlor display. Therefore, they reaped the greatest benefit from that endeavor.

Horticulture awakened women to the world outside the immediate sphere of their homes. Horticulture was a new stimulus in an entirely novel direction, and it provided grist for a mill that was not accustomed to grinding. New avenues were opened into unexplored realms of study, and they beckoned gardeners to delve into science, art and design.

Women first entertained the temptations of horticulture with mixed emotions. They scarcely knew how to view the desires that welled up in their breasts. Suddenly, they yearned to work out of doors. They wanted to share, compare and discuss their interests with like-minded ladies. And yet, those temptations were felt as slightly treasonous to a sex accustomed to devoting its days and nights solely to serving the family.

For the most part, women kept their internal battle quietly simmering in the background. However, a few brave souls had the courage to allow their emotions to surface. Most notably, Catherine Starbuck, the great grandmother of Garden Club member Mrs. K. H. Bragonier of Alexandria, Virginia, was one gardener who struggled with her horticultural inclinations and recorded her feelings. In a letter written in 1879 and published in 1961 in The Garden Club of America's anthology, *Our Garden Heritage*, Mrs. Starbuck described the anatomy of her personal turmoil,

Nantucket, November 11, 1879

I received today _____'s Illustrated Catalogue. I have pored over it all morning and neglected my house. I have no doubt you thought to do me a kindness, but why did you do it? You have upset me, you have unsettled me, you have undone me. I was plodding on in the orthodox and proper manner, and you have completely demoralized me. You have disinclined me to do my duty strictly in that line of life to which I am called. I want to do the things I can't do and I don't want to do the things I have to do. I don't want to be what I am; I want to be what I am not. I am no longer contented and have wants. I want an Antirrhinum. I want a Hunnimannia (Jack would say I had one now). I want a Kaulfaushcia, a Wareweskeii Ochrophalanca, a Manchizanthera tennacctifolia (must be sweetly pretty). I want to be an agriculturist, a florist and a horticulturist, and a pomologist and a botanist and an out of doorsist. I don't want to sweep and dust and make beds and blow the dust out of corners, and spill kerosene and chamois leather the mirrors and make children practice and stitch-stitch-stitch with the dreadful shirt woman. I want to dig and hoe and rake with Paul and water with Appolas and sow and scrape and weed and lay out and bed out and blossom out and *stay out*. I want to vegetate and germinate and radiate and foliate and bifoliate. I want to ramify and amplify and all the fies. I want to blossom like the rose and smell like a pink. I want to be a good runner, a good creeper and a good climber and a good bloomer. I am a good bedder already. I want to be "strong and hardy" and "satisfactory" and to "last well into frost". I would like to be "evergreen and perennial". But I know you. You are tired already and wish I was a tender annual you don't care how soon I "dry up" and "die out". I want people to say she "always gives good satisfaction and should be cultivated more generally", but you no doubt consider me a "free sucker". You think I "branch out too much" and you are out with your pruning knife this moment to trim me; but don't cut me off below the pen "just pinch off the top a little" for I have a few more words to tell you what a temptation I have for this agri-horti-flori-cultural mania.

Although Mrs. Starbuck was considerably more daring and vocal than the typical housewife, she expressed the inner yearnings secretly harbored by many of her contemporaries. Travel and communication had expanded late 19th Century women's sphere significantly. But nothing bolstered their personal sense of confidence like the warm glow of achievement. Horticulture offered a realm in which they could exercise their capabilities to the utmost.

If Mrs. Starbuck was one of the first women to give vent to her desires in the 1870s, a decade later she would be surrounded by kindred spirits. Women found that they had a knack for growing. Although they wisely left pomology and farming to the menfolk, women infiltrated all branches of ornamental horticulture. It was an avocation (and later a vocation) that seemed to suit them. And, since ornamental horticulture was a relatively new science, they were not confronted by any traditional role models. Most men readily and cheerfully conceded that flowers fell safely within the female's sphere of influence. As Henry Ward Beecher admitted in *Plain and Pleasant Talk About Fruits, Flowers and Farming* written in 1859, "A woman's perception of forms, of colors, of arrangements is naturally quicker than a man's."

Beecher's compliment may not thrill the ego of the modern reader, but those encouraging words from such a highly esteemed preacher must have been greatly valued by his Victorian female admirers. At the time, women were not accustomed to being praised for their creativity nor encouraged to pursue independent endeavors. According to tradition, women were not men's equals on any front—save perhaps in physical beauty and their ability to raise children. That stereotype was not held by men alone, women also had a very low opinion of the members of their own sex. Indeed, when the Empress of Austria was asked in 1882 why she preferred male company to that of her fellow females, she replied without a moment's deliberation, "Madame, I enjoy having these gentlemen, not because they are men, but because they are not women."

At a time when women possessed very little self-esteem, horticultural achievements provided precious encouragement. The creativity exercised in horticultural design and arrangement called forth new skills and rewarded the successful practitioner with a new sense of achievement. In addition, the study and research necessary to successfully fill a window with thriving houseplants also opened doors for women.

Success is of no consequence if the world remains ignorant of its existence. And so, the next step was for women to publicize their achievements. Many years elapsed before women's horticultural progress was acknowledged in any of the century's male-dominated periodicals. However, men finally took notice. One of the first to pay heed to the trend was Andrew Jackson Downing, who always made a point of being gracious in his compliments to the "fairer sex". He gallantly admitted that women had out-distanced men, at least in one realm,

> We write this especially for the eyes of the ladies. They are naturally the mistresses of the art of embellishment. Men are so stupid, in the main, about those matters, that if the majority of them had their way there would neither be a ringlet, nor a ruffle, a wreath, nor a nosegay, left in the world. All would be as stiff and as meaningless as their own meager black coats, without an atom of the graceful.

Downing's endorsement may have tickled the ladies, but it had little impact on his male readers. Unfortunately, Downing's reputation as a dandy made his opinion on such matters of little consequence. In truth, few men cared one way or the other whether there were ringlets or ruffles in the world. Although the average man was perfectly willing to admit that women grew exceptional flowers, most men were equally quick to avow that the achievement was singularly trivial.

Nonetheless, women had won a victory in their own eyes. And, with the confidence of success came independence. In the meantime, women had gained some autonomy on the home front when their husbands left cottage industries to work in centralized factories and businesses 10–12 hours a day. While they were absent, a woman had free reign in the house. She could exercise all of her creative talents and allow her imagination to wander without the constant check and challenge of a male opinion calling a halt to all of her "ruffle and ringlet" inclinations.

Women had also gained control of their daily schedule. As long as a wife kept the household in order, she was free to do as she wished with her spare time. She could take up any respectable hobby that she fancied in her home. And, eventually, she began to venture outside that fixed domain.

With the appearance of leisure time came new problems. Boredom was a previously unencountered malady. As a result, when the ugly head of ennui suddenly surfaced, people had no idea how to handle it. Due to the lightened housekeeping schedule, women were the victims most often afflicted with bouts of boredom. And, if mothers suddenly found themselves with extra hours to fill, then their daughters had even more excess time on their hands. Somehow, it had to be filled. Wilkie Collins described the problem and the most common solution in his novel, *The Moonstone*,

> Gentlefolks in general have a very awkward rock ahead in life—the rock ahead of their own idleness. Their lives being, for the most part, passed in looking about them for something to do, it is curious to see—especially when their tastes are of what is called the intellectual sort—how often they drift blindfold into some nasty pursuit. Nine times out of ten they take to torturing something—and they firmly believe they are improving their minds, when the plain truth is, they are only making a mess in the house. I have seen them (ladies, I am sorry to say, as well as gentlemen) go out, day after day, for example, with empty pill-boxes, and catch newts, and beetles, and

spiders, and frogs, and come home and stick pins through the miserable wretches, or cut them up, without a pang of remorse, into little pieces . . . Sometimes, again you see them occupied for hours together in spoiling a pretty flower with pointed instruments, out of a stupid curiosity to know what the flower is made of. Is its colour any prettier, or is its scent any sweeter, when they *do* know? But there! the poor souls must get through the time, you see—they must get through the time. You dabbled in nasty mud, and made pies, when you were a child, and you dabble in nasty science, and dissect spiders, and spoil flowers, when you grow up . . .

Boredom was a besetting problem for women suddenly faced with leisure time. Illustration from *The American Journal of Horticulture and Florists Companion.*

Idle pursuits did not remain a means of disposing of empty hours for long. There was a growing inclination to find more meaningful ways of filling time. One solution came in the form of a grassroots movement to school women in horticultural pursuits.

Although the Victorians harbored mixed views on the topic of female employment, the idea of training women for horticultural jobs sat well with society. After all, no one could deny that many women were forced to support themselves. At the time, the alternatives were mill work or sweat shop labor.

Compared to those arduous and demeaning disciplines, horticultural employment was a far more palatable solution. And, unlike other forms of hard, physical
labor, working with flowers did not rob a woman of her status as a "lady". Flower
related work was entirely lady-like.

A crusade began, dedicated to offering horticultural training for young
women who had scant prospects of marriage. The goal was to reach them early,
before they suffered from the wrack and ruin of infamous and loathsome
careers. If the horticulturally trained young lady happened to have the good fortune of marrying, then she would be a better housewife due to her schooling. If
not, she had found a means of self-support for the rest of her working life. *The
Gardener's Monthly* reported the trend in 1859,

> The benevolent ladies of our city [New York] are beginning to appreciate the value of
> horticulture as a female employment, and are about to establish a horticultural school
> for females upon Long Island, where poor orphan girls may be taught gardening as an
> art. In after years, these girls, saved as they will have been from the vicious influences
> of the large city and having a stock of robust health and an occupation that will keep
> their body and mind in active and pleasant exercise, will thank the lady, Mrs. Phelps,
> who founded it . . .

Besides the obvious economic consequences of Mrs. Phelps' school and the
other kindred institutions that followed its lead, there were also the sociological
advantages of women's employment to be considered. Prevailing Victorian
opinion held that an orphan who was deprived of the positive influences of a
nurturing mother and a supportive father would never be imbued with the
essential concepts of good and right unless she was somehow exposed to the
contagious goodness of nature. Crime, evil and misery might be staved off, and
the means of obtaining gainful employment might be won, merely by coaching a
young lady in the art of growing plants.

The burgeoning horticultural schools taught girls how to perform the menial
chores of plant care and the artistic tasks of floral design. However, other horticultural pursuits which did not entail soiling one's hands were also opening their
doors to women. Some of those occupations could be pursued discretely from
one's own home without venturing out into the controversial world of female
employment. One such occupation was freelance writing. Women frequently
contributed articles to plant periodicals, and they were occasionally offered
positions on the editorial staff of horticultural or women's magazines. This form
of employment was deemed appropriate for any woman, regardless of her class,
as long as she did not seek fame. In fact, Sarah Hale, the renown editor of *Ladies
Magazine* and *Godey's Lady's Book*, spent a great deal of time insisting that she
was just a simple widow, trying to support her family. She won fame, despite her
disavowals, while also securing financial security for her children.

Many women preferred greater discretion than Mrs. Hale about publicizing
the fact that fortune had forced them to earn their own way in life. Women's
magazines not only offered a lady the means of earning a little money by her

Young ladies benefitted from the contagious goodness of nature. Illustration from Edward Sprague Rand's *Flowers for the Parlor and Garden.*

pen, but she could also maintain desired anonymity by writing under a pseudonym such as "Daisy Eyebright" or "Fanny Fern". In fact, a number of prolific writers submitted material under several names and thus published multiple articles in the same magazine. Sarah Hale filled *Ladies Magazine* with letters to the editor and articles that were largely written by her own hand under a variety of assumed names.

Horticulture was also making an impact on the social front of society. One of the era's favorite pastimes was social calling, a custom which consisted of investing leisure hours paying visits back and forth. While visiting, women compared notes on their children, discussed the weather, and exchanged gossip gleaned from their weekly magazines. They also had a sterling opportunity to exhibit the tokens of their horticultural prowess. Since no one wanted to spend the afternoon immersed in such mundane subjects as the daily laundry or the morning chores, the conversation often turned to the houseplants that were proudly displayed in the front parlor patiently awaiting compliments. Women shared advice, recommended new plants and compared experiences. As Henry Ward Beecher noted, houseplants were a fascinating diversion,

> . . . what delightful subjects of gossip they furnish; and how many reputations have been spared when houseplants were at hand, with their various merits to be discussed.

An obvious off-shoot of all the visiting back and forth was the creation of societies. Societies were nothing new for men. In North America, male agricultural organizations had been in existence since 1785. However, those societies were primarily concerned with the nuts and bolts of farming. The average citizen wanted something with a broader appeal.

The first group founded to pursue general horticulture was the New York Horticultural Society which was originally chartered in 1818. The Pennsylvania Horticultural Society followed suit in 1827, and by 1835, there were flourishing horticultural societies in Geneva, Massachusetts, Albany, Charleston, Maryland, Tennessee and Washington, DC. Most of those societies were initially exclusively male with membership limited primarily to professional horticulturists and their wealthy patrons. But, as early as 1829, the Pennsylvania Horticultural Society set a precedent by welcoming female members. Apparently, however, the move was prompted more by the desire to add some temperance to the society's zesty debates rather than as a gesture of whole-hearted admiration for the feminine opinion. And the Pennsylvania Horticultural Society made no secret of its motives. After voting to admit ladies, the old members explained their function to the new,

> [Women] will give a tone and character to the society, will operate as a check to intemperate discussion, and will preserve us from that partisan spirit which too frequently works to the downfall of the most popular institutions.

Throughout the era, women played second fiddle in male dominated societies. In 1884, *Vick's Monthly* described one role that women were frequently called upon to perform,

> The time is near at hand when our agricultural and horticultural societies, all over the country, will be holding their annual meetings and appointing committees for the year . . . Many of these allow practices on their show grounds that are morally far below the standard of their membership, and which the officers are continually obliged to apologize for . . . As a probable improvement upon this condition of things, we ask that the lady members be associated in the standing committees as far as practicable—but especially on the executive committee . . . The effect will be wholesome.

However, in the case of the Pennsylvania Horticultural Society, a woman was not elected to the Executive Council until 1919.

If societies did not yet appreciate the horticultural input of their female members, they nonetheless provided a new means for women to bolster their confidence. Everyone, regardless of sex, was encouraged to exhibit and compete for prizes in seasonal shows and fairs. Women, children and members of all classes were given an equal opportunity to match skills with their fellow gardeners. Strict fairness in judging was considered to be a crucial ingredient for a successful show, as this item from the judge's rules in an 1860 issue of *The Gardener's Monthly* reveals,

> The handsomest half a dozen plants grown in cracked teapots in a mechanic's window should no more be forgotten than the best 10 orchids in a millionaire's hothouse.

Show competition was always stiffest in the potted plant divisions. As a result, women most often entered the flower arranging contests where they need not match expertise with professional growers. However, the Victorian rules of discretion prevented women from taking full credit for their artwork. Women rarely entered under their own name, particularly if they were unmarried. In fact, when the Royal Horticultural Society staged its first floral competition in 1861, a blue ribbon was awarded to a trio of arrangements exhibited by Thomas C. March. The arrangements were actually executed by his talented sisters, and he made no secret of that fact. But it was Mr. March who took home the ribbon and became a celebrity for the designs.

Women did not act hastily to develop their own societies. In 1868, the first general women's club was created for journalists and career women. However, it was not until the 1880s that women's groups, or women's clubs, as they were called, became popular. In addition to providing an opportunity to socialize, women's clubs often featured speakers on popular subjects to entertain and enlighten their members. Quite frequently, horticultural topics were addressed at the meetings and horticultural speakers were enlisted to lecture. Finally, in 1889, the first women's group dedicated solely to horticulture was chartered. The Cambridge Plant Club began meeting in that year, and it remains a strong organization to this day. The ranks of the Cambridge Club's membership continue to be filled with trend-setting ladies who are also ardent gardeners.

When women came together for purposes of fellowship, they discovered many common interests and concerns. They also found that there is power in numbers. It is incredible what a group of women can accomplish when they put their heads together to tackle an issue. In addition to the staid and noncontroversial societies devoted to home study and self-improvement, women began to organize societies dedicated to improving mankind.

One such society that quickly gained momentum from a rather unassuming beginning was the Flower Mission. Although generally considered to be a charitable organization rather than a horticultural society, the Flower Mission nonetheless spent its time solely in the labor of distributing flowers and plants.

The Flower Mission began in Boston in 1868. It was the brainstorm of a teacher whose daily commute from the suburbs to the classroom brought her through the poorest section of town. One day, she happened to bring a bouquet for her desk along on her daily trek, and was immediately surrounded by a crowd of slum children all begging for a blossom. After that experience, she made a habit of bringing flowers to hand out as she commuted to and fro. That was the humble beginning of what became the Flower Mission, dedicated to distributing flowers and plants to the sick, poor, orphaned and aged inhabitants of the city. It was a charity that spawned many kindred benevolent societies still in existence.

The enthusiasm which the Flower Mission generated provides an excellent example of the fervor that surrounded anything connected with nature. Twice a week, volunteers met to distribute 300,000 bouquets and plants to hospitals, insane asylums and orphanages "without distinction of religion or race." To the modern philanthropist, the mission's work might appear to be a blatant example of "let them eat cake" idealism. But the ladies of the Flower Mission were absolutely convinced that they were doing more to nurture goodness by distributing blossoms and living plants to the starving masses than they could accomplish by passing out bread. The mission was founded on the theory that blossoms up-lift the recipient's moral character and thus inspire him to improve his situation. If he was sick, the flower cheered him; if he was poor, the flower's beauty put the surroundings to shame and provided inspiration for improvement. Apparently, however, the Flower Mission's tactics had critics even among the idealistic Victorians. *Harper's Bazar* printed this defense of the Flower Mission for those who might be skeptical, "If any one doubts the subtle influence of this apparently trivial charity, they should follow the ladies of the Flower Mission through the wards of Bellevue."

Although the premise that nature can abolish poverty could be (and often was) challenged, the Flower Mission stood on more solid ground in their assertion that flowers aid in healing. For that aspect of the mission's work, the society had the firm endorsement of none other than the legendary Florence Nightingale, who assured the public that flowers were the best medicine for any ailment, especially fevers.

Aside from the effects that the Flower Mission had on poverty and sickness, that organization greatly benefited the ladies who served as volunteers. Not only did they receive the immense emotional satisfaction of donating the fruits of their hands for the betterment of mankind, but they also reaped rewards from the physical labor that the society's activities entailed. Although many were skeptical of the charity's effectiveness upon its recipients, everyone agreed that the Flower Mission was potent preventive medicine for the ladies who did the giving.

In general, plants worked wonders for the nation's health, and particularly for the health of middle class women. Although health proponents could not convince ladies to take exercise outdoors and ventilate their parlors for their own good, they could easily coax women to undertake those actions for the benefit of plants. Plants called forth the female's nurturing instincts while also introducing women to the value of physical fitness.

In Colonial times, there was little reason for concern about exercise and fresh air. Everyone was exposed to more than their minimum daily requirements of both those abundant commodities. But, with the proliferation of labor saving machinery and efficient heating devices in the 19th Century, lack of exercise and insufficient exposure to fresh air became issues of concern. The Western world watched as the health of its population deteriorated. Most noticeably, North American women were especially hard hit by an epidemic of previously unknown middle class maladies. Neuralgia, nervous debilitation, fits of swooning and scores of other nebulous ailments plagued women of all ages. Not only did those chronic complaints effect the quality of family life, but the general frailty of American women also had a very real effect on their child bearing capabilities. The situation became so dire that young men often traveled abroad in search of sturdier marrying stock. Catherine Beecher and Harriet Beecher Stowe were among the many period writers who noted the deplorable state of female health in mid-century,

> The fact that women of this country are unusually subject to disease, and that their beauty and youthfulness are of shorter continuance than those of the women of other nations, is one which always attracts the attention of foreigners.

A remedy had to be found, and gardening provided one rather enjoyable method of pursuing both exercise and fresh air. Gardening was among the first sanctioned forms of female exercise. And that recreation was widely practiced prior to the 1880s, when it was not normally considered lady-like to go gallivanting around in the pursuit of good health. As an 1887 *Scientific American* pointed out, in the early part of the century,

> Learning, philanthropy and religion were of consequence. To cultivate the body might be well enough for pugilists and circus riders, but was unworthy the serious thought of refined men and women.

Gardening was considered to be a mild form of exercise, primarily because it did not entail the donning of special garments. But, as anyone who has ever gardened either outdoors or indoors well knows, that pursuit can be rigorous at times, especially when there are huge pots to tote around and buckets of water to fetch back and forth. Although gardening may have been arduous work, it was endorsed by one and all as a suitable exercise for everyone, regardless of sex. Zenas Dane, editor of *Success with Flowers*, prescribed gardening to cure all of his readers' ills,

> Throw aside your books, your pen, your sewing, your duties of any sort that confine you to the house during all of your waking hours, and get out of doors into the air and

sunshine. The odor of the fresh upturned earth is a tonic in itself, and the physical effort required to turn it up will exercise muscles that many men and women never exercised. You may get tired, but you will sleep all the better for that, and your appetite will amaze your cook.

When a woman's sphere expanded, her family also felt the repercussions. The family shared in the pride of achievement when she took first place in a horticultural exhibition, and the family benefited from the uplifting influence that incumbent houseplants bestowed on their captive audience. Along more practical lines, husbands were saved the agony of nursing chronically ill wives simply by sending them outdoors for a few hours in the garden daily. Perhaps most importantly, women won self respect from their horticultural conquests, and in so doing, they also won the respect of their family.

What began as a seemingly inconsequential pursuit evolved into a significant influence. The horticultural renaissance eventually touched the lives of every North American man, woman and child. The world changed, and the parlor evolved to document those changes. Not only had the furniture and fenestrations altered, but the mood evolved from a stifling, haughty and haunting environment to one that was alive with possibilities. The parlor awakened to its surroundings. It was no longer a barricade between the family and the outside world. The parlor had become a portal opening to a new realm of possibilities.

Women won self-respect with horticultural conquests, and thus, they also won the respect of their family. Illustration from Margaret Sangster's *Home Life Made Beautiful.*

CHAPTER XIV

YESTERDAY, TODAY AND TOMORROW

FADS NEVER LAST FOREVER. Just as pteridomania and the cactus craze came and went, so the consuming fascination with houseplants eventually subsided. After monopolizing center stage for three quarters of a century, houseplants faded from the focus of attention. Interest turned elsewhere.

The waning was inevitable. Although tropicals had mesmerized the public for decades, they could not hold a captive audience forever. The novelty was bound to wear thin. After all, the pace of tropical discovery and horticultural introduction began to slacken dramatically as the century came to a close.

China was the last great frontier for plant exploration. And the era found an enthralling plant hunting hero in Robert Fortune (1812–1880), who botanized China immediately after it opened to trade. He kept the public's attention riveted on horticulture, playing the drama of his Chinese trips for all they were worth. The tales of his travels were published regularly in period magazines and never failed to attract an attentive audience. China held the public captive for a few more decades.

Interest in the Orient and its flora remained keen. Chinese exploration continued throughout the first half of the 20th Century, with expeditions conducted by such celebrities as Ernest H. Wilson (known to one and all as "Chinese" Wilson, a sobriquet he despised), George Forrest and Frank Kingdon-Ward. They all brought new plants back from the Orient, and wrote stirring accounts of their journeys. However, Robert Fortune captured most of the plants suitable for indoor cultivation, leaving his successors to retrieve the trees and shrubs of the Orient for introduction into the Western garden landscape.

The flow of new introductions has never come to a grinding halt. To this day, plant explorers journey to the ends of the earth in search of rare plant material, and they invariably discover plants that no man has collected before. However, by the turn of the century, most of tropica had been explored and the bounty of its flora was introduced.

Meanwhile, horticulturists back home had thoroughly sifted through the fruits of the jungles and identified those plants suitable for conservatories and windowsills. The influx of new plant material gradually diminished from a flood to a trickle. People were no longer overwhelmed by a wealth of new tropicals. In fact, by the turn of the century, horticultural magazines could scarcely devote a paragraph yearly to announcements of new species from abroad, whereas, in earlier days, several pages of fine print were required to publicize new introductions.

To take up the slack, nurserymen who had previously concentrated primarily on improving edible crops, set to work breeding the tropical plants on hand. Every worthy species that could be induced to set seed was encouraged to produce hybrids under the influence of the breeder's camel's hair brush. Horticulture was by no means dormant. But, somehow, the resulting hybrid variations on popular floral themes lacked the impact of the genuine article which had arrived straight from tropical jungles. The horticultural world was no longer bustling.

In the meantime, other concerns emerged to steal the limelight. As the 20th Century dawned, new interests came to the fore, upstaging the resident houseplants. The world was filled with news of the Women's Christian Temperance Union, women's suffrage, the motor car and moving pictures. The public was preoccupied elsewhere.

The sharp edges of the Victorian Era gave way to simpler, sleeker lines. In fashion, the heavily corsetted, highly curvaceous hour-glass figure melted into the long, lean garb of the flapper. As the frills and fussiness disappeared from the fashion scene, lifestyles also moderated. It was no longer either necessary or appropriate to blatantly advertise one's economic status for all the world to see. In keeping with that trend, the parlor and its decor were also pared down.

As the second decade of the 20th Century got under way, talk of war became front page news. Before long, accounts of World War I filled every paper from cover to cover leaving little room to be wasted on discussing the begonias that sat in the parlor. Horticulture took a back seat to topics of national urgency. Half a century before, horticulture could have withstood the competition. In fact, horticulture had survived the Civil War in salubrious health, acting as a common bond between a sundered population. When Southern agricultural papers fell as a casualty of the conflict, Southern gardeners begged Northern publishers to continue forwarding their issues in spite of the ban on communication between the Union and Confederate States. However, in 1917, horticulture was not as muscular an undertaking as it had been in the 1860s. It could not begin to compete with World War I.

The public's horticultural interests turned from ornamentals to Victory Gardens. Everyone, regardless of age or sex, no matter if they lived in the city or the country, grabbed a hoe and set to raising vegetables. Acreage and greenhouses that had formerly grown flowers were devoted to producing food for the war effort.

The ebbing interest in horticulture declined precipitously. Horticultural societies floundered and nearly failed. The Pennsylvania Horticultural Society, once a strong and healthy organization with 800 active members in 1844, could only claim a membership of 150 in 1915. In 1917, they sold Horticultural Hall and stored their library, neglected and unindexed, in locked crates. The scant business entailed in keeping the small society afloat was conducted from Room 606 of the Finance Building in Philadelphia. Many years would elapse before they regained their former prominence.

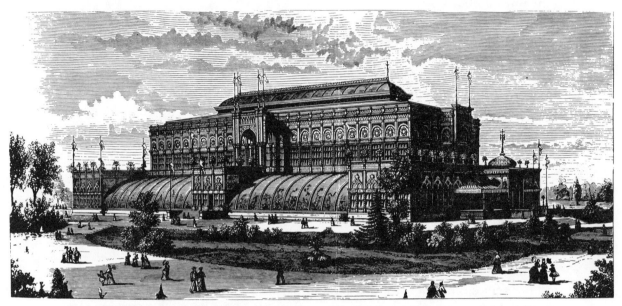

Interest in horticulture was sufficiently strong in 1876 to warrant the erection of this Horticultural Hall at the Centennial Exposition in Philadelphia.

Eventually, the war ended and the boys came home. But horticulture did not rally visibly until the 1930s. The economic angst of the Depression actually increased interest in horticulture. When times were bad, a relatively inexpensive bouquet of homegrown violets made all of the difference, lifting the spirits and easing the troubles of people faced by seemingly insurmountable woes. The florist trade began to see better days. But, things remained bleak for the horticultural enterprise as a whole.

Most large private conservatories and greenhouses fell into disuse as the wealthy, trend-setting class tightened their belts. Many tropicals were lost from cultivation, necessitating later recollection and reintroduction from the jungles. Among the notable losses were the Malaysian rhododendrons, which are tropical shrubs with huge, frequently fragrant umbels of pastel colored flowers; *Allamanda hendersonii*, once the most popular allamanda in cultivation with large, fragrant, yellow and maroon, trumpet-shaped flowers; and *Mitriostigma axillare*, a close relative of the gardenia with small but fragrant flowers. Horticulture suffered together with the people. But, when things began to look up, it was equally resilient.

What became of the front parlor? Throughout the war, Prohibition and Depression years, through all of the paring down, simplifying and tightening up, a few grand Victorian homes remained standing as an enduring testimony to a by-gone era. Thanks to the painstaking craftsmanship that went into their construction, those Victorian homes still stood, proudly lining the Main Streets.

Meanwhile, many of those big old houses were divided and subdivided so that several families might share their abundant space. But the inherent beauty built into the woodwork and molded into the mantel was scarcely diminished. The large, roomy bay windows still welcomed the sun's nurturing rays; and the sunporches survived and flourished. All of the essential ingredients for indoor gardening remained intact.

New homes were built. They had huge, bright windows and efficient heating systems which distributed warmth equally throughout their rooms. Modern technology made virtually every room of the home a haven for houseplants. Thus, other portions of the house began to share the parlor's burden of botanical duty, harboring all sorts of plants. Herbs took up residence in the kitchen, cool-loving plants came to dwell in sunporches, and living rooms harbored shade-loving ferns or philodendrons. Perhaps people were not as keen about their resident botanicals as the first indoor gardeners were in the 19th Century, but the tradition of growing houseplants never died.

Fashions move in cycles, and we seem close to reaching the zenith of another full circle. Interest in Victoriana is strengthening. Many a grand old Victorian has recently been restored and its front parlor reinstated in all its glory. This time around, the parlor typically holds but a fraction of the furniture, bric-a-brac and clutter of its former incarnation. It undoubtedly enjoys more human company than its little-used predecessor. Hopefully, the newly restored front parlor will not incur the wrath of the Edgar Allan Poes and Edith Whartons of the day.

Most importantly, we may hope that parlors, whether in restored Victorians or homes of more recent vintage, will once again harbor a multitude of houseplants—not simply a token Boston Fern keeping lonely vigil in the corner, but a luxuriant, verdant collection of diverse botanicals. The more, the merrier. For inspiration, we might turn to the words of Victorian tastemakers. Andrew Jackson Downing's sensibilities may be outdated, but his views relative to the incorporation of nature into home-life certainly remain relevant. Although time has marched on, botanicals have not lost their virtues of beauty, their intellectual interest or their ability to spark our appreciation for nature and its wonders. Houseplants are always tasteful in the parlor, as well as throughout the home. And, like our predecessors of two generations ago, there is no end to the possibilities. We possess today an equally incredible range of plants to adorn our homes. But, like the Victorians, we could use a little coaching on their usage, care and needs.

We might learn some lessons from the Victorians. The coldest, darkest parlor is infinitely enhanced by an ivy trained around the window frame. Taking a cue from the parlor's "dark ages", that room could easily entertain a few ferns sending their croziers showering downward, a palm, and a handful of the many foliage plants that were once so popular. Some narcissus or other forcing bulbs would be very comfortable sitting cozily on the mantel, just as they once sat by the belljar clock generations ago.

Or, in a warm room with an east or west exposure, the homeowner might profitably delve into the Victorian repertoire of foliage plants. Such a room would make a hospitable host for some begonias and a few fuchsias. While a brightly lit alcove with a south-facing window or a sunny bay window could certainly entertain some of the many flowering plants that the Victorians grew such as pelargoniums, clerodendrums, and perhaps some Flowering Maples.

One thing is certain, regardless of their temperature, exposure, vintage or design, our homes want plants and plenty of them. And, with the wealth of improved hybrids available today, our parlors, sitting rooms, studies, and living rooms can be far more resplendent than the display of a century ago, while retaining the virtues and character of the place.

After all, setting the stage is one of the primary functions of houseplants. Plants are as important to setting a mood as furniture and wallcoverings. Compact plants with simple, sleek lines fit well in a modern decor, while herbs and plants of culinary importance are comfortable in Colonials. But Victorian homes want appropriate period plants quietly coexisting with the ferny wallpaper and Oriental carpet. Thanks to the earnest efforts of 19th Century horticultural pioneers, houseplants have become an intrinsic part of the indoor scene.

We owe an enormous debt to the Victorians. Two generations ago, our ancestors had the ingenuity and foresight to invite plants into their homes. It was an idea of earth-shattering horticultural importance; and it continues to bear fruit.

We have grown accustomed to sharing our homes with houseplants, but, imagine living for at least two seasons of every year deprived of plants and their beauty. We are indeed indebted to the dreams envisioned and the goals set by those early gardeners who were driven by the times and their climate to lay the groundwork of indoor horticulture and begin a year-around association with plants. In their homes the first experiments with tropical plants were performed, and the primary skills of houseplant cultivation developed. In their front parlors, plants grew lush and luxuriant, tended by people with a burning desire to encourage a coexistence between man and nature. Whether living in a Victorian or in a modern dwelling, we all benefit from the lessons learned in the front parlor.

BIBLIOGRAPHY

Allen, David Elliston. *The Victorian Fern Craze: A History of Pteridomania*. London: Hutchison & Co, 1969.

Allen, Grant. *The Story of Plants*. New York: D. Appleton and Company, 1895.

Altick, Richard D. *Victorian People and Ideas*. New York: W. W. Norton & Co, 1973.

American Horticultural Annual. New York: Orange Judd & Co., 1868.

Anderson, Alice Sloan—editor. *Our Garden Heritage*: Articles from the Bulletins of the Garden Club of America. New York: Dodd, Mead & Company, 1961.

Bailey, L. H. *The Standard Cyclopedia of Horticulture*. New York: The Macmillan Company, 1935.

Ballard, Ernesta D. "The Organizations of Horticulture". *America's Garden Legacy: A Taste for Pleasure*. edited by George H. M. Lawrence. Philadelphia: Pennsylvania Horticultural Society, 1978.

Barber, Lynn. *The Heyday of Natural History*. Garden City, New York: Doubleday & Company, 1980.

Beecher, Catherine E. *Treatise on Domestic Economy*. New York: Harper & Brothers, 1848.

Beecher, Catherine E. and Stowe, Harriet Beecher. *American Woman's Home*. Watkins Glen, NY: American Life Foundation, 1979.

Beecher, Henry Ward. *Plain and Pleasant Talk about Fruits, Flowers and Farming*. New York: Derby & Jackson, 1859.

Bennett, Ida C. *The Flower Garden*. New York: McClure, Phillips and Company, 1903.

Benson, Albert Emerson. *History of the Massachusetts Horticultural Society*. Norwood, MA: Printed by the Massuchusetts Horticultural Society, 1929.

Berrall, Julia S. *The Garden*. New York: The Viking Press, 1966.

Boyd, James. *A History of the Pennsylvania Horticultural Society: 1827–1927*. Philadelphia: Printed for the Society, 1929.

Buist, Robert. *American Flower Garden Directory*. New York: Orange Judd & Company, 1854.

Buist, Robert. *The Rose Manual*. New York: Earl M. Coleman, 1978 reprint of the 1844 edition.

Carroll, Lewis. *The Annotated Alice*. New York: Times Mirror, 1960.

Carter, Tom. *The Victorian Garden*. Salem, NH: Salem House, 1985.

Clark, Francis E. & Harriet E. *Our Journey Around the World*. Hartford: A. D. Worthington & Co, 1894.

Coats, Alice M. *The Plant Hunters*. New York: McGraw-Hill Book Company, 1969.

Collins, Charles. *Greenhouse and Window Plants*. New York: MacMillan & Co., 1895.

Commission of Agriculture. *Report of the Commission of Agriculture for the Year 1866*. Washington: U. S. Government Printing Office, 1867.

Commissioner of Patents. *Report of the Commissioner of Patents for the Year 1854*. Washington: U. S. Government. A. O. P. Nicholson, Printer. 1855.

Cook, Clarence. *The House Beautiful*. New York: Scribner, Armstrong and Co., 1878. Reprinted by the North River Press.

Cook, E. T.—editor. "Carnations, Picotees and the Wild and Garden Pinks". *Country Life*. Covent Garden, 1905.

Copeland, Robert Morris. *Country Life: A Handbook of Agriculture, Horticulture and Landscape Gardening*. Boston: John P. Jewett & Company, 1860.

Corner, E. J. H. *The Natural History of Palms*. Berkeley: University of California Press, 1966.

Cushing, John. *The Exotic Gardener*. London: A. MacPherson, 1812.

Dalzell, Robert F., Jr. *American Participation in the Great Exhibition of 1851*. Amherst, MA: Amherst College Press, 1960.

Downing, Andrew Jackson. *The Architecture of Country Houses*. New York: Dover Publications, Inc., 1969. Originally published by D. Appleton & Company in 1850.

Downing, Andrew Jackson. *The Theory and Practice of Landscape Architecture*. From 1875 edition. Orange Judd. First published in 1841.

Downing, Andrew Jackson. *Victorian Cottage Residences*. New York: Dover Publications, Inc., 1981. First published in 1842.

Dubos, Rene J. "Tulipomania and the Benevolent Virus". *The Garden Journal*. The New York Botanical Garden. Vol. 10, No.2. (March-April 1960): 41–43, 66–67.

Dulles, Foster Rhea. *The United States Since 1965*. Ann Arbor. The University of Michigan Press. 1971.

Duval, Marguerite. *The King's Garden*. Charlottesville, VA: University of Virginia Press, 1977.

Eley, James N. *The American Florist* or *A Guide to the Management and Cultivation of Plants in Conservatories, Greenhouses, Rooms and Gardens*. Hartford: Elihu Greer, 1845.

Elsmere, Jane Shaffer. *Henry Ward Beecher*. Indianapolis: Indiana Historical Society, 1973.

Faulkner, Harold U. *Politics, Reform and Expansion 1890–1900*. New York: Harper & Row, 1959.

Favretti, Rudy F. & DeWolf, Gordon P. *Colonial Gardens*. Barre, MA: Barre Publishers, 1972.

Fawkes, F. A. *Horticultural Buildings*. London: Swan Sonnenschein & Co., no copyright.

Fessenden, Thomas G. *The New American Gardener*. Boston: Otis, Broaders & Co., 1840.

Field, F. E. *The Greenhouse as a Winter Garden*. New York: G. P. Putnam & Sons. 1870.

Gothein, Marie Louise. Edited by Wright, Walter P. Translated from the German by Mrs. Archer-Hind. *The History of Garden Art*. New York: Hacker Art Books, 1966.

Green, Harvey. *The Light of the Home*. New York: Pantheon Books, 1983.

Hadfield, Miles. *Pioneers in Gardening*. London: Routledge & Kegan Paul, 1955.

Handlin, David P. *The American Home*. Boston: Little, Brown & Company, 1979.

Hassard, Annie. *Floral Decorations*. New York: MacMillan & Co., 1876.

Hedrick, U. P. *A History of Horticulture in America to 1860*. New York: Oxford University Press, 1950.

Heinrich, Julius J. *The Window Flower Garden*. New York: Orange Judd Co., 1887.

Henderson, Peter. *Practical Floriculture*. New York: Orange Judd Company, 1879.

Henderson, Peter. *Henderson's Handbook of Plants*. New York: Peter Henderson & Co, 1881.

Henderson, Peter. *Garden and Farm Topics*. New York: Peter Henderson & Co., 1884.

Hereman, Samuel (Assisted by a Nobleman's Gardener). *Blight on Flowers*. London: T. M. Cradock, 1840.

Hibberd, Shirley. *The Fern Garden*. London: W. H. & L. Collingridge, no copyright.

Hibberd, Shirley—editor. *The Floral World*. London: Groombridge and Sons, 1867.

Hillhouse, Lizzie Page. *House Plants and How to Succeed with Them*. New York: A. T. De La Mare, 1897.

Hix, John. *The Glass House*. Cambridge, MA: MIT Press, 1974.

Houghton, Walter E. *The Victorian Frame of Mind 1830–1870*. New Haven: Yale University Press, 1957.

Huxley, Anthony. *An Illustrated History of Gardening*. New York: Paddington Press, Ltd., 1978.

Ingram, J. S. *The Centennial Exposition Described and Illustrated*. Philadelphia: Hubbard Bros, 1876.

Irving, Washington. *The Sketch Book of Geoffrey Crayon, Gent.* 1819.

Jackson, Mary Elizabeth. *The Florist's Manual*. London: Henry Colburn & Co., 1822.

Johnson, Edwin. *Winter Greeneries at Home*. New York: Orange Judd Co., 1878.

Johnson, Louisa. *Every Lady Her Own Flower Gardener*. New York: A. O. Moore, Agricultural Book Publisher, 1858.

Jönsson-Rose, N. *Window and Parlor Gardening*. New York: Charles Scribner's Sons, 1895.

Jones, C. S. & Williams, Henry T. *Beautiful Homes*. New York: Henry S. Allen, 1885.

Keays, Mrs. Frederick Love. *Old Roses*. New York: The MacMillan Co., 1935.

Kohlmaier, Georg & Van Sartory, Barna. *Houses of Glass*. Cambridge, MA: MIT Press, 1986.

Koppelkamm, Stefan. *Glasshouses and Wintergardens of the Nineteenth Century*. New York: Rizzoli International Publications, Inc., 1981.

Leighton, Ann. *American Gardens of the Nineteenth Century*. Amherst, MA: The University of Massachusetts Press, 1987.

Leighton, Ann. *American Gardens in the Eighteenth Century*. Boston: Houghton Mifflin Company, 1976.

Leuchars, Robert B. *A Practical Treatise on the Construction, Heating and Ventilation of Hot-Houses*. Boston: John P. Jewett & Co., 1851.

Lonsdale, Edwin. *The Management of Greenhouses*. Commonwealth of PA. Dept. of Agriculture Bulletin No. 97. Wm. Stanley Ray, State Printer of PA, 1902.

Lothrop, D. & Co. *Wonders of the Plant World*. Boston: D. Lothrop & Co. 1872.

Loudon, Mrs., edited by Downing, A. J. *Gardening for Ladies*. New York: John Wiley, 1849.

Loudon, J. C. *The Greenhouse Companion*. London: Harding, Triphook and Lepard, 1825.

Lynes, Russell. *The Tastemakers*. New York: Grosset & Dunlap, 1949.

Macoboy, Stirling. *The Colour Dictionary of Camellias*. Sydney: Lansdowne Press, 1981.

MacSelf, A. J. *The Horticultural Exhibitor*. London: Thornton Butterworth Ltd, 1924.

Maling, Miss. *The Indoor Gardener*. London: Longman, Green, Longman, Roberts & Green, 1863.

Marx, Leo. *The Machine in the Garden*. New York: Oxford University Press, 1964.

McIntosh, Charles. *The Greenhouse, Hothouse and Stove*. London: Wm. S. Orr, 1838.

McMahon, Bernard. *McMahon's American Gardener*. 11th Edition Revised by J. Jay Smith. New York: Funk & Wagnall's, 1976. (originally published in 1806, 11th edition 1857)

Metcalf, C. L. and Flint, W. P. *Destructive and Useful Insects*. New York: McGraw-Hill Book Company, Inc., 1928.

Mitchell, Eugene. *American Victoriana*. New York: Van Nostrand Reinhold Co, 1983.

Morton, A. G. *History of Botanical Science*. New York: Academic Press, 1981.

Neil, Patrick. *The Practical Fruit, Flower and Vegetable Gardener's Companion*. New York: A. O. Moore Agricultural Book Publishers, 1858.

Newton, John. *Culture of the Chrysanthemum as Practiced in the Inner Temple Gardens*. London: The Gardener's Lodge at Inner Temple by John Newton, 1890–91.

Nicholson, George. *Encyclopedia of Horticulture*. New York: J. Arnot Penman, 1886–1889.

Oliver, John W. *History of American Technology*. New York: The Ronald Press Company, 1956.

Olmsted, Frederick Law. *Public Parks and the Enlargement of Towns*. Cambridge, MA: American Social Science Association, 1870.

Parkman, Francis. *The Book of Roses*. Boston: J. E. Tilton & Co., 1866.

Parsons, Samuel. *The Art of Landscape Architecture*. New York: G. P. Putnam's Sons, 1915.

Parsons, S. B. *The Rose*. New York: Wiley & Putnam, 1847.

Paul, William. *The Rose Garden*. New York: Earl M. Coleman, Publisher, 1978. Reprint of 1848 edition.

The Pennsylvania Horticultural Society. *From Seed to Flower*. Philadelphia: The Pennsylvania Horticultural Society, 1976.

Periam, Jonathan. *The Home and Garden Manual*. New York: Greenwich House, 1984. Originally published in 1884.

Perl, Philip. *The Time-Life Encyclopedia of Gardening: Ferns*. Alexandria, VA: Time-Life Books, 1977.

Peterson, Harold L. *Americans at Home*. New York: Charles Scribners, 1971.

Price, Sadie F. *The Fern Collector's Handbook and Herbarium*. New York: Henry Holt & Co, 1897.

Rakeman, Steven J. and Berg, Donald. *The 1870 Agriculturist*. Rockville Centre, NY: Antiquity Reprints, 1980.

Rand, Edward Sprague, Jr. *Flowers for the Parlor and Garden*. Boston: J. E. Tilton & Company, 1868.

Randolph, Cornelia J. *The Parlor Gardener*. Boston: J. E. Tilton & Company, 1861.

Ray, Richard & Walheim, Lance. *Citrus*. Tucson, AZ: HP Books, 1980.

Rexford, Eben E. *Home Floriculture*. New York. Orange Judd Company. 1911. First published in 1890 by James Vick.

Rexford, Eben E. *Indoor Gardening*. Philadelphia: J. B. Lippincott Company, 1910.

Ridley, Anthony. *At Home*. New York: Crane Russak, 1976.

Saxton, C. M. *The American Rose Culturist*. New York: C. M. Saxton, 1852.

Sayers, E. *Treatise on the Culture of the Dahlia and Cactus*. Boston: Weeks, Jordan & Co., 1893.

Scott, William. *The Florists' Manual*. Chicago: Florist's Publishing Co, 1899.

Scott, Frank J. *Suburban Home Grounds*. New York: D. Appleton & Co., 1870 reprinted in 1982 by the American Life Foundation, Watkins Glen, NY.

Singer, Charles et al—editors. *A History of Technology*. London: Oxford University Press, 1958.

Strasser, Susan. *Never Done*. New York: Pantheon Books, 1982.

Taft, L. R. *Greenhouse Construction*. New York: Orange Judd Company, 1894.

Tannenbaum, Edward R. *1900: The Generation Before the Great War*. Garden City, NJ: Anchor Press/Doubleday, 1976.

Tergit, Gabriele. *Flowers Through the Ages*. London: Charles Skilton, Ltd., 1972.

Thaxter, Celia. *An Island Garden*. Ithaca, NY: Bullbrier Press, 1985. Originally published in 1894.

Thorburn, Grant. *Life and Writings of Grant Thorburn*. New York: Edward Walker. 1852.

Thorburn, Grant. *Forty Years Residence in America*. Boston: Russell, Odiorne & Metcalf, 1834.

Tice, Patricia M. *Gardening in America, 1830–1910*. Rochester, NY: The Strong Museum, 1984.

Trollope, Anthony. *North America*. New York: Alfred A. Knopf, 1951. Originally published in 1862.

Trollope, Mrs. Frances. *Domestic Manners of the Americans*. New York: Vintage Books, 1960. Originally published in 1832.

Van Ravenswaay, Charles. *A Nineteenth Century Garden*. New York: The Main Street Press, Universe Books, 1977.

Ward, Charles Willis. *The American Carnation*. New York: A. T. De La Mare Printing & Publishing Co., 1903.

Warner, Charles Dudley. *My Summer in the Garden*. Boston: Houghton Mifflin & Company, 1890.

Watson, Alexander. *The American Home Garden*. New York: Harper & Brothers, 1864.

Williams, Henry T. *Window Gardening*. New York: Henry T. Williams, Publisher, 1873.

Wilson, Helen Van Pelt. *The Joy of Geraniums*. New York: M. Barrows and Company, Inc., 1965.

Wilson, Ernest H. *Plant Hunting*. Boston: The Stratford Company, 1927.

Withner, Carl L. "The Houses and Tools of Horticulture" a lecture given in 1978.

Woloch, Nancy. *Women and the American Experience*. New York: Alfred A. Knopf, Inc., 1984.

Wolsely, E. Hon. Frances. *Gardening for Women*. London: Cassell & Company, Ltd., 1907.

Wright, Richardson. *The Story of Gardening*. New York: Dodd, Mead and Company, 1934.

INDEX